The economics of imperfect information

The economics of imperfect information

Louis Phlips

Center for Operations Research & Econometrics
Université Catholique de Louvain

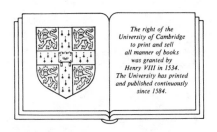

The right of the
University of Cambridge
to print and sell
all manner of books
was granted by
Henry VIII in 1534.
The University has printed
and published continuously
since 1584.

CAMBRIDGE UNIVERSITY PRESS

Cambridge
New York   New Rochelle   Melbourne   Sydney

Published by the Press Syndicate of the University of Cambridge
The Pitt Building, Trumpington Street, Cambridge CB2 1RP
32 East 57th Street, New York, NY 10022, USA
10 Stamford Road, Oakleigh, Melbourne 3166, Australia

First published 1988

Printed in the United States of America

Library of Congress Cataloging-in-Publication Data
Phlips, Louis.
The economics of imperfect information / by Louis Phlips.
    p. cm.
Bibliography: p.
Includes index.
ISBN 0-521-30920-4.   ISBN 0-521-31381-3 (pbk.)
1. Information theory in economics. 2. Uncertainty. 3. Decision
making. 4. Game theory. 5. Institutional economics. I. Title.
HB133.P48 1988
330.1–dc19   88-15096

British Library Cataloguing in Publication applied for.

Contents

Figures and tables

Preface

These are my lecture notes for a course on the economics of information, which I have been teaching at the Université Catholique de Louvain for a number of years. They aim at introducing the students to the recent literature which studies the implications of incomplete information and informational asymmetries for microeconomic theory. The purpose is to show how recognition of the incompleteness of information available to market agents allows the capture of some of the richness of behavior that marks real world markets. These notes should therefore, hopefully, be of some use to those students of industrial economics who wish to get acquainted with what the economics of information has to contribute to their field.

Since this literature is growing in all directions, I did my best to emphasize the common logic. Chapter 1 should be useful in this respect. The reader is especially requested not to skip the outline of the book at the end of the chapter, where this logic is spelled out in a few pages.

The students taking this course at Louvain-la-Neuve are advanced undergraduates and beginning Ph.D. students with very different backgrounds. I therefore tried to avoid unessential technicalities and to concentrate instead on basic concepts and tools. Inevitably, this implied introducing some (elementary) game theory, which in turn required a minimum of sophistication. The insights gained seemed to compensate the special effort this may have imposed on some. At any rate, at the end of the course all had to admit that microeconomics, seen from the informational point of view, is much more fascinating and more relevant to the understanding of the working of real world markets than they could have imagined. I should add, though, that despite my efforts toward simplification some sections are definitely more technical or just more difficult than I had hoped for. I have adorned these sections with an asterisk to indicate that they should not be covered in a first course. (Let me confess that I cannot resist the temptation of skipping some of them in my own teaching.)

I have greatly benefited from unpublished lecture notes by Martin Hellwig in preparing Chapter 5. Section 6.4 reproduces my 1987 contribution "Information and Collusion" in *The Economics of Market*

Dominance, Blackwell, Oxford, edited by Donald Hay and John Vickers. Dr. Dieter Schwarz of the Commission of the European Communities insisted that I should look into the forbidding problem of predatory pricing. He made me discover what I now consider as one of the most fascinating topics in the economics of imperfect information. My report for the Commission, which circulated as a discussion paper of its Directorate-General "Competition," is reproduced as Chapter 7.

I am grateful to Colin Day, Editorial Director of Cambridge University Press, Bob Marshall (Duke University), Margaret Slade (University of British Columbia), and an anonymous referee for a critical reading of parts of the manuscript. Above all, I wish to thank those students who helped improve these notes by their questions, remarks, or term papers, and to single out the contributions by Cathy Cieslik, Christian Gollier, Emmanuelle Havrenne, Valérie Jacob, Bénédicte Noël, and Gérard Schmets.

Once again, the secretarial staff of CORE provided cheerful and efficient secretarial assistance.

De Haan, September 1987

Acknowledgments

The author gratefully acknowledges permission to reprint the following material:

Figure 2.2 – reprinted by permission from Varian, "A Model of Sales," *AER* 70, no. 4.

Figures 3.1, 3.2, 3.3 – reprinted by permission from Cooper and Ross, "Product Warranties and Double Moral Hazard," *Rand Journal of Economics* 16 (Spring 1985).

Figure 3.4 – reprinted by permission from Braverman, Guasch, and Salop, "Defects in Disneyland," *Review of Economic Studies* 50, p. 126.

Figures 3.7, 3.9, 3.10 – reprinted by permission from C. Wilson, "The Nature of Equilibrium in Markets with Adverse Selection," *Bell Journal of Economics* 11 (Spring 1980).

Figure 3.8 – reprinted by permission from C. Wilson, "Equilibrium and Adverse Selection," *AER* 69 (May 1979).

Figure 3.11 – reprinted by permission from Kim, "The Market for 'Lemons' Reconsidered," *AER* 75 (1985), no. 4.

Figures 4.5, 4.6 – reprinted by permission from Reece, "Competitive Bidding for Offshore Petroleum Leases," *Bell Journal of Economics* 9, pp. 379, 381.

Figure 4.7 – reprinted by permission from De Brock and Smith, "Joint Bidding, Information Pooling, and the Performance of Petroleum Lease Auctions," *Bell Journal of Economics* 14 (Autumn 1983).

Figures 5.1, 5.2 – reprinted by permission from M. Spence, *Market Signaling* (Cambridge, Mass.: Harvard University Press, 1974).

Figure 5.3 – reprinted by permission from Hirshleifer and Riley, "The Analytics of Uncertainty and Information," *Journal of Economic Literature* 17, no. 4.

Figures 5.4, 5.5 – reprinted by permission from Rotschild and Stiglitz, "Equilibrium in Competitive Insurance Markets," *Quarterly Journal of Economics* 90 (1976), pp. 633, 635.

Figures 5.9, 5.10 – reprinted by permission from Jaffee and Russell, "Imperfect Information, Uncertainty and Credit Rationing," *Quarterly Journal of Economics* 90 (1976), pp. 659, 661.

Figures 6.2, 6.3, 6.4 – reprinted by permission from Osborne, "Cartel Problems," *AER* 66 (1976), pp. 835, 838, 840.

Figure 6.5 – reprinted by permission from Friedman, *Oligopoly Theory* (Cambridge University Press, 1983).

Figures 7.4, 7.5, 7.6 – reprinted by permission from Easley, Masson, and Reynolds, "Preying for Time," *Journal of Industrial Economics* 33 (1985), p. 452.

Figures 7.7, 7.8 – reprinted by permission of the authors and the University of Chicago Press from Isaac and Smith, "In Search of Predatory Pricing," *Journal of Political Economy* 93 (1985), pp. 335, 341.

Tables 7.1, 7.2, 7.3, 7.4 – reprinted by permission from Salop and White, "Private Antitrust Litigation: An Introduction and Framework," in White (ed.), *Private Antitrust Litigation: New Evidence, New Learning* (MIT Press, 1988).

Figure 8.2 – reprinted by permission of the authors and the University of Chicago Press from Plott and Sunder, "Efficiency of Experimental Security Markets," *Journal of Political Economy* 90 (1982), p. 679.

CHAPTER 1

Preliminaries

Before we embark upon our analysis of the problems that arise in market situations when some of the agents involved are imperfectly informed, it may be wise to start with a brief overview of the main concepts, assumptions, and tools involved. This preliminary chapter will not only introduce the reader to the somewhat esoteric terminology that has come to be generally adopted in the field, but will also delimit the areas to be covered. The outline of the book, which concludes this chapter, shows the many directions in which the "economics of imperfect information" has developed, and it should help the reader to understand the logical coherence of these directions.

1.1   Information structures[1]

The basic concept is that of an "information structure." In each market situation to be discussed, we shall have to define what the information structure is, since this structure will determine, together with the decision rules followed by the sellers and buyers, what the market outcome will be, whether there is an equilibrium – or many equilibria – and what its properties are.

The information structure of a market situation simply gives a precise meaning to the intuitive idea of imperfect or incomplete or imprecise information. Consider the classic case of "uninformed buyers" examined in Stigler's seminal 1961 paper. The potential buyers of a commodity (a particular camera, say) wish to know which shop in town sells it at the lowest price. Before one is able to find out how they will search for it, and what the outcome of the search will be, one has to define their information structure. Stigler supposes that each potential buyer knows all the shops in town, but does not know which shop charges which price. Instead, each potential buyer knows a distribution function, which gives the probability that a price observed after a given

---

[1] For more details, see Nermuth (1982, chaps. 1, 2), whose exposition is in the spirit of Marschak and Radner (1972).

number of searches (i.e., visits of different shops) is below some minimum.[2]

In this setup, there is an "unknown true state of the world," namely the shop which charges the lowest price in town. The price observed during the shopping trip after a number of searches is a "signal." The signal and the true state are related through the probability that the signal is below some minimum. In general, we could say that an information structure contains three elements: the set of possible states of the world, the set of possible signals, and the probability that a signal is observed given that a state prevails. The signal is thus a random variable.

In our example, information would be *complete* if each potential buyer knew which shop charges which price. Then the cheapest shop would be known with probability 1 (and the probability that any other shop is the cheapest would be 0).

Complete information is also *noiseless*, in the sense that for every state there is a signal such that this signal is observed *with certainty* (probability 1) when the state prevails. However, incomplete information may also be noiseless: There may be a signal observed with certainty for every state, but this signal may be less informative than when there is a different signal for every different state (as is the case under perfect information). If, in our example, the buyers knew with certainty that the minimum price lies within a certain range, their information would be noiseless but incomplete. In fact, Stigler supposed the buyers' information to be *noisy*, since they know only the probability that an observed price lies below some minimum. However, if after two searches two different prices are observed, it is certain that the true minimum price in town lies below the highest of these two prices, so the buyers should be able to define a range within which the true minimum price lies with certainty and to narrow it down as search proceeds. This suggests that it is possible to redefine a problem with noisy information as a problem with noiseless information, and vice versa, so that the choice of the formalization is a matter of convenience.

In what follows, the information structure will always be *asymmetric*, in that complete information prevails on one side of the market (e.g., on the selling side) while incomplete information characterizes the other side (e.g., the buying side), or in that some agents have information which other agents on the same side of the market do not have.

Milgrom and Roberts (1987, p. 184) provide a particularly well-cho-

---

[2] For more details, see Chapter 2.

sen illustration of three different information structures: one with complete information, one with incomplete information but no asymmetry, and one with asymmetric information. The example shows that it is the informational asymmetry which leads to interesting forms of strategic behavior and helps us to understand why asymmetric information is essential in the economic literature discussed in this book. It is worth quoting Milgrom and Roberts:

To get an idea of the role of informational asymmetries in strategic behavior, consider three simple card games. In the first, each player is dealt five cards face up, the players make any bets they want, and then the best hand wins. In the second, each player receives five cards, some of which are dealt face up and the rest face down. Without looking at their hole cards, the players make their bets, then the cards are turned face up and the best hand wins. Finally, the third game is like the second except that players can look at their hole cards. Again there is betting, the hidden cards are revealed, and the best hand wins.

The first game is one of complete [. . .] information. Everyone knows everything, and as long as we assume that people prefer more money to less, it is fairly trivial to figure out what will happen: there will certainly be no betting, and probably no one will bother to play! Clearly, not all games of complete information are either so uninteresting (witness chess) or so lacking in explanatory power [. . .]. However, in its informational structure, this game typifies both the sort of game theory that is discussed in intermediate micro texts and, indeed, most of standard microeconomic theory itself.

The second game has uncertainty/informational incompleteness, but no information asymmetries. Its informational structure puts it in the domain of decision theory and the economics of uncertainty. Games of this sort are useful models for studying such issues as insurance, risky investments, and learning (especially if we revise the game to have the hole cards revealed one at a time, with betting after each is shown). However, its play would not generate any interesting forms of strategic behavior.

The third game involves informational asymmetries: while there is some publicly available information, each player is privately informed about his or her hole cards. (In fact, the informational structure of this game, in which the probability distribution over what the particular private information of the various players could be is common knowledge, corresponds very closely to that in the asymmetric information game models used in most applications to industrial organization.) The existence of this private information can obviously lead to interesting strategic play: bluffing, signaling, reputation building, etc. It is also the reason why poker is of enduring popularity.

As this example is meant to suggest, recognition of informational asymmetries and the strategic possibilities they engender can yield models that begin to capture the richness of behavior that marks the real world. This is the great advantage of these methods: they permit us to model, and thereby start to understand, phenomena that made no sense in terms of complete information analyses or one based on incomplete but symmetric information (uncertainty).

It should thus be clear that the "economics of uncertainty" and the "economies of imperfect information" are two different fields, and it should also be clear why this book is concerned only with the latter. Both study the implications of incomplete information and of the resulting uncertainty. But the former focuses on its implications for the decision making of an individual consumer or firm. It may go further and derive consequences for the market as a whole, but always under the assumption that uncertainty is the same for all market participants. It is natural therefore for theories of insurance decisions or investment decisions to postulate competitive markets in which there is no strategic interplay between the agents. On the contrary, when the focus is on informational asymmetries, then strategic interplay becomes essential and the application naturally concerns markets characterized by monopolistic competition or oligopoly. The economics of imperfect information is therefore an integral part of the theory of industrial organization.

In their survey of the two fields, Hirschleifer and Riley (1979) suggest that decision making under uncertainty is concerned with "event uncertainty," while our topic is "market uncertainty." Market uncertainty occurs when economic agents are unsure about the supply–demand offers of other economic agents. For example, buyers are unsure about the prices charged or the qualities offered by the sellers. Buyers may be consumers or they may be firms hiring new employees, so the uncertainty is about the latters' productivity. Or sellers are unsure about the prices buyers are ready to pay. Sellers may be producers of consumer goods, but they are also job applicants who wonder what salary to accept, or insurance companies wondering about the risk they are covering, or banks trying to ascertain the solvency of potential borrowers. Or sellers may be oligopolists that are badly informed about the prices or the production rates or the costs of production of their competitors. Going through these examples makes it obvious that informational asymmetry is what characterizes "market uncertainty" as opposed to "event uncertainty."

1.2.   Decision rules or strategies

Given an information structure, we assume that economic agents will choose an action (with certainty or with some probability) when a signal is observed. That is, we assume they will follow a decision rule.

In Stigler's uninformed buyers case, the action consists in following a particular deterministic search strategy. In his 1961 paper, Stigler used a very simple decision rule: The buyers simply determine the number of shops to visit after comparing the expected gain of an additional search with its cost. The expected gain is the expected reduction in price. The search cost is the cost of the time spent searching.

Other decision rules could be and were used to analyze the same situation, as will be shown in greater detail in Chapter 2. Why should one determine the number of shops before starting the shopping trip? Why not use the information that becomes available at each visit of a new shop and revise that number accordingly? Why define the expected gain in terms of a price reduction rather than a gain in utility? And why should the action be deterministic (i.e., why should the strategy be "pure," in the jargon of game theory) instead of being chosen with a certain probability so as to become a "mixed" strategy: Shouldn't the buyer's search be defined in probabilistic terms to allow for random events that may occur during the shopping trip?

The decision rule will turn out to be as essential as the information structure, because it is their combination that will determine the final outcome.

1.3.   Market outcomes

Market outcomes will be described as properties of a market *equilibrium*. Several equilibrium concepts are available in the literature, but they are not all equally compatible with the postulated asymmetric information structures.

Let me note, right from the start, that a *competitive equilibrium with a given market price* is hard to reconcile with informational asymmetries, even if the market price is uncertain. Attemps to reconcile perfect competition with consumer search illustrate this difficulty.[3] In Fisher's 1970 model, for example, firms know that they are in a competitive market – and therefore that their demand curve is flat, at "the" market price – but they are uncertain about the exact value of this market price. Buyers are also uncertain about this, but not too much: They search just enough for a low-price firm to attract more customers than a high-price firm, but without attracting all customers. What will firms do? Fisher postulates that they will try to find "the" market price by lowering their price in case of net excess supply and raising it in case of net excess demand, with the end result that the distribution of prices will degenerate to the perfectly competitive price. But why would firms do this, rather than take advantage of the fact that their

---

[3] See Hey (1979, chap. 25).

individual demand curve *is* downward sloping? Why do they refuse to see this obvious fact?

In Diamond's 1971 analysis, a dynamic competitive model with consumer search and well-informed firms leads to another degenerate distribution, at the monopoly price! However, to prevent the development of goodwill, which is not compatible with perfect competition, Diamond is led to suppose that each period each consumer in the market searches just one firm at random, so the price history of firms has no effect on the number of consumers who buy from it in any one period!

Rather than trying to save the concept of a perfectly competitive market and the "law of supply and demand" which is supposed to clear this market, a lot of energy is saved if one simply admits that this law is inadequate. As already hinted at by Arrow (and stressed by Gordon (1981)) in his seminal 1959 article on price adjustment, there are two problems with it. First, dynamic adjustment to the equilibrium price may take a substantial length of time. During this time one cannot assume that firms believe that the market is clearing or that they have an incentive to find out what the market clearing price could be. Second, and perhaps more important, the competitive equilibrium model is unable to tell us who decides to change the equilibrium price. This is the "problem of the missing auctioneer." One alternative, which I prefer, is to study the functioning of auctions under incomplete information with a small number of sellers or buyers, to see how the bidding process leads to information transmission and to equilibrium prices that are *not* given (see Chapters 4 and 8).

When the number of firms is large but each has a downward-sloping demand curve (there is no given market price), we are in a world of monopolistic competition. Here, the traditional concept of a *free entry zero-profit equilibrium* has been used with success in combination with asymmetric information structures. Early attempts at deriving price dispersion as a property of market equilibrium or at explaining sales as contributing to the persistence of such equilibrium price dispersion proceeded that way (see Chapter 2). The same is true for the pioneering analysis of how separation of high-risk from low-risk types obtains in insurance markets (see Chapter 5).

At the other extreme – when a market is controlled by a monopolist – the market equilibrium coincides with the *profit-maximizing position* of the monopolist. However, the presence of an informational asymmetry makes it necessary for the monopolist to take its consequences explicitly into account. If some of its customers have lower search costs than others, for example, and are therefore ready to search longer, then the monopolist should use its customers' equilibrium conditions as constraints in its maximization problem. A similar case arises when some customers care more than others about getting protection against quality uncertainty.

However, as we already stressed, informational asymmetries typically lead to situations in which strategic interplay is essential. Here, the concept of a *noncooperative Nash equilibrium* turns out to be most useful. This equilibrium is defined under the assumption that there is no (explicit or tacit) collusion among producers: Each firm behaves as "competitively" as possible in the sense that it maximizes its own profit individually, without trying to form a cartel, yet without ignoring its competitors' actions.

Each firm i is treated as a player in a game,[4] so its profit function Π_i is called its *payoff function*. The strategy space Q_i describes the set of actions available to a player. When each player has chosen a strategy, the resulting n-tuple $q = (q_1, \ldots, q_n)$ is a joint strategy for all n players. A noncooperative Nash equilibrium is then a joint strategy $q^* = (q_1^*, \ldots, q_n^*)$ such that for *each* player i ($i = 1, \ldots, n$) its strategy q_i^* is a "best reply" to the others' strategies or, equivalently,

$$\Pi_i(q^*) = \max_{q_i} \Pi_i(q_i, q_{N-i}^*) \tag{1.1a}$$

for all i, or

$$\Pi_i(q^*) \geq \Pi_i(q_i, q_{N-i}^*) \qquad \text{for all} \quad q_i \in Q_i, \tag{1.1.b}$$

where $q_{N-i} = (q_1, \ldots, q_{i-1} \cdot q_{i+1}, \ldots, q_n)$. A "best reply" for firm i is a strategy that maximizes $\Pi_i(q_i, q_{N-i})$; it is the best player i could do if he knew the strategy choices q_{N-i}, and is thus the result of an ordinary maximization problem. A Nash equilibrium is a collection of *simultaneous* best replies. As a result, it is characterized by the fact that no player has an interest to change it unilaterally, since player i cannot increase its profit by changing its q_i^*, given the strategies of all the other players, and since this is true for all other players.[5] Nermuth (1982, p. 49) remarks that

while it does not explain how the players should arrive at an equilibrium, at least it does explain why they should stick with it once they are there. Certainly one can argue that a strategy combination that is not an equilibrium cannot represent a state of affairs in which each player acts rationally: there must be

---

[4] A very brief summary of noncooperative game theory can be found in Nermuth (1982, chap. 3). For more detailed presentations see Friedman (1977, 1983) or Shubik (1982).

[5] L. Johansen (1982) discusses and convincingly rejects a number of critiques of the Nash equilibrium concept, showing that these critiques are based on a misunderstanding of its simultaneous nature.

at least one player who could improve his own payoff simply by altering his own strategy, an act nobody can prevent him from committing.

To illustrate, consider the case where $n = 2$ and q_i is firm i's rate of production. We then have Cournot's duopoly model in which the duopolists react in quantities. Cournot's solution[6] turns out to be a noncooperative Nash equilibrium.

The Nash equilibrium is interesting not only because it captures the essential features of oligopolistic (small n) competition, but also because the strategies involved can be of very different nature. In Cournot's duopoly model, they are production rates giving rise to a unique market price. But nothing prevents us from defining the strategies as prices (one for each firm), or as different product qualities (one for each firm), or as types of labor contracts (the players being hiring firms and job applicants). Quite surprisingly, and rather paradoxically, we will discover (in Chapter 6) that a set of noncooperative Nash equilibrium strategies could give collusive outcomes, when the game is not a one-period ("single-shot") game as given here but is supposed to be repeated over time. In fact, such strategies give a precise meaning to what is often loosely referred to as "tacit collusion."

The reader will also discover, as we proceed, that the Nash equilibrium is a quite general concept whose use is not restricted to the analysis of oligopoly. It can be used whenever one has to find a set of strategies such that no player has an interest to deviate from it. For example, a set of bids made by potential buyers at an auction can be interpreted as a Nash equilibrium (see Chapter 4). Let me also pinpoint the terms of a warranty contract, which simultaneously create an incentive for the buyer of a durable to use it with care and for the seller to provide good quality (see Chapter 3).

In addition to the equilibrium concepts just discussed, the economics of information created its own specialized equilibria, such as "signaling equilibria," "reactive equilibria," or "rational expectations equilibria." These concepts will be defined and discussed later on as the need arises.

1.4.   Imperfect versus incomplete information

Game theory makes a useful and important distinction between games with "imperfect" information and games with "incomplete" information. This distinction aims at drawing the model builder's attention

---

[6] See Chapter 6.

to the difference between the actual decisions made by the players and the rules which define the game itself.

The players are said to have "imperfect" information when there is uncertainty about the actual behavior of the players or, more generally, when the evolution of the play until the point in time when a new decision is to be made is not known. For example, a member of a price cartel cannot observe the past or present prices of the other members, or the members of a production cartel cannot observe each others' actual production rates.

On the contrary, information is "incomplete" when the players do not know some of the elements which define the rules of the game itself. These rules include the set of payoffs, the set of strategies, and the number of players. An auction in which the bidders do not know what value the other bidders attach to the auctioned object is thus a "game with incomplete information," because the players do not know each others' payoffs. The same is true for a duopoly game in which one producer does not know the demand function or the cost function of his competitor, so there is uncertainty about the competitor's profit. (The uncertainty may also apply to one's own payoff, needless to say.)

For a long time, game theorists did not know how to handle games with incomplete information. In 1967, however, the pioneering work of Harsanyi (1967–68) has shown a way out. It amounts to redefining the game in such a way that each player knows the probability distribution of the variable that is uncertain. In a sense, the game is thus transformed into a game with complete information about the probability distribution. The properties of this distribution should be chosen with care and be well defined.

We will come across several examples[7] of this analytical device, which is by now very common. The earliest example in economics is perhaps Vickrey's treatment of a "Dutch" auction (in which the offer price is lowered by an auctioneer or a clock device until one of the bidders accepts the last price offer). Vickrey (1961) supposed that the unknown reservation values of the bidders are drawn from a rectangular distribution, the same of all bidders and known by all bidders (see Chapter 4). In Chapter 5, employers are supposed to know the distribution of the innate abilities of job applicants. In Chapter 6, duopolists are supposed to know the joint distribution of the unknown intercept of their market demand function and of the signal that provides information about this intercept. In Chapter 7, potential entrants

---

[7] See also Selten (1982).

into a market know the distribution of different types of established firms and the actual unknown type they are facing is supposed to be drawn from this distribution. In each case, an additional fictitious player ("Nature") is supposed to draw the actual values of the unknown variable from the postulated distribution. The actual players find their equilibrium strategies by maximizing their expected payoffs.[8]

1.5.   Organization and information

Natural questions for an economist to ask are: How can a given information structure be improved? Is it profitable to improve the structure? What is the efficient information structure? These questions were raised in Marschak's pioneering 1954 paper "Towards an economic theory of organization and information" and extensively studied in Marschak and Radner's *Economic Theory of Teams* (1972). See also Radner (1983).

Attention is directed toward the determination of information structures inside firms, which are treated as "teams." A team is defined as an organization whose members have the same interests and beliefs but do not share the same information. The question is, how should the tasks of inquiring, communicating, and deciding be allocated among the members of the team so as to achieve results that would be best from the point of view of their common interests and beliefs?

Just to illustrate the type of approach, consider the one-person case (this is thus *not* a team) of a monopolist who sets the price p of its product and produces just enough for the demand, which is specified as $2x - p$, where x is a random variable reflecting the public's taste (Marschak 1974, Essay 20, pp. 44–45). The monopolist knows the mean μ and the variance σ^2 of x. Its profit is equal to $p(2x - p)$ minus the cost of production, which is supposed to be independent of the amount produced and can be disregarded. How much will this monopolist pay a market research agency for keeping the monopolist informed of current public tastes (i.e., of the actual value of x)?

In the absence of further information, the monopolist will choose the price p so as to maximize expected profit $Ep(2x - p) = p(2\mu - p)$. This price is $p = \mu$, and the expected profit is $\Pi_0 = \mu^2$. If the monopolist is informed of the actual value of x, it will choose every

---

[8] This analytical device doesn't tell us anything about how players with incomplete information manage to find their equilibrium strategies in real-life situations. The theory of "bounded rationality" developed by Simon (1955, 1956) gives a clue as to how satisfactory approximations to game-theoretic solutions can be found in practice. See also March (1978).

$\text{Max } p(2\mu - p)$
$\quad p$

$\dfrac{d(p(2\mu - p))}{dp} = 1(2\mu - p) + p(-1) = 2\mu - 2p = 0$
$\Rightarrow p = \mu$

$J_0 \; \Pi_0 = \mu(2\mu - \mu) = \mu^2$. This is not a random variable, so $E\Pi_0 = E\mu^2 = \mu^2$

time the price so as to maximize the current known profit $p(2x - p)$, and its best decision rule is $p = x$. This yields an expected profit $\Pi_1 = Ex^2 = \mu^2 + \sigma^2$. Hence, the value of the inquiry is $\Pi_1 - \Pi_0 = \sigma^2$. (This is always positive: in this example, because a variance is positive; in general, because Π_1 is the average of maxima, Π_0 is the maximum average, and the average of maxima cannot be smaller than the maximum average.) It pays to buy information, and the services of the market research agency are the most valuable as the variability of tastes gets stronger.

However, this book focuses on markets, not on what happens inside firms. The Marschak–Radner analysis is thus not directly applicable to the market situations analyzed here: sellers and buyers cannot be said to have the same interests and beliefs. When interest and beliefs are different, then information efficiency and market efficiency are linked in a special way. Our problem is: Can one organize markets in such a way that the agents have an incentive to reveal their true preferences or costs?

This question was raised by Vickrey in his pioneering 1961 paper on the optimal organization of auctions and competitive sealed tenders. Vickrey assumed that an exclusive public market agency is established to handle all sales of a commodity for which either buyers or sellers or both are too few in number to ignore the repercussions of their actions on the market price and do not collude for some reason (for example, they are too numerous). This agency (or control planner) is supposed to maintain an efficient resource allocation and thus to fix the equilibrium competitive price. Vickrey remarks:

The trouble with this as a workable solution is that much of the information that the marketing agency would need in determining the competitive equilibrium price would have to come from reports and actions of buyers and sellers, who would have an incentive to understate prospective demands and supplies or to curtail their actual sales and purchases in the hope of inducing the marketing agency to change the price in their favor. [. . .]

What the marketing agency needs, in order to determine the optimum pattern of transactions in its commodity, is an unbiased report of the marginal-cost (= competitive supply) curves of the sellers and of the marginal-value (= competitive demand) curves covering a range of prices that will be sure to contain the equilibrium price. The problem is then for the marketing agency to behave in such a way as to motivate the buyers and sellers to furnish such unbiased reports. One method, though an expensive one, is to arrange to purchase the commodity from suppliers and to sell it to purchasers on terms that are dependent on the reported supply and demand curves in such a way that the suppliers and purchasers will maximize their profits, individually at least, by reporting correctly, so that any misrepresentation will subject them to risk of loss (or at least offer no prospect of gain).

This problem has given rise to a vast literature in public economics and in game theory, most of which is outside the scope of this book. The interested reader is referred to Green and Laffont (1978) for the public decision-making aspects and to d'Aspremont and Gérard-Varet (1979) and Laffont and Maskin (1983) for a game-theoretic treatment. We shall be satisfied with a discussion of auctions as demand-revealing mechanisms (Chapter 4) and of the informational efficiency of double auctions (Chapter 8).

1.6.   Cognitive dissonance

The assumption that economic agents prefer to have better information if they can acquire it without cost is implicit in models determining efficient information structures and even in models of optimal search: In these models, the costs of information acquisition and transmission and the costs of search are the only factors that limit the quest for more information. But do economic agents always wish to be better informed? In game-theoretic models, players are given subjective probability distributions and are supposed to consistently revise these as new information becomes available. But do players actually perform these revisions in real-life situations?

Economic theory postulates they do, and we shall stick to this postulate throughout. For the type of problems to be discussed, this seems indeed to be an adequate methodology, even if the postulate is not entirely realistic. There are, however, economic problems for which it may be necessary to postulate another type of behavior or at least to take some contradictory results from social psychology into account. This is the point made by Akerlof and Dickens (1982). It may be worthwhile to note their arguments briefly before proceeding on the assumption that new information is indeed consistently made use of whenever it becomes available.

In special circumstances, the theory of "cognitive dissonance," taken from psychology, might be relevant. In economic terms, this theory can be reduced to three propositions (Akerlof and Dickens, 1982, p. 307):

First, persons not only have preferences over states of the world, but also over their beliefs about the state of the world. Second, persons have some control over their beliefs; not only are people able to exercise some choice about belief given available information, they can also manipulate their own beliefs by selecting sources of information likely to confirm "desired" beliefs. Third, it is of practical importance for the application of our theory that beliefs once chosen persist over time.

The theory is supported by experiments showing that (1) groups of persons with the same information have systematically different beliefs so that they interpret a given information differently, (2) groups of persons with different beliefs display differences in receptivity to new information, and (3) persons who justify to themselves some difficult undertaking are likely to have a strong and persistent belief that the undertaking is a good one.

These findings are relevant for a number of economic problems. Akerlof and Dickens thoroughly discuss the case of workers in *dangerous jobs*. Workers in atomic power plants typically fail to wear the safety badges that measure radiation exposure, because they prefer to believe that their work is safe and they make a choice about whether to believe the job is safe or not safe. Cognitive dissonance is also (potentially) useful in explaining the *sources of innovation*: Resistance to new information that contradicts prevailing beliefs may explain why minor innovations mainly come from existing laboratories, whereas major innovations mainly come from outside. *Advertising* often conveys very limited or even irrelevant information about the product, but is nevertheless effective. Why? Akerlof and Dickens (1982, p. 317) suggest the following:

> As the advertising practitioners point out, people do have needs and tastes and they do buy goods to satisfy them. Some of these needs and tastes are quite obscure or subtle; it may be hard to tell when the needs are being met. In such cases people may *want* to believe that what they have just bought meets their needs. Advertising gives people some external justification for believing just that. People like to feel that they are attractive, socially adept, and intelligent. It makes them feel good to hold such beliefs about themselves. Ads facilitate such beliefs – if the person buys the advertising product.

Similarly, compulsory *social security* may be necessary because persons left to their own devices would prefer not to foresee that they might get old, that they might get very sick, and so on, and would therefore tend to purchase too little insurance.

1.7. Outline of the book

I hope that the preceding sections have put our topic into perspective. I now wish to give a systematic survey of the different directions in which the economics of imperfect information has developed and of the main results obtained.

Part I treats static problems in which information structures are related to current variables. Information is asymmetric throughout, but the nature of the asymmetry changes from chapter to chapter.

Chapters 2 and 3 discuss implications of the fact that the demand side of the market for a commodity is badly informed about either its price or its quality. This is the, by now, traditional type of asymmetry on which the pioneering papers in the economics of information concentrated.

Chapter 2 considers the main implications of asymmetric information about prices. To obtain price information, consumers have to search and therefore incur search costs, which mainly reflect the value of time. For some these costs are higher than for others, so search behavior differs from customer to customer. Equilibrium conditions are derived which determine either the number of searches to be made or a stopping rule giving a reservation price below which any observed price is considered acceptable. It is then shown how sellers can incorporate their customers' equilibrium conditions as constraints in their profit maximization. In doing so, sellers may find it in their interests to generate "noise" (to organize random sales, for example) in order to separate the high-cost from the low-cost customers and charge lower prices to the latter.

In a market with many sellers and free entry, the informational asymmetry about prices leads to two typical outcomes. First, it explains the presence of price dispersion, different sellers charging different prices for the same commodity at (zero-profit) equilibrium. Second, it creates an incentive for the sellers to make sure that price dispersion persists over time. Since consumers learn by experience, they will discover, as time elapses, which shops persistently have low prices. For price dispersion to persist, it is necessary therefore that the price image of a shop be blurred over time. A typical way to obtain this is for the sellers to (a) organize sales of a limited duration from time to time *and* (b) to substantially reduce prices during these periods. The latter result is obtained by characterizing the (zero-profit) equilibrium density function from which sellers draw their sales prices.

Does an equilibrium price dispersion also arise when the number of sellers is small? Take a duopoly. With two sellers, the same commodity can indeed be sold at two different prices in equilibrium when and because some consumers are better informed about one firm than about the other. Such an informational asymmetry with respect to a particular firm arises automatically when the consumers and the duopolists have different locations in space. It is natural therefore to do the analysis in the framework of the so-called Hotelling model. Its Nash equilibrium displays two different prices. As a by-product, it is discovered that, when the two sellers are free to choose their location, they will tend to locate not too far from each other. This is a weak form of what is known as Hotelling's principle of minimum differentiation.

Chapter 3 discusses some implications of asymmetric information about the quality of a durable good. Buyers can discover its quality only by using it, and sellers cannot directly observe how buyers use it.

The seller–buyer relationship is analyzed first. If in case of product failure a third party (an expert) can objectively evaluate the causes and extent of the failure, then the seller can provide some protection by offering a warranty contract to the purchaser of a new durable. In doing so, however, this seller runs into two problems. On the one hand, the terms of the warranty may create an incentive for the buyer to use the durable with less care or to give it insufficient maintenance. On the other hand, they may give the seller an incentive to modify the quality produced, a lower protection implying a lower quality. The Nash equilibrium warranty contract is such that less than full protection is provided, so it is in the buyer's interest to take care of the durable. However, both the level of care taken by the buyer and the quality offered by the seller are below what they would have been if they had been observable. And it may be profitable again for the seller to generate "noise," that is, to voluntarily produce a proportion of defective units and to offer an optional warranty at a price.

In general, nonoptional warranties offered free of charge promote good quality compared to a situation in which no protection against product failure and no expert advice is available, as is the case for a number of markets of used durables. In such markets, the average quality tends to be too low compared with the price. This is the "lemons principle": If you buy a used car from a private owner (or from a dealer who refuses to give a warranty), you may expect it to be a "lemon," that is, a car of bad quality. A more careful analysis of the used-car market leads to further insights. First, price dispersion *not* related to search costs shows up in equilibrium (with better cars getting a higher price, while some sellers of better-quality cars may not find a buyer). Second, the lemons principle may be contradicted if allowance is made for the fact that the quality of a car is not exogenous (but depends on the care with which it was treated by its owner) and if one introduces the special circumstance that a car owner can change his or her position from buyer to seller at little cost.

Finally, the role intermediaries (retailers) play in the transmission of quality information is brought into the picture. It is discovered that resale price maintenance may be rationalized as a protection of the dealer's margin given by the seller to induce his or her retailers to provide either product-specific special services or more general quality certification.

Chapter 4 introduces a different type of informational asymmetry. A monopolist is selling a unique object (an individual is selling a painting, say) or a monopsonist is buying a particular service (a government is contracting out the construction of a highway). Because they do not know how much the potential buyers value the object or at what cost the potential contractors can produce the service, they choose to sell or buy by auction rather than by posting a price. Indeed, auctions offer the advantage that the participants reveal their valuations or their costs to some extent through the bidding mechanism.

Two polar cases are examined. The independent-private-values model postulates that each bidder knows with precision how much the item is worth to him or her but is ignorant about the others' private values. Each of these private values is independent of the reservation values of the others, so it conveys no information about any other buyer's value. Under these assumptions, the English auction and the "second-price" sealed-bid auction appear as games with incomplete information which are perfect demand-revealing mechanisms (leading to a Pareto-efficient allocation). The individual utility-maximizing bids are dominant strategies and thus automatically have the Nash equilibrium property. On the contrary, two other types of auctions, the Dutch auction and the "first-price" sealed-bid auction, are games with incomplete information which do not have these properties. Their Nash equilibrium bids can be found if additional assumptions are made, the basic assumption being that the reservation values of all bidders are drawn from a probability distribution. Nevertheless, all four types of auctions provide the same expected price. But it is in the seller's interest to announce that no bids below some minimum price will be accepted. These results are confirmed by a number of experimental games which are discussed in some detail.

The other polar case is the common value model, in which the item to be auctioned has a single objective value but no one knows it. Bidders have differing estimates based in part on private information, and these estimates are not independent of those of the other bidders. Hence the "winner's curse": winning the auction is itself informative, since it reveals that all others had a lower estimate of the true value so that the winner should revise his or her estimate.

Chapter 4 ends with a short discussion of how, in the case of a procurement auction, the government can design a contract that shares the risk related to cost uncertainty in order to give bidders an incentive to reduce their bids, and of how the latter can collude to misinform the government and, thus, to manipulate its forecasts.

Auctions generate information about values, whether private or common. Signaling generates information about individuals (their abilities, their attitude toward risk, their creditworthiness) and transmits it to the other side of the market. When the agents who receive these signals use them to their advantage, an equilibrium may emerge. These signaling equilibria are analyzed in Chapter 5. The discussion centers on the labor market, in which the equilibria take the form of wage schedules which link wages to education received. They encourage job applicants to "select themselves" in the sense that more able applicants will turn up with more or better diplomas and thus separate themselves from the less able ones. In general, there are many signaling equilibria, some of which may be noncooperative Nash equilibria. The alternative and more restrictive concept of a reactive equilibrium is therefore introduced. This is an equilibrium from which firms will not deviate (a) because reactions by other firms to possible deviations make the latter unprofitable and (b) because such reactions are always to be expected.

Chapter 5 also includes a short discussion of the special features of signaling equilibria in insurance and credit markets. In insurance markets, high-risk and low-risk customers are separated in equilibrium: Each type gets a different contract. The separation implies that the former receive full risk coverage, whereas the latter obtain only partial coverage. Again, an alternative concept of a reactive equilibrium is introduced. Finally, it is shown how the difficulty of separating high-risk from low-risk borrowers can lead to rationing of individual borrowers in credit markets. Here, a separating equilibrium with different contracts appears to the extent that collateral requirements are brought into the picture.

A new type of informational asymmetry is the unifying theme of Part II. It is the asymmetry that results from the fact that private information is available to some market agents and not to others which are on the same side of the market, such as competing firms, potential entrants, or simply other sellers or buyers. How will this asymmetry affect the market outcome? Will they want to keep this information private, or will they share it? Will the market mechanism itself disseminate the information?

The three topics discussed are such that dynamics are essential. In collusive situations, the detection and deterrence of cheating implies that the temporal sequence of events must explicitly be taken into account. Predatory pricing implies the entry of a new competitor into the market followed by a sequence of price cuts. The transmission of private information through the bidding mechanism in double auctions implies a sequence of adjustments of prices and expectations over time.

Chapter 6 starts from the observation that the policing of a collusive agreement is a problem in the theory of information, since deviations from the agreement (such as secret price cutting or shipments in excess of production quotas) must be detectable for retaliation to be possible and for a threat of retaliation to be credible. It is also a central problem in oligopoly theory, since "the prisoner's dilemma" shows that if one member of the agreement cheats it is better for the others, taken individually, also to cheat. One way to police an agreement is to adopt a rule saying that if one member deviates, all the others will also deviate (in such a way that each member keeps its market share or that all will shift to a noncooperative Nash equilibrium). Since such a rule is itself a set of equilibrium strategies, it is a credible deterrent to individual cheating. However, it can be effective only to the extent that there is perfect and complete information among the members, who should therefore have an incentive to share the relevant information.

When information is incomplete or imperfect, collusive agreements must break down. The results of experimental games with quantity strategies suggest that the noncooperative Cournot–Nash equilibrium is the typical outcome when information is limited and the number of players is small. It is of some importance, therefore, to show theoretically that Cournot–Nash equilibrium can indeed exist under incomplete information and that players do not wish to share their private information in such equilibria.

These conclusions tend to give a theoretical foundation to the distrust with which antitrust policy treats the transmission and sharing of information about market variables among oligopolists. However, the current EEC policy is based on the presumption that the transmission of information to a competitor (and the simultaneity of price moves over time which is deemed to result from it) is per se evidence of collusion. It is argued that this presumption is stretching the theoretical conclusions too far.

Chapter 7 is based on the rather recent and perhaps surprising insight that predatory pricing is also a problem in the theory of information. Common sense suggests that predatory price cutting is irrational, at least in the framework of a single-market monopoly situation. In addition, "the chain store paradox" – which gives a game-theoretic treatment of multimarket monopoly – suggests that predation cannot occur in equilibrium under complete information. As long as both the potential predator and the potential prey know each other's situation (in terms of foregone profits) and each other's moves, and as long as it is clear to both that the issue is one of predatory pricing, the potential prey will enter the market without fear and the established firm will prefer normal competition, that is, a noncooperative Nash equilibrium with both firms in the market.

However, if the potential victim has incomplete information and is, as a result of it, in doubt whether predation could occur, then its entry can meet a predatory response in equilibrium. One approach supposes that the entrant entertains the possibility (however small) that the established firm may be irrational (a fanatic predator or a fanatic pacifist). The established firm may then risk to prey in order to establish a reputation of aggressiveness, since if it ever fails to prey the entrant will conclude that it will never prey. The drawback of this approach is that it implies predation, once begun, to continue forever. An alternative approach uses less restrictive assumptions and supposes that the entrant entertains the possibility that a price cut by the established firm could be either predatory or an implication of a noncooperative Nash equilibrium. It is not sure, therefore, whether there is room for it in the market it entered in. By cutting its price, a predator then makes it look as if, indeed, there is no room for an additional firm in the market, when in fact there is. This seems to be the characteristic feature of the majority of actual cases of alleged predation.

The implications for antitrust policy are clear. To begin with, one cannot conclude, as is often done, that the best policy is no policy at all. It is also clear that none of the policy standards presented in the literature (such as pricing below marginal cost, an increase of output above the preentry level or a price increase after the entrant has been forced to cease operations) can be used as evidence of predation. Each case has to be evaluated on the basis of all evidence relevant to the question whether there is room for the alleged victim in the market in a noncooperative Nash equilibrium.

Chapter 8 is devoted to the transmission of private information by the market mechanism in double auctions, in which both sides of the market make bids and market prices equate aggregate supply and demand. This is the celebrated question of the "efficiency" of capital markets and futures markets. It will be argued that even in a rational expectations equilibrium private information cannot be made fully public by the market mechanism – contrary to a rather widespread misconception. For such markets to exist and to operate well, some of the participants have to be misinformed at the start. And a fraction of these have to remain misinformed for an equilibrium to be possible.

A final comment is in order. After going through this list of results, one is happily surprised to discover that a number of real-life phenomena, which appear as "frictions" or "disequilibria" in theories based on complete information, become properties of the market equilibrium when informational asymmetries are taken into account. These phenomena include price (or wage) dispersion, wage schedules not related to productivity, credit rationing, and price wars. Admittedly, "adverse selection" may occur, in that good quality may vanish from the market. But even this "market failure" helps to understand the emergence of warranties, service contracts, and collateral requirements. Asymmetric information also explains the why and how of auctions, sales, and resale price maintenance. In this sense, the literature surveyed in this book contributes to a "new institutional economics."

Statics

Asymmetric price information

2.1. Consumer search

Historically, the first studies of markets with imperfect information considered situations in which buyers are badly informed about sellers' prices. It is natural, therefore, to first consider the behavior of consumers under price uncertainty, leaving quality uncertainty for a later chapter.

2.1.1. The cost of information

Consumers are supposed to maximize their "consumer surplus," that is, the difference between the utility of a good expressed in monetary units – the "reservation price" – and its selling price. On the simplifying assumption that each customer buys at most one unit, he or she will choose the brand and the shop that gives the highest surplus and thus wishes to know which shop sells a given brand at the lowest price.

But what if the customer does not know which shop sells at which price? He or she will then have to use some a priori knowledge, based on past personal experience and common knowledge. For example, a probability distribution of the prices in a shopping area (a town, for example) may be common knowledge: Expensive high-quality shops are known to be located in particular streets; low-quality inexpensive brands are known to be available in some department stores.

Getting information on prices charged for particular brands by particular shops then involves costs of information, which depend on the information technology (the existence of consumer reports, specialized journals, advertising, etc.), the number of brands and shops available and one's a priori knowledge. These costs are mostly in terms of the cost of the time spent searching: Time is more valuable for the "rich" than for the "poor." Rich customers are therefore said to be "high cost," and poor customers are said to be "low cost." Other things equal, the former should search less than the latter.

In a loose way, perfect information is sometimes equated with zero costs of information. This makes sense if one means to say that perfect information can be obtained at zero cost. When the costs of information are positive, then information is imperfect in the sense that the customer must compare the marginal cost of an additional piece of information with the expected marginal gain in terms of increased surplus, and some may thus be led to stop searching before the lowest price is found, even if by paying the cost perfect information can be obtained. The marginal cost of search is often assumed constant in order to simplify things and because of lack of empirical and theoretical work on its shape.

2.1.2. Price search

The seminal paper on price search is Stigler's (1961) *The Economics of Information*. Stigler starts by emphasizing the fact that price dispersion is ubiquitous even for homogeneous goods,[1] and comments on it as follows:

> Price dispersion is a manifestation – and, indeed, it is the measure – of ignorance in the market. Dispersion is a biased measure of ignorance because there is never absolute homogeneity in the commodity if we include the terms of sale within the concept of the commodity. Thus, some automobile dealers might perform more service, or carry a larger range of varieties in stock, and a portion of the observed dispersion is presumably attributable to such differences. But it would be metaphysical, and fruitless, to assert that all dispersion is due to heterogeneity.

Suppose then, for the sake of clarity, that the consumer faces a distribution of prices for the same good on a local market and tries to find the retail outlet that charges the lowest price. Suppose, further, that the consumer knows the distribution of prices but has no means of knowing, without searching, which outlet charges the lowest price. The problem then is to determine how long he or she will search before buying – that is, how many sellers he or she will canvas, given that search has a cost in time and foregone earnings and that, after some point, to continue the search may be more costly than the gain that is to be expected from it.

Stigler models this search (visit to another retail outlet) as a drawing from a particular random distribution (a normal and a uniform distribution, in fact), and argues that consumers will visit a fixed number, n, of stores and then buy from the store with the lowest price.

---

[1] See Table 16 of the EEC's Eighth Report on Competition Policy, Brussels, April 1979. Out of 503 products on the Dutch market, for example, 166 had a dispersion between 10 and 40%, 89 had a dispersion larger than 40%, and 248 had less than 10% dispersion. Dispersion was measured as the difference between the maximum and the minimum prices, divided by the maximum price. Further empirical work can be found in Jung (1960), Marvel (1976), and Pratt, Wise, and Zeckhauser (1979).

To determine this number of searches n, one does not have to specify a particular distribution. All one has to do is to suppose that there is a known (continuous) distribution function $F(m)$ giving the probability that the price observed at the ith search is below some minimum m, or

$$\text{Prob}(p_i \leq m) = F(m). \tag{2.1}$$

For n searches, we have[2]

$$\text{Prob}[\min(p_1, p_2, \ldots, p_n) \leq m] = 1 - \text{Prob}(p_i \geq m, \text{ all } i),$$

or, since we suppose independent random drawings,

$$\text{Prob}[\min(p_1, p_2, \ldots, p_n) \leq m] = 1 - \prod_i \text{Prob}(p_i \geq m).$$

However, $\text{Prob}(p_i \geq m) = 1 - F(m)$, so

$$\text{Prob}[\min(p_1, p_2, \ldots, p_n) \leq m] = 1 - [1 - F(m)]^n. \tag{2.2}$$

This is the distribution function of the minimum price after n searches. We can then find the expected price the consumer pays by taking the expected value[3] of that minimum price, after n searches; that is,

$$E(m) = \int_0^\infty [1 - F(x)]^n \, dx. \tag{2.3}$$

Clearly, the expected minimum price decreases as n increases, since $1 - F(x)$ is always between 0 and 1.

What is the expected gain, g_n say, of searching one more time (given that n searches have been completed)? We have

$$g_n = \int_0^\infty [1 - F(x)]^n \, dx - \int_0^\infty [1 - F(x)]^{n+1} \, dx,$$

that is, the difference between two successive expected minimum prices, or

$$g_n = \int_0^\infty \left\{ [1 - F(x)]^n - [1 - F(x)]^{n+1} \right\} dx$$

$$= \int_0^\infty [1 - F(x)]^n [1 - (1 - F(x))] \, dx$$

$$= \int_0^\infty [1 - F(x)]^n F(x) \, dx, \tag{2.4}$$

[2] I am following the nice presentation given in Deaton and Muellbauer (1980, pp. 410–11).

[3] By definition, the expected value is the integral of $[1 - F_x(x)]$, where $F_x(x)$ is the distribution function. Here, it amounts to taking the integral of $1 - 1 + [1 - F(m)]^n$ $= [1 - F(m)]^n$.

which is again a decreasing function of n. Searching longer is less and less productive. With a positive (and possibly increasing) cost of search, the consumer will have an equilibrium point at some positive value of n, possibly zero. This point is such that the expected gain is equal to the cost of search.

Before continuing let us take a critical look at Stigler's assumptions and results. The basic assumption is that the consumer knows the distribution of prices but does not know which shop posts which price. I wonder whether in real-life situations the opposite is not often true: A consumer may know which shops are expensive and which shops are cheap, but have only very vague ideas about the distribution of prices in town. If, in addition, it is well known that the expensive shops are located in this part of town and the nonexpensive shops in that part of town (as is the case in Brussels), then the assumption of independent random drawings may be questioned. Note also that, in Stigler's formulation, the gain is simply the expected reduction in price. It may be of some interest to reason in terms of increased utility as a consequence of price reductions and to generalize the analysis to multiproduct search, as in Burdett and Malueg (1981). Further insights can also be obtained by introducing a budget constraint, as in Manning and Morgan (1982), Aharon and Veendorp (1983), and Veendorp (1984).

On the other hand, Stigler started his analysis by emphasizing that price dispersion is the measure of ignorance in the market. Yet, his analysis leaves price dispersion unexplained. Section 2.3 will give some clues as to why price dispersion is related to imperfect information and about how it can be maintained over time.

Finally, Stigler's rule determines the number of searches to be made before the search actually starts. As soon as a consumer has started a shopping trip, new information becomes available. Shouldn't this new information lead to a revision of the optimal number of searches? This is the question raised by theories of sequential search.

2.1.3. *Sequential search*

Stigler notes that equalizing the expected gain and the cost of search is an unambiguous rule when a unique purchase is being made – a used grand piano. If purchases are repetitive, one has to take the evolution of prices over time into account. The initial number of searches is the only one that need be undertaken, if the correlation of asking prices of dealers over successive time periods is perfect. If it were zero, search in each period is independent of previous experience. If it is positive but not perfect, then consumer search is larger in the initial period than in subsequent periods.

Yet, these remarks should not hide the fact that Stigler's search rule determines the number of searches *prior to searching*. What he or she actually finds does not affect the number of searches, which was determined before the visits to different outlets. This supposition is unrealistic and sometimes quite silly. For example, a person who follows Stigler's rule will, even after being quoted a price less than the cost of search, keep on sampling until his or her predetermined quota of price quotations is fulfilled. Several authors (e.g., Nelson 1970 and Rothschild 1973, 1974b) have argued that Stigler's decision rule is not optimal, since it ignores the fact that the consumer can learn during a search and that a better strategy is to use the information of the search as it comes to hand.[4] The optimal rule is *sequential*: After receiving each price quotation, the consumer decides whether to continue searching or accept the quoted price.

Indeed, a consumer who knows the distribution function can recognize a good price when one presents itself. Let m therefore be redefined as the minimum price *so far observed*. Then the expected gain from another search is to be redefined as

$$E[m - x] = \int_0^m (m - x)f(x)\,dx = \int_0^m F(x)\,dx = g(m),$$

$$(2.5)$$

where the second integral is derived by integrating by parts. Now it pays to search as long as $g(m)$ is larger than the cost of search, and to stop searching as soon as a price is found that is below R, where R is the solution to

$$g(R) = \text{cost of search} \qquad (2.6)$$

(at least when the search cost is constant). The parameter R is called the reservation price, and is a function of both search costs and the shape of the distribution of prices. This reservation price is such that the searcher will accept any price less than or equal to R, but will reject a price higher than R.

Rothschild (1974b) notes that this sequential rule has the same properties as Stigler's (fixed-sample-size) rule:

1. If all its potential customers follow one of these rules, then a firm faces a well-behaved (downward-sloping) demand function.

---

[4] Nelson (1970) analyzes the case where quality information is gathered by experience rather than by search, because experience is less expensive. Experience implies evaluating quality by actual purchase rather than by search. Nelson also derives the implications of this phenomenon for the competitive structure of markets for quality goods.

2. Customers' search behavior is a function of the cost of search and the distribution of prices.
3. In particular, if the cost of search increases, the amount of search decreases. (With the sequential rule, R increases with search costs, so the intensity of search is lower.)
4. If prices become more dispersed, expected total costs decrease, because the expected minimum price as well as the reservation price decreases. Other things equal, customers prefer to draw from riskier distributions!

The sequential rule also implies that increased price dispersion increases the intensity of search.[5]

Rothschild (1974b) emphasizes that these results depend on the assumption that the consumer behaves as if he or she knew the distribution of prices. From an economic point of view, this assumption is hard to accept. How could a consumer know this distribution, when most professional economists have no idea about the actual dispersion of prices and when studies on this problem are in their infancy? On the other hand, since the sequential search rule *is* optimal, it is important to know whether it could be followed,[6] even by a person who (explicitly or implicitly) uses the wrong distribution, or more generally what a person should do when the price distribution is not known.

Rothschild (1974b) managed to derive and characterize optimal-search rules from unknown distributions. He concludes that, under special but not unreasonable assumptions, these rules have the same qualitative properties as those listed above for rules from known distributions. Without great loss, we can thus assume that rich people have a high cost of search and a high reservation price and therefore search less than poor people, who have a low cost of search and a low reservation price.

*2.2.   The noisy monopolist

A natural question is whether a seller might not deliberately use this knowledge and introduce price dispersion in order to split up the market and make price discrimination possible. Why not charge high prices to individuals who have high search costs and thus do *not* seek out the low-price outlets, while charging low prices to consumers who have low search costs, and thus do seek out the low-price outlets? This price policy would increase profits, if the submarket with high-cost con-

---

[5] Further properties are derived in Rosenfield and Shapiro (1981).
[6] Telser (1973) explores the properties of reasonable rules of thumb.

sumers is more price inelastic. And the fact of charging different prices would separate the buyers and thus make price discrimination feasible, since those who search less will stop searching at the higher price, while the others will continue their search until the lower price is found. In what he calls "the noisy monopolist," Salop (1977) analyzes the conditions under which this type of dispersion is profitable. Note that it appears in practice under the disguise of unadvertised specials, random sales, changes in packaging, and so on.

Since he wants to determine the noise to be created as the solution of an optimal control problem, Salop starts by reformulating the theory of sequential search in a way that facilitates the use of optimal control techniques. The stopping rule defined by equation (2.6) requires that an optimal reservation price $\hat{R}$ be found such that any price less than or equal to it is accepted, and no further search occurs. Salop finds this reservation price by minimizing the expected cost of buying 1 unit of a commodity; that is,

$$\pi = p(R) + \sigma(R)c \tag{2.7}$$

with respect to R. The expected purchase price is denoted $p(R)$, $\sigma(R)$ is the expected number of searches, and c is the (constant) unit search cost. Differentiating π with respect to R gives

$$p'(R) + \sigma'(R)c = 0 \tag{2.8}$$

or

$$-p'(\hat{R}) = \sigma'(\hat{R})c.$$

This result has the same interpretation as equation (2.6). The value of $\hat{R}$ must be such that the expected marginal gain of search $(-p'(R))$ is equal to the marginal cost of search $(\sigma'(\hat{R})c)$. In other words, $\hat{R}$ must be such that a small change in it decreases the expected purchase price and increases search costs by equal amounts.

The noise to be created is measured by the number of searches, which is therefore treated as the control variable, whereas the total cost of a purchase, π, is treated as a state variable. Both depend on c, and so does $\hat{R}$. Let us then differentiate π with respect to c, to find

$$\pi'(c) = p' \frac{d\hat{R}}{dc} + \sigma' \frac{d\hat{R}}{dc} c + \sigma$$

$$= (p' + \sigma'c) \frac{d\hat{R}}{dc} + \sigma$$

$$= s(c) \geq 0 \tag{2.9}$$

using the fact that, at the consumer's equilibrium, $p' + \sigma'c = 0$ according to equations (2.8) and redefining σ as $s(c)$ to stress that, again at the consumer's equilibrium, the number of searches depends on c (through $\hat{R}$). Although $s(c)$ is positive, its derivative is negative, or

$$\pi''(c) = s'(c) \leq 0. \tag{2.10}$$

Salop's idea is to use these two properties of consumer search as constraints on the seller's pricing policy. Constraint (2.9) says that the increase in total cost, as a result of an increase in search cost, just equals the number of searches; constraint (2.10) says that total cost rises with search costs at a decreasing rate.

Of course, the seller receives only $p(c) = \pi(c) - s(c)c$. (Indeed, $\pi(c)$ is analogous to a delivered price in spatial economics, and the total search cost $s(c)c$ implied in the purchase of 1 unit of the good is analogous to a transport cost paid by the buyer. $p(c)$ is thus the net price received by the seller, equal to the asking price.)

The seller will want to choose the price $p(c)$, the number of searches $s(c)$, and the total cost $\pi(c)$ which maximize profits. To do that, the seller must act in accordance with the conditions of consumer equilibrium, that is, equations (2.8) to (2.10). On the other hand, these conditions facilitate the task, since the seller has to maximize only with respect to the number of searches $s(c)$ – the noise to be created. This number is determined by $\pi'(c)$, which can be obtained by differentiating the profit-maximizing $\pi(c)$. The difference between $\pi(c)$ and $s(c)c$ finally gives $p(c)$. More formally, $s(c)$ thus appears as the only control variable in the following optimal control problem:

$$\max_{s(c)} \int_0^z [\pi(c) - s(c)c]X(\pi(c), c) \, dc$$

subject to $\pi'(c) = s(c)$,

$$s'(c) \leq 0,$$

$$\pi(c), s(c) \geq 0. \tag{2.11}$$

In this formulation, c is supposed to vary between zero and some maximum z. Consumers with search cost c are supposed to have a gross demand function $X(\pi(c), c)$, which has both $\pi(c)$ and c arguments.

The solution[7] implies, inter alia, that if the seller forces type c consumers to search, the marginal value of an increase in their data-gath-

---

[7] The reader should consult Salop (1977) for a more rigorous discussion of the problem and of the solution. $\lambda(c)$ is the costate variable, and $\pi(c)$ is the state variable. The cost of production is ignored for simplicity.

ering time $\lambda(c)$ equals the marginal deadweight loss of the search time cX. Indeed, the Hamiltonian is

$$\mathcal{H} = (\pi - sc)X - \lambda(\pi' - s)$$

and the Pontryagin conditions are $\partial \mathcal{H}/\partial s = 0$, which imply $-cX + \lambda = 0$ or

$$\lambda(c) = cX, \tag{2.12}$$

and $\lambda'(c) = \partial \mathcal{H}/\partial \pi$ or

$$\lambda'(c) = -[(\pi - sc)X_\pi + X] \tag{2.13}$$

where $X_\pi = \partial X/\partial \pi$. The right side of (2.13) is the marginal revenue of increasing p.

To find the profit-maximizing $\pi(c)$, we combine equations (2.12) and (2.13) in the following way. Differentiate (2.12) to get

$$\lambda'(c) = X + cX_c + cX_\pi \pi'(c) \tag{2.14}$$

and set this equation equal to (2.13), recalling that $\pi'(c) = s$. This gives

$$2X + \pi X_\pi + cX_c = 0 \tag{2.15}$$

which describes the profit-maximizing $\pi(c)$.

To illustrate, Salop specifies the demand function as

$$X(\pi, c) = \alpha - \beta\pi + \gamma c,$$

where $\alpha > 0$, $-\beta = X_\pi$, and $\gamma = X_c$. Substituting into equation (2.15), we obtain

$$2[\alpha - \beta\pi + \gamma c] - \beta\pi + \gamma c = 0$$

and

$$\pi(c) = \frac{2}{3}\frac{\alpha}{\beta} + \frac{\gamma}{\beta}c.$$

Differentiating with respect to c, we have

$$s(c) \equiv \pi'(c) = \frac{\gamma}{\beta}, \qquad \text{a constant.}$$

Since $s(c)$ must be nonnegative, it is clear that a necessary condition for this sort of price dispersion, based on noise, is that $\gamma > 0$ (i.e., that demand rises with unit search costs). This implies that at any price π, there are more high-cost (rich) customers than low-cost (poor) customers, with the result that price elasticity declines with increases in unit search costs.[8] The seller then wishes to charge a higher price to buyers with more inelastic demand.

2.3.   Market equilibrium

In a market with many sellers and free entry, the informational asymmetry about prices leads to two typical outcomes. First, it explains why different sellers charge different prices for the same commodity. Those who search more get a better price, and vice versa, hence the title "Bargains and Ripoffs" of the pioneering paper by Salop and Stiglitz (summarized in Salop 1976). Second, it creates an incentive for the sellers to organize sales of a limited duration from time to time and to substantially reduce prices during these periods.

2.3.1.   Price dispersion

Let there be n firms (n may be very large) producing a physically homogeneous commodity. Differences in the geographical location of the firms lead to price uncertainty on the demand side. Each producer has the same fixed cost and the same increasing marginal cost of production, so they all have the same U-shaped average cost function with a minimum at p^*. There are L potential customers, each with the same given reservation price R^*. They are thus ready to purchase 1 unit of the commodity at any price smaller than R^*. However, the effective purchase depends on the search cost, which determines the minimum price below which they stop searching.

If information were perfect and if there were only one seller, the monopoly price p^m would be $p^m = R^*$. With free entry, the price would fall to its competitive level p^*. With imperfect information on the demand side, the market equilibrium has three properties: (a) There is price dispersion – there are k different equilibrium prices $\hat{p}_1, \hat{p}_2, \dots,$ $\hat{p}_k$, each charged by a proportion $\beta_1, \beta_2, \dots, \beta_k$ of the total number of firms; (b) each firm maximizes its own profit, given its demand curve (whose slope is determined by the behavior of its customers and of its competitors); (c) no new firm wishes to enter the market, so realized profits are zero. Figure 2.1 depicts such an equilibrium, with $\hat{p}_1 = p^*$ and $\hat{p}_k \leq R^* = p^m$.

To demonstrate this, consider a special case in which the information structure is drastically simplified: Suppose the L customers know the prices and the corresponding proportions β, but do not know which

---

[8] A linear demand curve that shifts upward becomes less price elastic at any given price. This is what a positive γ does.

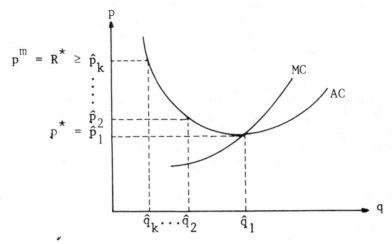

Figure 2.1. Equilibrium price dispersion.

firm charges which price. Suppose furthermore that with a search cost c_i, consumers belonging to group i obtain *perfect* information.[9] Finally, there are only two groups of customers ($i = 1, 2$): A proportion α has a cost $c_1 \geq 0$, and the rest $(1 - \alpha)$ incur a cost c_2 strictly larger than c_1.

Notice that if $c_1 = c_2 = 0$, there will be a unique equilibrium price equal to p^*. Notice also that if $c_1 = 0$ and α is large, that is, if there is a large group of perfectly informed consumers, one can also have a unique equilibrium price equal to p^*, notwithstanding the fact that c_2 is positive. For the informed, α group produces an information externality, in the sense that the badly informed do not need to bother about getting informed.

Suppose therefore that both groups have a positive cost ($c_1 > 0$ and $c_2 > c_1$). First of all, an equilibrium at the unique price p^* is impossible, because any firm could raise its price somewhat above p^* without losing any customer. A unique equilibrium price remains a possibility, though, but only if both costs were prohibitive for the customers (any price $\bar{p}$ such that $\bar{p} - p^* \leq c_1 < c_2$). Otherwise, the equilibrium will imply *two* prices. The α group is paying $p_1 = p^*$, because its members will want to obtain perfect information as soon as $p_1 - p^* > c_1$ and will buy only at the lowest price, with free entry, so p_1 must be equal to p^* at equilibrium. The low price p_1 is charged by some proportion

---

[9] In contradiction with search theory, really!

(say β) of firms. The other firms can charge a higher price p_2 as long as $1 - \alpha$ of the population remains uninformed; that is, as long as $p_2 - p_1 < c_2$ or $p_2 < p^* + c_2 \leq p^m = R^*$ and α is small enough. However, these firms will attract only a proportion $1 - \beta$ of the uninformed, because a proportion β of the uninformed customers will do business with a low-price firm by pure chance.

What if there are more than two types of information costs (i.e., more than two types of customers)? You might think there will be more than two prices at equilibrium. This is wrong, as long as each of these costs gives access to *perfect* information: Whoever decides to incur a cost (of whatever size) gets perfectly informed and will request a price as low as p^*; whoever finds the cost prohibitive (whatever its size) gets no information. With access to perfect information, there cannot be more than two groups at equilibrium, one group buying at p_1, and the others buying at price p_1 if they are lucky and otherwise at some price $p_2 < p^m$.

It is only when positive search costs do not lead to perfect information that there will be as many prices as types of customers at equilibrium, as is the case when consumers go on a "shopping tour" (in the Salop–Stiglitz model, there is no shopping, really) and learn progressively in visiting a number of shops. Price dispersion with more than two prices is the equilibrium result in models by Butters (1977), who supposes that information is transmitted by advertising, and by Schwartz and Wilde (1979, 1982a), who introduce shopping explicitly. The role of informational intermediation is studied in Hänchen and von Ungern-Sternberg (1985).

2.3.2. Sales

Implicit in the foregoing discussion is the idea that, once an equilibrium price dispersion is reached, it will persist over time. One may then wonder how such a persistence can be justified. Consumers can go on shopping tours repeatedly, talk to other consumers, and thus learn which shops consistently have low prices. Persistence of price differences then seems implausible. It would be plausible only if consumers were prevented from learning by experience, that is, if the high-price image of a shop was blurred over time. One way of obtaining this result is to have sales from time to time. Paradoxically, perhaps, price differences could thus persist over time as the result of a marketing device which consists in organizing sales of limited duration.

Varian (1980, p. 651) makes this point in the following words:

Most of the models of price dispersion referred to above are concerned with analyzing "spatial" price dispersion; that is, a situation where several stores contemporaneously offer an identical item at different prices. [. . .]

In the Salop and Stiglitz model – as in all the models of spatial price dispersion – some stores are supposed to *persistently* sell their product at a lower price than other stores. If consumers can learn from experience, this persistence of price dispersion seems rather implausible.

An alternative type of price dispersion might be called "temporal" price dispersion. In a market exhibiting temporal price dispersion, we would see each store varying its price over time. At any moment, a cross section of the market would exhibit price dispersion; but because of the intentional fluctuations in price, consumers cannot learn by experience about stores that consistently have low prices, and hence price dispersion may be expected to persist.

One does not have to look far to find the real world analog of such behavior. It is common to observe retail markets where stores deliberately change their prices over time – that is, where stores have *sales*. A casual glance at the daily newspaper indicates that such behavior is very common. A high percentage of advertising seems to be directed at informing people of limited duration sales of food, clothing, and appliances.

Varian suggests to model these sales as a strategy where stores randomize their prices. Suppose each store has to fix one price each week (it advertises this price in the weekly newspaper). The randomization then consists in choosing this price at random from a density function which gives the probability of drawing a particular price. And the problem is to characterize this density function at equilibrium, on the assumption that it is the same for each store and that each store follows the same strategy.

To solve this problem, Varian uses the same basic assumptions about the structure of the market as do Salop and Stiglitz (1977), except that, since the analysis refers to retail trade, the n firms are now stores characterized by identical, strictly declining average cost curves. Indeed, retail stores typically have fixed costs of rent and sales force plus constant variable costs, the wholesale price, of the item being sold. Otherwise the commodity is supposed to be homogeneous, and all consumers have the same reservation price R^*. They desire to purchase at most 1 unit.

Again, there are two types of consumers, the uninformed and the informed. The uninformed choose a store at random and purchase the good if its price is less than R^*. The informed go to the store with the lowest price and purchase there, since they know which store charges which price: I is the number of informed consumers, and M is the number of uninformed consumers. The number of uninformed consumers per store is therefore $U = M/n$.

Each store has the same pricing strategy, that is, advertises a price p chosen at random from a density function $f(p)$ in the weekly newspaper. The informed consumers read this newspaper, and the uninformed consumers do not. The sale is "successful" if the advertised price turns out to be the lowest of the n prices being offered: The store attracts $I + U$ customers. Otherwise this store gets only its share U of the uninformed: The sale is a "failure." There is a "tie" if two or more stores happen to advertise the lowest price, and these each get an equal share of the informed customers.

What is the equilibrium density function from which each store will draw its price? The answer to this question will indicate which prices are likely to be drawn: Will these be the highest possible, the lowest possible, some average price, or the highest and the lowest possible? Equilibrium is again characterized by zero profits, because entry occurs until profits are driven to zero.

Notice, first, that no price above the reservation price will be charged, because demand is zero at that price. On the other hand, the lowest possible price is the one that is equal to the average cost incurred with the largest possible quantities sold, $q = I + U$. The total cost curve being $c(q)$, this average cost is $c(I + U)/(I + U)$. Let the lowest price be $p^* = c(I + U)/(I + U)$. Any price below p^* would result in negative profits.

Notice also that, at equilibrium, all stores cannot charge the same price. If all were charging a price larger than p^*, one store could deviate, attract all the informed customers, and make a profit. If all were charging p^*, all would make a negative profit. Indeed, p^* is the cost associated with the *maximum* number of customers a store could get, whereas under the present assumption each store would get a smaller number (an equal share) and therefore incur a larger cost.

In models of "spatial" price dispersion of the Salop–Stiglitz type, several stores typically charge the same price at equilibrium: There is a positive probability of a tie. In the present model, each store's equilibrium strategy on the contrary involves zero probability of a tie.[10] The intuition is as follows. If a store could charge a slightly lower price, say $p - \epsilon$, with the same probability with which other stores charged p, it would make a profit (if ϵ is small) when the other stores tie. This is not compatible with equilibrium. The implication is that we can work

---

[10] In technical terms, there are no "point masses" in the equilibrium pricing strategies. A price p is a point mass of a density function $f(p)$ if there is positive probability concentrated at p.

with a continuous cumulative distribution function $F(p)$ such that $f(p) = F'(p)$.

The expected profit of a store is thus an integral defined over the values p can take, namely the interval (p^*, R^*), with as arguments the profits in case of a successful sale or a failure, weighted by their probabilities. If the sale at price p is a success, the store gets $U + I$ customers and its profit is $\Pi_s = p(U + I) - c(U + I)$. Success implies that all other stores charge prices higher than p, an event which has probability $(1 - F(p))^{n-1}$. If the sale is a failure, the store only attracts U customers and its profit is $\Pi_f = pU - c(U)$. The associated probability is $1 - (1 - F(p))^{n-1}$, the probability that p is higher than the lowest price.

The maximization of the expected profit implies

$$\Pi_s(1 - F(p))^{n-1} + \Pi_f[1 - (1 - F(p))^{n-1}] = 0$$

when $f(p) > 0$, or

$$(\Pi_f - \Pi_s)(1 - F(p))^{n-1} = \Pi_f,$$

or

$$F(p) = 1 - \left(\frac{\Pi_f}{\Pi_f - \Pi_s}\right)^{1/(n-1)}.$$

The equilibrium density function is the derivative of this function. It can be computed as soon as the profit functions are specified.

Varian gives the following example. Suppose the stores' cost function has fixed cost k and zero marginal cost. Then $\Pi_s = p(I + U) - k$ and $\Pi_f = pU - k$, so $\Pi_f - \Pi_s = -pI$ and

$$F(p) = 1 - \left(\frac{k - pU}{pI}\right)^{1/(n-1)}.$$

This expression can be rewritten in terms of p and R^* if we remember that the profit is zero when $p = R^*$, or $R^*U - k = 0$, so $U = k/R^*$. (Since $U = M/n$, we then also have $n = R^*M/k$.)

The distribution function can now be written as

$$F(p) = 1 - \left(\frac{k - pk/R^*}{pI}\right)^{1/(n-1)}$$

or as

$$F(p) = 1 - \left[\frac{k}{I}\left(\frac{1}{p} - \frac{1}{R^*}\right)\right]^{1/(n-1)}.$$

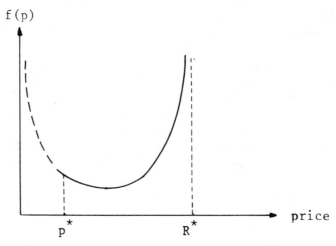

Figure 2.2. Graph of $f(p) = 1/p(1 - p/R^*)$.

The equilibrium density function is the derivative of this distribution function, that is,

$$f(p) = F'(p) = \frac{(k/I)^{1/(n-1)}}{n-1} \frac{(1/p - 1/R^*)^{1/(n-1)-1}}{p^2}$$

$$= \left[\frac{k(k/I)^{1-m}}{(R^*M - k)} \right] \frac{1}{p^{2-m}(1 - p/R^*)^m},$$

if we let

$$m = 1 - \frac{1}{n-1} = \frac{n-2}{n-1} = \frac{R^*M - 2k}{R^*M - k}$$

so that

$$\frac{1}{n-1} = \frac{k}{R^*M - k}.$$

For a large number of stores, n is large and m is approximately 1, so the equilibrium density function is proportional to $1/p(1 - p/R^*)$. It is illustrated in Figure 2.2. Its striking feature is that the probability for stores to charge extreme prices (very high or very low) is higher than the probability for stores to charge intermediate prices. This is plausible, because stores would like to charge informed customers p^* and charge uninformed customers R^*. Varian (1980, p. 658) concludes

The form of the resulting pricing strategy as given in Figure [2.2] does not seem out of line with commonly observed retailing behavior. Large retail chains such as Sears and Roebuck and Montgomery Ward sell appliances at their regular price much of the time, but often have sales when the price is reduced by as much as 25 percent. However, we rarely observe them selling an appliance at an intermediate price. Although this casual empiricism can hardly be conclusive, it suggests that the features of the model described here may have some relevance in explaining real world retailing behavior.

2.4.*   Oligopoly and consumer search

The implications of imperfect information about prices are rather well understood, when sellers are many, that is, when the market is characterized by monopolistic competition. What if sellers are few? Do the same conclusions carry over to oligopolistic markets? In particular, will price uncertainty also lead to price dispersion? What is the impact of search on the geographical concentration of the sellers in equilibrium? Studies analyzing the oligopolistic equilibria that emerge are themselves few and based on rather extreme assumptions. This is not surprising, since new ground has to be explored at each step.

The modeling can be done in a number of ways. A natural starting point is to suppose that there are just two firms and that they are producing a homogeneous commodity, to make sure that if, in equilibrium, a price difference (price dispersion) were to show up, this dispersion could not be explained away by product differentiation.

When sellers are many (monopolistic competition), it is natural to postulate a U-shaped average cost curve, the same for each firm (see Section 2.3), in order to derive a zero-profit industry equilibrium. Here we are looking for a noncooperative Nash equilibrium with positive profits. If the duopolists were producing for inventory, it would be essential to suppose U-shaped average cost curves, implying increasing marginal production costs at equilibrium, so the carrying of inventories may affect the equilibrium prices.[11] When the quantities sold are equal to the quantities produced, as assumed here, not much seems to be lost when marginal costs are assumed constant or zero.

On the demand side, the first thing to do is to postulate an information structure. It seems wise to keep this information structure as simple as possible, and to avoid complicated sequential search behavior and corresponding stopping rules. In the present state of the art, it is preferable to stick to some simple price search model and to adopt a de-

---

[11] On this, see Phlips and Richard (1986).

cision rule saying, for example, that a consumer will buy from the duopolist with the lowest price, taking search costs into account.

The information structure and the decision rule may be symmetric or not. It is symmetric when consumers do not discriminate between the two firms a priori and when there are no systematic differences in the information the consumers have about the two firms. In Nermuth's words (1982, p. 71), this

excludes "goodwill", in the sense that the household *prefers*, cet. par., to buy from, say, store 1 rather than from any other store. It also excludes the possibility that there may exist more or less "obscure" firms, in the sense that all households are relatively better informed about the price, say, at store one than about store two (the "obscure" store).

In the absence of symmetry, the

households may be better informed about one firm than about another, and/ or their decision rule may exhibit some bias, reflecting, for example, the good reputation of a certain firm . . . the average potential customer will probably have a less accurate idea about the price and quality standards of an obscure restaurant in some dark street than about one in the main square, etc. (p. 90).

Biased decision rules may be due to pure prejudice or to a better location or some other advantage. In a spatial context, where each consumer has a given location and the two duopolists are located at some distance from each other, asymmetries of this sort naturally arise: A customer will more easily get information about and may have a positive bias for the seller that is closest to his or her own location.

Finally, one has to model demand. One possibility is to give each customer a continuous demand function which determines the quantity he or she will buy after having chosen one of the two firms. The alternative is to suppose that each customer buys at most 1 unit of the commodity. The latter assumption is particularly handsome in spatial models. If, for example, there is one customer located at each point in space (a flat distribution), then the number of customers who patronize a particular firm is equal to the total quantity sold by that firm. This assumption is at the heart of the so-called Hotelling model.

2.4.1. Information structures and oligopoly

Nermuth (1982, chaps. 4–6) chose to work with continuous demand functions. Given two firms producing a homogeneous commodity at zero cost, Nermuth considers both symmetric and asymmetric information and decision structures.

On the assumption, in the symmetric case, that all customers have the same downward-sloping demand function $f(p_j)$, where j is the firm of choice, Nermuth writes the profit of this firm simply as

$$\Pi_j = B(p_j)N_j(p_1, p_2) \tag{2.16}$$

where $B(p_j) = p_j f(p_j)$ and $N_j(p_1, p_2)$ is its expected number of customers and also its market share, the total number of customers being normalized to 1. In fact, B is the profit per customer. If the firm had the monopoly of the market, its price would be determined by equating the first derivative of B, B', to zero. Under perfect competition, the price would be zero, with the implication that B would also be zero. The symmetry assumption implies that $N_j(p_1, p_2) = \frac{1}{2}$. Even without making the information and decision structure explicit, one can immediately see that there exists a unique symmetric equilibrium at which each duopolist charges the same price p^*, which must lie between the monopoly price (p^m) and the competitive price (p^c) and is defined by

$$\Pi'_j(p^*) = B'(p^*)N_j(p^*) + B(p^*)N'_j(p^*) = 0$$

$$(j = 1, 2). \tag{2.17}$$

Indeed $\Pi'_j(p^c) = \frac{1}{2}B'(p_c)$ is positive and $\Pi'_j(p^m)$ is negative. A deviation from p^* can never be profitable.

Of course, the information and decision structures can be made explicit. Nermuth supposes, for example, that the prices are signaled with an evenly distributed error ϵ, which is the same for all firms and all consumers, to arrive at the same type of unique equilibrium price, which tends to the competitive price if $\epsilon \to 0$ (perfect information) as $n \to \infty$ (many firms) and to the monopoly price as $\epsilon \to \infty$ (no information). However, when different consumers have differing error margins, which are still symmetric with respect to firms, and if these errors differ enough (so that, in the limit, some have perfect information and others have no information), then no equilibrium exists. Basically, this follows from the fact that with zero production costs (or constant unit costs) each firm could profitably deviate from a unique price.[12]

The main interest of these results is to indicate that if one wants to derive equilibria with price dispersion one should introduce some asymmetry in the information structure with respect to firms. When he postulates that consumers are better informed about one firm than about the other, Nermuth (1982, chap. 6) indeed finds that a price

---

[12] Note that, in the monopolistic competition case discussed in Section 2.3, a (zero-profit) equilibrium at the competitive price exists when a large number of customers is perfectly informed, because a price increase implies higher costs and price differences between firms are limited by the cost of search.

dispersion equilibrium may exist. The "obscure" firm charges a higher price, except possibly if consumers have an a priori prejudice in favor of one firm.

The needed assumptions and the proofs are too technical for my present purpose. Rather than trying to simplify these, I prefer to abandon the assumption of continuous demand curves and follow the alternative route, which is simpler, easier to visualize, and allows a spatial interpretation. It supposes that each consumer buys 1 unit of the commodity, has a particular location, and is therefore closer to one of the two firms. Asymmetry of the information structure with respect to firms thus arises quite naturally.

2.4.2. The Hotelling model

It is well known that a spatial approach facilitates the analysis of oligopolistic equilibria.[13] Giving the oligopolists and their customers a particular location in space has the advantage of concreteness and makes it easier to visualize what is going on. In addition, a reinterpretation in terms of quality differentiation is often possible, with geographical locations corresponding to different varieties of a commodity so that the choice of a location corresponds to the choice of a particular brand, for example. Hotelling's seminal 1929 paper "Stability in Competition" is based on this idea. Since many recent contributions still explicitly refer to it, it may be worthwhile to start with a brief presentation of what has become known as "the" Hotelling model.

Hotelling supposes that the customers of an homogeneous commodity are evenly distributed along a line of length L. There are two sellers: firm 1 and firm 2. They produce the commodity at zero cost and are located at respective distances a and b from the ends of this line (see Figure 2.3). Each customer buys 1 unit of the commodity from the firm, whose mill price (p_1 or p_2) is such that the sum of this price plus the "cost of transportation" to the customer's location is the smallest. The cost of transportation per unit of distance is c. (In Hotelling's presentation, this cost represents the dissatisfaction of having to buy a variety of the commodity that differs from the preferred one, which is defined by the customer's location. It can be interpreted as the cost incurred by the customer when it is the latter who takes care of the actual transportation, as is the case when a customer has to drive to a shopping center.[14] Figure 2.3 represents the situation with given locations of the two firms and two prices such that their difference is

[13] See the Symposium on Spatial Competition and the Theory of Differentiated Markets in the *Journal of Industrial Economics*, 31, September–December 1982.

[14] Pricing is then done on a "fob-mill" basis. On this, see my 1983 book *Economics of Price Discrimination*.

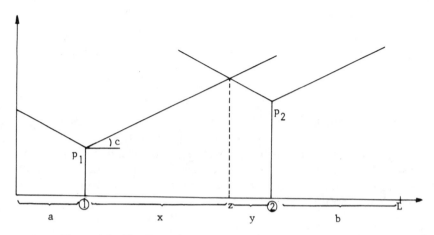

Figure 2.3. The Hotelling model.

smaller than the total transportation cost between the two locations
($|p_1 - p_2| \le c(L - a - b)$).

The customers located at point z are indifferent between buying from
firm 1 at price p_1 and buying from firm 2 at price p_2. This point is at
distance x from firm 1 and at distance y from firm 2. Since, at z,

$$p_1 + cx = p_2 + cy \tag{2.18}$$

while $L = a + b + x + y$, it follows that

$$x = \frac{1}{2}\left(L - a - b + \frac{p_2 - p_1}{c}\right),$$

$$y = \frac{1}{2}\left(L - a - b + \frac{p_1 - p_2}{c}\right). \tag{2.19}$$

Consequently, the profits of the two firms are

$$\Pi_1 = p_1 q_1 = p_1(a + x) = \frac{1}{2}(L + a - b)p_1 - \frac{p_1^2}{2c} + \frac{p_1 p_2}{2c},$$

$$\Pi_2 = p_2 q_2 = p_2(b + y) = \frac{1}{2}(L - a + b)p_2 - \frac{p_2^2}{2c} + \frac{p_1 p_2}{2c}.$$

$$\tag{2.20}$$

Putting the first partial derivatives $\partial\Pi_1/\partial p_1$ and $\partial\Pi_2/\partial p_2$ equal to zero,
one finds the (Nash) equilibrium prices

$$p_1^* = c\left(L + \frac{a - b}{3}\right), \quad p_2^* = c\left(L - \frac{a - b}{3}\right) \tag{2.21}$$

and the equilibrium quantities sold

$$q_1^* = a + x = \frac{1}{2}\left(L + \frac{a - b}{3}\right),$$

$$q_2^* = b + y = \frac{1}{2}\left(L - \frac{a - b}{3}\right). \quad (2.22)$$

With symmetric locations (that is, $a = b$) the two equilibrium prices are equal, and each firm serves half of the market.

From here, Hotelling determines the optimal locations a^* and b^* by inserting the equilibrium prices and quantities in the profit functions and determining the values of a and b that give the highest profits. The equilibrium profits are

$$\Pi_1^* = p_1^* q_1^* = \frac{1}{2}c\left(L + \frac{a - b}{3}\right)^2,$$

$$\Pi_2^* = p_2^* q_2^* = \frac{1}{2}c\left(L + \frac{b - a}{3}\right)^2 \quad (2.23)$$

and $\partial\Pi_2^*/\partial b = c(L + (b - a)/3)/3$, for example. This derivative is positive for any value of a and b (and increasing in b). The same is true for $\partial\Pi_1^*/\partial a$ (which is increasing in a). Clearly, it is in each firm's interest to increase its distance from the end of the line and to locate in the center. (In terms of product differentiation, this means that both firms find it profitable to put close varieties on the market. Hotelling therefore calls this result the principle of minimum differentiation.)

However, Hotelling's reasoning is erroneous in that it supposes equilibrium prices to exist for any value of a and b. D'Aspremont, Gabszewicz, and Thisse (1979) pointed this out and derived the necessary and sufficient conditions for an equilibrium to exist. They show that, if the two firms are located in the same point, that is, for $a + b = L$, the only equilibrium point is $p_1^* = p_2^* = 0$. For $a + b < L$, an equilibrium exists if and only if a and b are such that

$$\left(L + \frac{a - b}{3}\right)^2 \geq \frac{4}{3}L(a + 2b),$$

$$\left(L + \frac{b - a}{3}\right)^2 \geq \frac{4}{3}L(b + 2a). \quad (2.24)$$

When the locations are such that these conditions are met, then the unique equilibrium implies the prices derived in equations (2.21).

Notice that, with symmetric locations (that is, $a = b$), the inequalities (2.24) reduce to $a = b \leq L/4$. In general, therefore, Hotelling's equilibrium can be valid only for locations *away* from the center, so his principle of minimum differentiation is not valid. On the other hand, under conditions (2.24) $\partial \Pi_1^* / \partial a$ and $\partial \Pi_2^* / \partial b$ remain positive, so firms will tend to move toward the center; thus no simultaneous equilibrium of prices *and* locations is possible in the Hotelling model.

2.4.3. Price dispersion

How does one have to modify the model just described in order to be able to study the effects of imperfect price information? Gabszewicz and Garella (1987) suggest the following very simple information structure. There are two shops with different locations, as in Figure 2.3. The consumers know their average price, but do not know which shop quotes which price. In order to identify the individual prices, they must contact the shops. No shop has the reputation of being cheaper than the other, so the probability of observing a particular price is the same. The asymmetry in the information therefore arises only from the fact that one shop's location is closer to a particular customer. To minimize search costs, a consumer first solicits the shop that is closest to him or her.

Let t denote a particular customer on the line. The assumption just made then implies formally that all customers located between zero and $(L + a - b)/2$, which defines the point halfway between the location of shop 1 and the location of shop 2, will first call shop 1. All customers located between $(L + a - b)/2$ and L will first canvass shop 2.

To accentuate the asymmetry, suppose further that the visit to the closest shop is costless, but to canvass the other shop implies a cost $c(t)$ equal to

$$c(t) = \begin{cases} c[(L - b) - t] & \text{if } 0 \le t < \dfrac{L + a - b}{2}, \\ \\ c(t - a) & \text{if } \dfrac{L + a - b}{2} \le t \le L. \end{cases} \qquad (2.25)$$

The cost per unit of distance, c, is thus reinterpreted as the cost of placing an order. Consequently, firms are supposed to deliver the commodity at home at no cost.

The decision rule is then, for consumer t, to buy from shop 1 if this consumer is located to the left of $(L + a - b)/2$ and if $p_1 \le p_2 + c(L - b - t)$. A consumer t located at or to the right of $(L + a - b)/2$ buys from shop 2 if $p_2 \le p_1 + c(t - a)$. Consumers can compute these

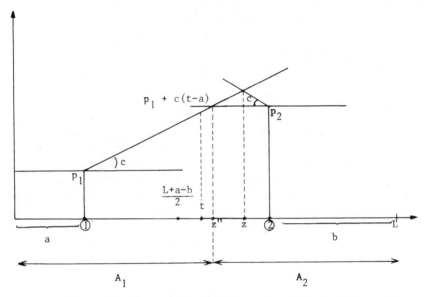

Figure 2.4. Asymmetric price information in the Hotelling model.

inequalities, because as soon as the price of one shop is known the price of the other shop is also known (given that the average price was known from the start). Visiting the closest shop thus provides perfect price information. Strictly speaking, no search costs are incurred.

Figure 2.4 represents the situation of a consumer t located to the right of $(L + a - b)/2$ and, thus, closer to shop 2, who finds it nevertheless profitable to buy from firm 1. In the situation depicted, the demand for shop 2 is equal to the interval A_2. For the consumer located at z'', $p_2 = p_1 + c(z'' - a)$; hence,

$$z'' = \frac{p_2 - p_1 + ac}{c}.$$

The demand for shop 2 is equal to interval A_1 or z''. If p_1 were higher than p_2, keeping the same value of c, the reverse could happen, with interval A_1 smaller than $(L + a - b)/2$ and extending until $p_1 = p_2 + c(L - b - z')$, that is, until

$$z' = \frac{p_2 - p_1 + c(L - b)}{c}.$$

In general, all consumers to the right of $(L + a - b)/2$ would buy at shop 2 if z'' coincided with $(L + a - b)/2$, or

$$\frac{p_2 - p_1 + ac}{c} = \frac{L + a - b}{2}, \tag{2.26}$$

that is, if the price of shop 1 (solving equation (2.26) for p_1) is equal to or higher than

$$\overline{p}_1 = p_2 - \frac{c(L - a - b)}{2}. \tag{2.27}$$

Similarly, all consumers to the left of $(L + a - b)/2$ would buy at shop 1 if

$$\frac{p_2 - p_1 + c(L - b)}{c} = \frac{L + a - b}{2}, \tag{2.28}$$

that is, if the price of shop 1 is equal to or lower than

$$\overline{\overline{p}}_1 = p_2 + \frac{c(L - a - b)}{2}. \tag{2.29}$$

In other words, as long as, given p_2, p_1 is between $\overline{p}_1$ and $\overline{\overline{p}}_1$, demand for shop 1 is equal to $(L + a - b)/2$ and totally inelastic to p_1. A similar analysis can be done for p_2, given p_1. It gives

$$\overline{p}_2 = p_1 - \frac{c(L - a - b)}{2} \tag{2.30}$$

and

$$\overline{\overline{p}}_2 = p_1 + \frac{c(L - a - b)}{2}. \tag{2.31}$$

The resulting demand curve and the corresponding revenue function for shop 1 are depicted in Figure 2.5. The revenue has a linear segment connecting two quadratic parts.

We are looking for a Nash equilibrium in prices. Such an equilibrium is defined as the pair (p_1^*, p_2^*) such that $R_1(p_1^*, p_2^*) \geq R_1(p_1, p_2^*)$ for all p_1 and $R_2(p_1^*, p_2^*) \geq R_2(p_1^*, p_2)$ for all p_2. If it exists, it implies that p_1^* is different from p_2^*. At equilibrium, there must be price dispersion.

It is clear that the two equilibrium prices cannot lie in the ranges where the two demand curves are flat, because the highest prices are revenue maximizing, or $p_1^* = p_2^* + c(L - a - b)/2$ and simultaneously $p_2^* = p_1^* + c(L - a - b)/2$ (see equations (2.29) and (2.31)), which

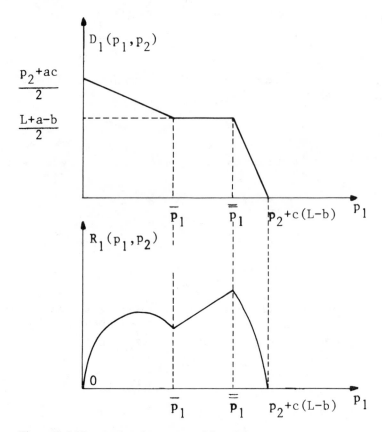

Figure 2.5. Demand and revenue of firm 1.

is impossible. Similar contradictions result when one price lies in the flat range on one demand curve and the other lies outside the flat range on the other curve, or if the two prices lie above $\bar{\bar{p}}_1$ and $\bar{p}_2$, respectively, or below $\bar{p}_1$ and $\bar{p}_2$, respectively.

Consequently, the equilibrium prices must be such that either

(I) $p_1^* < \bar{p}_1$ and $p_2^* > \bar{\bar{p}}_2$

or

(II) $p_1^* > \bar{\bar{p}}_1$ and $p_2^* < \bar{p}_2$.

To find these equilibrium prices, one has to maximize the revenues simultaneously. When the equilibrium is of type I, p_1^* is the lower price, so z'' is the demand of shop 1 and $L - z''$ is the demand for shop 2.

The equilibrium prices must then solve the system

$$\underset{p_1}{\text{Max}} \left(\frac{p_2^* - p_1 + ac}{c} \right) p_1,$$

$$\underset{p_2}{\text{Max}} \left(L - \frac{p_2 - p_1^* + ac}{c} \right) p_2 \tag{2.32}$$

since $z'' = (p_2 - p_1 + ac)/c$. Putting the first derivatives equal to zero and solving the two-equation system gives

$$\text{(I)} \quad p_1^* = \frac{c}{3}(L + a), \qquad p_2^* = \frac{c(2L - a)}{3}. \tag{2.33}$$

When the equilibrium is of type II (z' and $L - z'$ are the respective demands), the first-order conditions give

$$\text{(II)} \quad p_1^* = \frac{c(2L - b)}{3}, \qquad p_2^* = \frac{c}{3}(L + b). \tag{2.34}$$

Notice that an equilibrium of type II is simply an equilibrium of type I with a replaced by b.

Comparing these equilibrium prices of types I and II with those of the original Hotelling model, given in equations (2.21), we see that the former are systematically lower. Paradoxically, perhaps, imperfect information may thus lead to lower prices. This occurs because c is reduced to zero for any consumer who canvasses the shop closest to his or her location (see the two horizontal lines at levels p_1 and p_2 in Figure 2.4). Hence the appearance of a flat segment in the demand functions of the two shops, so either $p_1^* < \bar{p}_1$ or $p_2^* < \bar{p}_2$. With c affecting the buying decision in one direction only, the *two* equilibrium prices of any type end up being lower.

We noticed that symmetric locations ($a = b$) imply equal prices in the original Hotelling model. In that model, price dispersion results from asymmetries in the location. In the present model, b does not determine the equilibrium prices of type I. (Consider Figure 2.4 again and suppose p_1 and p_2 are equilibrium prices. The location of shop 2 inside the interval A_2 is immaterial.) Similarly, a does not determine the equilibrium prices of type II. Here, price dispersion does not result from locational asymmetries but from asymmetries in the cost of canvassing a shop. It is the informational asymmetry that drives the model.[15]

---

[15] Since the firms' revenue functions are not concave, the conditions under which the equilibrium prices exist have to be examined carefully. The revenue functions have two quadratic parts and therefore display two local maxima. A careful examination

The analysis conducted so far was based on the assumption that the locations of the shops are given (a and b given). What if the shops are allowed to choose their locations in addition to price? They will consider the effect of alternative locations on the corresponding price equilibria.

Assume a price equilibrium of type I ($p_1^* < p_2^*$) and a given location b for shop 2. Shop 1 has an interest in moving closer to its competitor, that is, to increase a, since this (see Figure 2.4) will move z'' to the right and thus increase its sales A_1. That this increases profits can be seen algebraically by inserting the equilibrium prices in the revenue function of shop 1 defined in equation (2.30):

$$R_1(a) = p_1^* q_1^* = \frac{c}{3}(L + a)\left(\frac{p_2^* - p_1^* + ac}{c}\right) = \frac{c}{3}(L + a)^2.$$

The parameter R_1 appears as a function of a and increases monotonically in a. A similar result holds for $R_2(a)$ when the equilibrium is of type II ($p_2^* < p_1^*$). This procedure, initially used by Hotelling (as explained earlier) is now valid, because we know price equilibria exist as long as $a < L/2$ or $b < L/2$, depending on the type of equilibrium.

The two shops will tend to locate not too far from each other. In this sense, a weak form of Hotelling's principle of minimum differentiation appears as valid under the kind of asymmetric information postulated here. Identical locations, however, are excluded from the analysis from the start, because then no asymmetry in the information structure is possible.

2.4.4. A spatial game with search

Casual observation suggests that in real life retail shops do tend to locate at the same spot.[16] In European towns, shoe shops are typically located in the same street. The same is true for many consumer durables such as electronics equipment, furniture, and clothing. These commodities are characterized by the fact that they are imperfect substitutes. An oligopoly model with nonhomogeneous commodity and imperfect information about the product varieties offered might be ca-

---

of these functions allows Gabszewicz and Garella to conclude that there always exists a nonnull set of b values for which an equilibrium of type I exists, if $a < L/2$. Similarly, if $b < L/2$, there always exists a nonnull set of a values for which an equilibrium of type II exists. But no equilibrium exists if the shops are symmetrically located ($a = b$). In addition, no equilibrium of type I exists if $b < a$, and no equilibrium of type II exists if $a < b$. Consequently, whenever one of the two types of equilibria exists, it is unique.

[16] See the empirical evidence reported by Nelson (1970).

pable of explaining this clustering and thus validating Hotelling's principle of minimum differentiation in its strict sense. This is the intuition behind the model constructed by Stahl (1982), which also takes Hotelling's approach as its starting point.

To avoid the equilibrium existence problem we have discussed, which characterizes the Hotelling model when prices are endogenous, Stahl supposes that prices are exogenously given and identical for N varieties of a differentiated commodity. The analysis thus concentrates entirely on the choice of geographical location by firms and on the consumers' decision to visit a "marketplace" and to buy or not to buy one of the available varieties. Let us make this more precise.

The geographical space considered is the nonempty interval $[\bar{y}, y]$ on a line with y denoting a consumer's location. The interval can be thought of as representing a (linear) town. There are N given firms, each selling one commodity i at the same cost (location rents have not yet had time to arise). These firms are perfectly informed about the varieties offered by their competitors and about consumers' preferences.

Each firm has to select the location l_i that maximizes its sales (payoff) given l_{-i}, the collection of locations of all other firms. Let $\Pi_i(l_i, l_{-i})$ be the payoff of firm i when it locates at l_i. A noncooperative Nash equilibrium of the game is a set of locations $\{l_1^*, \ldots, l_i^*, \ldots, l_N^*\}$ such that no firm finds it profitable to relocate on its own, that is, such that

$$\Pi_i(l_i^*, l_{-i}^*) \geq \Pi_i(l_i, l_{-i}^*) \tag{2.35}$$

for all $i, i = 1, \ldots, N$.

Stahl defines a "marketplace" as a location with an assembly of one or more firms. Its size is the number of firms assembled at that marketplace, s_k. Its composition, e_k, is the set of firms assembled in it. Thus if firms i and j are included in e_k, then $l_i = l_j$. To the equilibrium set of locations therefore corresponds a collection $\{e_1^*, \ldots, e_K^*\}$, which describes the equilibrium configuration of marketplaces, where K is the number of marketplaces ($K \leq N$).

There are N types of consumers (as many types as varieties). Each consumer is perfectly informed about the locations and the sizes of the marketplaces, but not about their composition. *A consumer does not know, therefore, which varieties are offered in a particular marketplace.* In order to find out, he must visit it at a cost which is linear in distance and increases at the constant rate c. However, each consumer visits at most one marketplace, so *search is restricted to one marketplace only.* If a consumer decides to visit a marketplace, no additional costs result from the sampling of all stores located there. The decision to visit or not to visit a marketplace is based on expected utility maximization, in which the consumer assigns *equal probability* to finding any variety in that marketplace. There is thus a known uniform probability distribution, and it is the same for all consumers. This information structure is very special indeed.

In addition, there is a numeraire good, available everywhere, of which consumer i buys a quantity x_i. A subset of the available varieties, m_i, provides positive utility to consumer i. Consumer preferences are described by a utility function $u_i(j_i, x_i)$, where j denotes a particular variety $(j = 1, \ldots, m_i)$. These preferences are strictly transitive over the varieties in m_i, and the utility functions are additive and linear in x_i. Under these assumptions, consumer i decides to visit market k if

$$\sum_{j=1}^{m_i} \pi_j(s_k)[u_i(j) - u_i(0)] > cd_k, \tag{2.36}$$

where $\pi_j(s_k)$ is the probability that the first $j - 1$ preferred varieties are not but the jth preferred variety indeed is offered in marketplace k of size s_k. The distance between the consumer's location and marketplace k is denoted by d_k, so cd_k is the cost of transportation to the marketplace. The function $u_i(0)$ is the utility of consuming only x_i when no acceptable variety is found, and $u_i(j)$ is the utility of variety j.

2.4.5.   *Aggregate demand increases with the size of the marketplace*

An important feature of the model is the following: The more firms are located in a marketplace, the more customers will want to visit it. In other words, aggregate demand observed at a marketplace increases with the size of it. Indeed, a larger number of stores implies a larger number of varieties. This in turn increases the probability of finding a preferred variety, with the result that a consumer of a given type i is willing to travel a longer distance.

To see this, notice that the distance a consumer is willing to travel increases when s increases if the expected utility, defined in inequality (2.36) also increases with s, that is, if

$$\sum_{j=1}^{m_i} \pi_j(s')[u(j) - u_i(0)] > \sum_{j=1}^{m_i} \pi_j(s)[u_i(j) - u_i(0)], \tag{2.37}$$

with $s' > s$.

However, when inequality (2.37) is written out in detail, it implies

$$[\pi_1(s') - \pi_1(s)][u_i(1) - u_i(2)]$$

$$+ [\pi_1(s') + \pi_2(s') - (\pi_1(s) + \pi_2(s))][u_i(2) - u_i(3)]$$

$$+ \cdots + [\pi_1(s') + \cdots + \pi_{m_i}(s') - (\pi_1(s) + \cdots + \pi_{m_i}(s))]$$

$$\cdot [u_i(m_i) - u_i(0)] > 0.$$

Since the preferences are transitive, $[u_i(1) - u_i(2)] > 0$, $[u_i(2) - u_i(3)] > 0$, and so on, so that inequality (2.37) is satisfied if

$$\sum_{j=1}^{m_i} [\pi_j(s') - \pi_j(s)] > 0. \tag{2.38}$$

This is indeed the case, for

$$\sum_{j=1}^{m_i} \pi_j(s_k) = \text{Prob}\{1 \in e_k\} + \text{Prob}\{1 \notin e_k, 2 \in e_k\}$$

$$+ \cdots + \text{Prob}\{1, 2, \ldots, m - 1 \notin e_k, m \in e_k\}$$

$$= 1 - \text{Prob}\{1 \notin e_k, 2 \notin e_k, \ldots, m \notin e_k\}$$

$$= 1 - \frac{\binom{N - m}{s}}{\binom{N}{s}},$$

for any k. With $s' > s$,

$$1 - \frac{\binom{N - m}{s'}}{\binom{N}{s'}} > 1 - \frac{\binom{N - m}{s}}{\binom{N}{s}}.$$

For example, let $N = 6$, $m = 3$, $s' = 2$, and $s = 1$. Then

$$1 - \frac{3!/(3 - 2)!2!}{6!/(6 - 2)!2!} = 1 - \frac{3}{15} > 1 - \frac{3!/(3 - 1)!1!}{6!/5!1!} = 1 - \frac{3}{6}.$$

When the size of the marketplace increases, the probability of finding any variety in it also increases.[17]

---

[17] $\binom{N}{s} = N!/(N - s)!s!$ is the number of different combinations of s varieties drawn from the total number of varieties. $\binom{N - m}{s}$ is the number of different combinations of s varieties drawn from the $N - m$ unwanted ones. The ratio of the two is the probability that only the unwanted varieties are available in a marketplace with s firms located in it.

The implications for the choice of location are important. Stahl (1982, pp. 98–99) writes the following:

> Therefore a seller, upon choosing a profit maximizing location, is confronted with the alternative either to establish a local monopoly with a small market area and a larger share of consumers purchasing, by lack of alternative, his variety; or to join other firms in a competitive marketplace with a larger market area in which he fetches the demand from only the small subset of consumers not substituting away towards the other alternatives available there. More precisely, the change in our seller's market demand when joining the latter marketplace may be decomposed into two effects: a negative *substitution effect* generated from competition about consumers' demand, and a positive *market area effect* generated from the joint location of sellers. Despite a fiercer competition, our seller will join the larger marketplace if the reduction in the demand due to the substitution effect will be more than outweighed by the increase in demand due to the market area effect. Furthermore, if joining the large market that seller will, by increasing its demand drawing power, confer an *external benefit* to the sellers already there. This external benefit is exclusively due to consumers' imperfect information as to which products are offered where.

2.4.6. *Geographical concentration in marketplaces*

Let us now examine the properties of the noncooperative Nash equilibria of the game we have described. Stahl first gives conditions under which there is no equilibrium involving locational monopolies, and then gives conditions under which all sellers will locate at the same marketplace in equilibrium.

Suppose consumer i has the additive utility function

$$u_i(j_i, x_i) = u_i(j_i) + x_i$$

and gets the highest utility from variety i. Suppose also that consumer i's preferences over the other varieties are strictly transitive, so $u_i(j_i) > u_i(j + 1)_i$. Also suppose that, up to the choice of the most preferred variety i, all consumers' preferences are identical, in the following sense. Each type of consumer has a different most preferred variety, each of which gives the same utility. Otherwise the preference ordering is the same. Preference orderings are thus the same up to a translation. An example will make this clear.

Let there be four varieties (firms) and four types of consumers, so $N = 4$. Let $m = 3$, so three out of the four varieties are useful to a consumer. Then the varieties are ordered as in the table.

Consumer type	Most preferred variety	Variety in second position	Variety in third position
1	1	2	3
2	2	3	4
3	3	4	1
4	4	1	2

If now firms 2 and 4 (selling varieties 2 and 4) choose the same location, consumer types 1 and 2 will buy from firm 2 while consumer types 3 and 4 will buy from firm 4. Similarly, in a marketplace with firms 1 and 3 located in it, consumer types 1 and 4 will patronize firm 1 while consumer types 2 and 3 will patronize firm 3. Each firm has $N/2 = 2$ types of customers. On the contrary, if each firm had chosen an isolated location, it would have had $m = 3$ types of customers.

The example implies that there is the further assumption that all consumers are distributed along the line with equal densities: At each location, the share of consumer type i located there is $1/N$.

Under these conditions, there exist values of m for which at least two firms will choose the same location at equilibrium. In other words, at least one firm j will chose $l_j^* = l_i^*$, and the two firms will have equal sales.

A sufficient condition for $l_i^* = l_j^*$ is that sales be larger when firms i and j locate together than if they choose different locations, or if

$$\frac{N}{2}\, \tilde{d}(2) > m\tilde{d}(1), \tag{2.39}$$

where $\tilde{d}(s)$ is the maximal distance a consumer is willing to travel to a marketplace of size s. Indeed, the distance $\tilde{d}(2)$ multiplied by $N/2$ measures total sales of a firm located together with another. The distance $\tilde{d}(1)$ multiplied by m measures total sales of an isolated firm. In the example, I assumed $m > N/2$. But we also know that $\tilde{d}(1) < \tilde{d}(2)$. For some values of m, inequality (2.39) can thus be satisfied. In fact, *all* firms will form marketplaces at least pairwise under the conditions that preference orderings are the same up to a translation and that consumers are distributed with equal densities. One can also conclude that *some* firms will gain from a spatial association as long as the commodity is differentiated. It is only if all commodities were considered perfect substitutes by all consumers that spatial concentration would never take place.

Notice also that if the commodity is differentiated and all consumers are choosy enough to desire, at given prices, one and only one variety (so that $m_i = 1$), then concentration of all firms at *one single* marketplace is the only equilibrium possible. Since there is no competition between them, all firms must gain from spatial association if consumers are imperfectly informed about the varieties offered. Such an equilibrium may also obtain if consumers consider several varieties acceptable (that is, $m_i > 1$), if m_i is small enough. A concentration of all sellers in one marketplace is thus an equilibrium configuration that is very likely to arise.

CHAPTER 3

Asymmetric quality information

We now turn to a situation where buyers are imperfectly informed about the quality of the seller's product. The product is a durable good such that buyers will discover its quality only by using it. How will the seller, who knows the quality of its product, react to this circumstance?

If the quality cannot be verified by an objective test or by a third party, the question is a difficult one and the object of current research. (Laffont and Maskin (1987) argue that the most profitable policy for the seller is *not* to reveal the quality.) But if verification is possible, then the seller will provide some protection against bad quality by offering a warranty contract. This will, in turn, affect the quality offered.

3.1. Product warranties

Product warranties have several interesting features. First of all, they provide insurance against product failure. The product will be replaced or repaired or reimbursed. Sometimes the warranty is optional. Often it is not.

Second, product warranties have incentive properties. Since they imply a cost for the seller, they create an incentive to improve quality. When they give partial protection, it is in the buyer's interest to take care of the product, for example by having his or her car serviced regularly. The warranty may be conditional on regular service and control by the seller, especially if it is of limited duration.

Third, product warranties have informational properties. They convey the message that the product is of good quality: Who would guarantee good quality when it is in fact bad? And a better protection, because it is costly to provide, gives an indication of better quality.

Fourth, product warranties are a means to establish and maintain seller reputation (Shapiro 1982a). They make the buyer expect good quality, and the seller will want these expectations to be confirmed to ensure his or her credibility.

Finally, optional warranties can be used to price discriminate against less elastic market segments. At a higher price, these buyers are given the opportunity to buy additional protection. To make this discrimination effective, lower quality may be simultaneously offered to more elastic market segments.

3.1.1. *Moral hazard problems*

Car producers typically offer warranties of a limited duration (one year, say, on mechanical deficiencies and five years on corrosion). However, special clauses limit the protection to deficiencies in the production process. That is why the car should be serviced exclusively by recognized dealers and why only original spare parts may be used. In particular, negligence, bad driving, or lack of experience of the buyer are not covered. In other words, the origin of the failure must be identified as being on the seller's side. The service booklet allows the seller to check the regularity of the service and can be used (possibly in court) as objective evidence. Optional contracts for free service and repair can be purchased at a price. Sometimes, the price is the cost of repairing a first failure, after which any further repair is free.

On the market for television sets and radios, the typical warranty covers spare parts and repair costs during the first six months of operation. The starting date is fixed with precision and the warranty may be limited to the first buyer (in contrast with the car market). A series of clauses exclude all cases in which the product has been tampered with. Contracts offered by competing producers all have the same basic features.

The situation is similar in the market for consumer durables (refrigerators, vacuum cleaners, etc.), except that the buyer generally has to pay part of the costs of repair. Clearly, the purpose is to limit abuses on the buyer's side.

These examples highlight one essential aspect: There are *moral hazard* problems. Moral hazard arises when an agent can influence the occurrence of an event (here product failure) against which the agent is insured, but the seller of the insurance policy cannot monitor or detect this action. In the case of a warranty, the terms of the warranty may create an incentive for the buyer to give his car insufficient maintenance or to drive without care. This is a first moral hazard problem. A similar problem, however, arises on the seller side, when the actual quality is not observable by the buyers. When the seller has provided low protection, she may be tempted not to maintain high quality, and conversely. There is thus a "double moral hazard": Warranties act as incentive mechanisms for both sides of the market. It is double, because information is imperfect on both sides: Buyers are imperfectly informed about product quality, but sellers are imperfectly informed about the way in which buyers will subsequently use their product.

Although there is an obvious analogy with the insurance market, the analogy is far from perfect. Some insurance is provided, but it is provided by the seller, not by an insurance company, because the latter has no technical control over the way in which the product is used by the buyer. On the other hand, one observes that sellers of more reliable brands of a particular product offer more, equal, or even less warranty protection than sellers of less reliable brands. Third, warranties do not provide full insurance against possible unsatisfactory performance of the product. These three features cannot be captured when a warranty contract is analyzed as a regular insurance policy. In such an approach (see Heal 1977), one finds that insurance should be complete. And one cannot, of course, explain why insurance companies are not active in the "warranty market," nor why the degrees of protection are not perfectly correlated with quality.

For the same reasons, giving warranties a signaling role does not capture the essence of the problem. If good warranty protection signals[1] good quality, as in Spence (1977), then perfect correlation between the two and full insurance is the outcome, a result that contradicts all available evidence.

3.1.2. Warranties with double moral hazard

The model developed by Cooper and Ross (1985) is capable of explaining the particular features of the warranty problem.[2] Their basic insight is that the impact of double moral hazard depends critically on whether care and quality are complements or substitutes in determining the probability that a product will work. Technically speaking, the sign of π_{eq} must be crucial, where $\pi(e,q)$ is the probability that a product will work, depending on the level of care or effort expended by the buyer, e, and on the quality level, q, chosen by the seller. The term π_{eq} is the cross partial derivative whose sign determines whether e and q are complements or substitutes. The probability of breakdown is $1 - \pi$. Suppose also that $\pi_e > 0$, $\pi_q > 0$, $\pi_{ee} \leq 0$, and $\pi_{qq} \leq 0$.

Consider a seller and a buyer who are both risk neutral, to remove any concern about risk sharing. They sign a contract stipulating that 1 unit of a product is sold at price p and that the degree of warranty

---

[1] On signals, see Section 5.1.   [2] See also related work by Kambhu (1982).

protection against product failure will be s. If the product fails, this can be observed by everybody without further discussion.

When there is perfect information about the effort the buyer will expend and about the quality the seller will provide, then the contract can also stipulate e and q in addition to p and s.

Let the buyer's utility function be

$$u(p, s, e, q) = y - p + \pi z + (1 - \pi)sz - g(e). \tag{3.1}$$

The buyer spends $y - p$ on other goods, has a utility worth πz dollars if the product works and $(1 - \pi)sz$ if the product fails, because the warranty provides a compensation sz. The function $g(e)$ measures the disutility of the care or effort expended by the buyer and has the following properties: $g'(0) = 0$, $g'(\cdot) \geq 0$, and $g''(\cdot) > 0$.

The seller's expected profits are then

$$\Pi(p, s, e, q) = p - C(q) - (1 - \pi)sz, \tag{3.2}$$

where the cost of production $C(q)$ is such that $C'(0) = 0$, $C'(\cdot) \geq 0$, and $C''(\cdot) > 0$. Note that the choices of e and q affect both parties directly through $g(e)$ and $C(q)$, respectively, and indirectly through $\pi(e, q)$.

Under full information, it is possible to make a first-best contract that sets the four elements (p, s, e, q) in such a way that total welfare

$$u + \Pi = y + \pi z - g(e) - C(q)$$

is maximized. The elements p and s drop out of this sum and are indeterminate. The first-best contract (e^*, q^*) satisfies

$$\pi_e z = g'(e), \tag{3.3a}$$

$$\pi_q z = C'(q) \tag{3.3b}$$

simultaneously. The marginal benefits to both parties are equal to the marginal costs to each. For a given quality, the optimal effort is the solution $e^*(q)$ of equation (3.3a). For a given effort, the optimal quality is the solution $q^*(e)$ of equation (3.3b).

These two optimal inputs must be made enforceable. That is possible when the parties can observe e and q. In that way, any incentive that may exist to deviate from e^* and q^* can be neutralized.

When both e and q are unobservable, such an enforcement is not possible. The agreement must then be such that neither party has an incentive to deviate from the agreed-upon inputs: The agreement must be self-enforcing. A Nash equilibrium would have such a property.

To model this, Cooper and Ross consider a two-stage game. In the first stage, the seller and the buyer sign a binding contract determining the price p and the degree of warranty protection s. In the second stage, with p and s given, the players choose the Nash equilibrium values of e and q.

The buyer maximizes u with respect to e, given s and a conjecture about q. The seller maximizes Π with respect to q, given s and a conjecture about e. (The equilibrium is independent of the price, because p enters linearly in both u and Π.) The Nash equilibrium is the pair of values of $\hat{e}(q; s)$ and $\hat{q}(e; s)$, the reaction functions, that solves

$$\pi_e(1 - s)z = g'(e), \qquad \pi_q sz = C'(q). \qquad (3.4)$$

The reaction functions are positively sloped when $\pi_{eq} > 0$ and negatively sloped when $\pi_{eq} < 0$. An increase in the degree of warranty protection increases $\hat{q}$ and decreases $\hat{e}$.

Comparing system (3.4) with system (3.3), we see that none of the parties receives the full marginal benefit of a greater effort or an increased quality, when $0 < s < 1$, and that $\hat{q} < q^*$ and $\hat{e} < e^*$, because g is increasing in e and C is increasing in q. It is clear also that system (3.4) is the same as system (3.3) when $s = 0$ in the equation determining $\hat{e}$ and $s = 1$ in the equation determining $\hat{q}$. The reaction functions are therefore related as follows:

$$e^*(q) = \hat{e}(q; 0), \qquad q^*(e) = \hat{q}(e; 1). \qquad (3.5)$$

This gives a benchmark with which to compare the Nash equilibrium for $0 < s < 1$. It also implies that the first-best contract cannot be implemented as a noncooperative equilibrium, since s cannot simultaneously be equal to 0 and 1.

When quality and care are complements, $\pi_{eq} > 0$ and the reaction functions are positively sloped as in Figure 3.1, taken from Cooper and Ross (1985, p. 107). Point K is the full-information first-best equilibrium, and A is a Nash equilibrium for a given degree of warranty. Both inputs are smaller as a result of double moral hazard.

The same is true when quality and effort are independent, as shown in Figure 3.2.

When effort and quality are substitutes, a reduction in the quality offered makes the efforts of the buyer more productive in terms of avoiding a breakdown. Conversely, a reduction in the buyer's effort increases the contribution of quality to the probability that the product will work. We already know that both $\hat{e}$ and $\hat{q}$ cannot be higher than the first-best solution. But here either $\hat{e}$ or $\hat{q}$ can be. Figure 3.3(b) illustrates the case where $\hat{e}$ is higher than e^*, because the same given q implies a higher effort. The result of the comparison is ambiguous.

The second stage of the game being solved for given s, it remains to

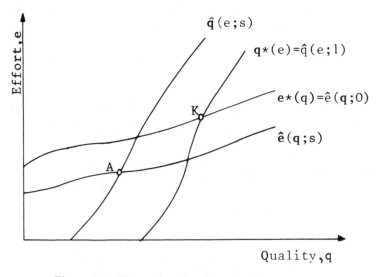

Figure 3.1. Warranties: Quality and effort are complements.

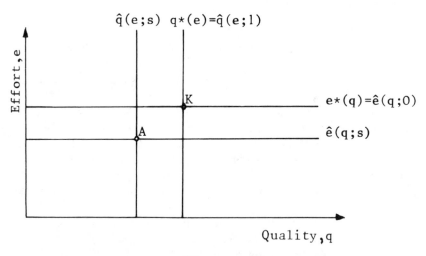

Figure 3.2. Warranties: Quality and effort are independent.

solve the first stage, given the Nash equilibrium pair $(\hat{e}, \hat{q})$, in order to determine the equilibrium value of s. The foregoing reasoning was based on the assumption that s is between zero and 1. It now turns out that the equilibrium value of s^* is, indeed, between 0 and 1: At equi-

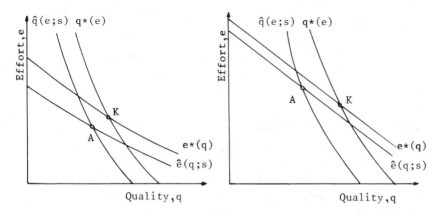

Figure 3.3. Warranties: Quality and effort are substitutes.

librium, less than full protection is in the parties' mutual interest, because this will provide incentives for the provision of positive levels of both e and q.

To see this, maximize the sum of the benefits of both parties, that is,

$$\pi z - g(e) - C(q)$$

with respect to s, subject to $e = \bar{e}(s)$ and $q = \bar{q}(s)$, where $\bar{e}(s)$ and $\bar{q}(s)$ denote the Nash equilibrium of the second-stage game for given s. The first-order condition is

$$(\pi_q z - C')\bar{q}_s + (\pi_e z - g')\bar{e}_s = 0,$$

or, using equations (3.4),

$$\bar{q}_s \pi_q z(1 - s) + \bar{e}_s \pi_e zs = 0. \tag{3.6}$$

For this to hold, s^* must be between 0 and 1.

We started with the observation that sellers of better quality offer higher *or* lower protection. That is, s and q may be positively or negatively correlated. In the framework of the Cooper–Ross model, a positive correlation can result from the fact that buyers with higher maintenance costs demand higher quality and higher protection. A negative correlation can result from the fact that sellers may have cost advantages in building quality and suffer cost disadvantages in providing warranty protection. Japanese car producers selling in the U.S. market apparently are in this situation: The cost of building up parts inventories and dealer networks raises the cost of providing warranty protection. Cooper and Ross compare the equilibrium values of s and q with a linear specification of $\pi(e, q)$ and a quadratic specification of $g(e)$ and $C(q)$, to show that both a positive and a negative correlation can indeed happen.

The entire analysis is done for a contract between one seller and one buyer. The extent of competition between sellers determines the price, which remained exogenous throughout.

3.2.*   The noisy monopolist again

We saw in Section 2.2 that it can be profitable for a monopolist to create noise in order to separate customers with high search costs (and less elastic demands) from customers with low search costs (and more elastic demands) when there is imperfect price information. Intuition suggests that an analogous possibility arises when there is imperfect quality information. Wouldn't it be profitable to *voluntarily* produce a proportion of defective units, even if a zero-defect rate could be achieved at no additional production cost, and to offer an *optional* warranty? The presence of defective units would induce some customers to take the guarantee at a price. The monopolist would thus be able to price discriminate between those who take the warranty and the others and extract some additional surplus. That this intuition is correct was shown by Braverman, Guasch, and Salop (1983).

We concentrate on their graphical comparison of conventional monopoly pricing with such an optional warranty strategy. Consider Figure 3.4. Let $x(p)$ be the monopolist's demand function. The marginal cost of production (MC) is equal to c. The conventional monopoly price is p_m and the corresponding quantity sold is x_m. There are no defective units produced.

Suppose now that the monopolist holds the price p_m constant, but produces defective units at the rate $1 - q$. Let $b = 1/q$. Then the effective price a consumer has to pay is bp_m, because to have x nondefective units he must buy b more units. And since $b > 1$, the price of a nondefective unit increases. At the price bp_m, he would buy x_b units in the absence of a guarantee contract, and his surplus would fall by the shaded area bp_mDAp_m. Call this $G(b)$. The monopolist may charge up to $G(b)$ for the optional warranty.

To see whether this strategy is profitable, one has to look at the cost side. With a warranty contract, the monopolist must replace all the defective units and therefore produce bx for every x sold. The effective unit cost of production therefore rises to bc. Total costs rise by the shaded area $bcFBc$. Call this $\Delta C(b)$. It is profitable to offer an optional warranty if $G(b) > \Delta C(b)$.

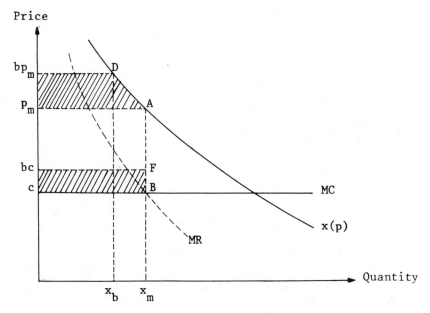

Figure 3.4. Optional warranty contract.

This condition is satisfied even if the defect rate is very small (or b close to 1). To see this, suppose the demand curve is linear in the neighborhood of point A ($b = 1$). Then (see Figure 3.4)

$$G(b) = (bp_m - p_m)x_m - \tfrac{1}{2}(bp_m - p_m)(x_m - x_b)$$

$$= p_m(b - 1)x_m - \tfrac{1}{2}p_m(b - 1)(x_m - x_b)$$

$$= p_m(b - 1)x_m \left[1 - \frac{1}{2x_m}(x_m - x_b) \right],$$

$$\Delta C(b) = (bc - c)x_m = c(b - 1)x_m,$$

or

$$\frac{G(b)}{\Delta C(b)} = \frac{p_m[1 - \tfrac{1}{2}(b - 1)\epsilon]}{c}$$

where

$$\epsilon = \frac{p}{x}\left(\frac{\Delta x}{\Delta p}\right) = \frac{p_m}{x_m}\left(\frac{x_m - x_b}{bp_m - p_m}\right) = \frac{x_m - x_b}{x_m(b - 1)}.$$

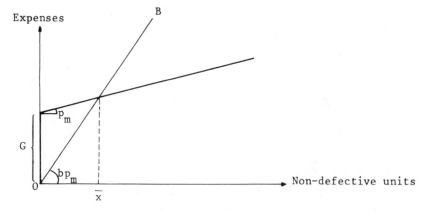

Figure 3.5. Two-part tariff with optional warranty.

This ratio is larger than 1 if b is near 1, because p_m is larger than c. The warranty contract is more profitable than pure monopoly pricing.

The result is a two-part tariff, with an "entrance fee" equal to G (which gives the right to have defective units replaced) and a marginal price p_m. This tariff is illustrated in Figure 3.5.

Without the guarantee contract, the consumer would pay the effective price bp_m for a nondefective unit with a total expense represented by the ray OB. The monopolist must make sure that the consumer buys at least $\bar{x}$ units, since otherwise she would prefer not to take the warranty contract. The value of $\bar{x}$ depends on the slope of OB, that is on b. The higher b is, the smaller q is, the higher the proportion $1 - q$ of defective units is, and the smaller $\bar{x}$ is. In other words, the monopolist must make sure that there are enough defective units.

Note that these results do not depend on any risk-aversion characteristics of the consumer. (They depend only on the monopoly price exceeding the marginal cost and the price elasticity of demand being finite, both of which are inherent characteristics of a monopolistic market.) If the consumer were risk averse, this strategy would be even more profitable because a risk premium could then be added to G.

3.3.   Market equilibrium

We have been discussing warranties offered by the producer of a new durable. In practice, these warranties are given to an individual buyer through a recognized dealer. In most cases, the durable is brand new. However, the dealer may have used the durable for demonstration purposes, as is the case with "demonstration cars" used by the dealer to give potential buyers a ride. After a number of kilometers (up to 10,000 km in some cases), such a car can nevertheless be sold at a relatively small discount, because the dealer can still attach the producer's warranty to it. It is treated in this respect as if it were new.

A private buyer who just bought a new car and wants to sell it after driving it for a few kilometers is in a completely different situation. Even if it is in perfect shape, this car owner will have to accept a substantial price difference and may lose up to 20%. Why is this? This is the question raised by Akerlof in his celebrated 1970 article "The Market for Lemons." His answer is that an asymmetry in available information has developed. Although this car owner knows that the car is in perfect condition and in no way different from a new car on display in a dealer's showroom, potential buyers do not know this. They have every reason to suspect that something is wrong with it. And this car owner, not being a recognized dealer, cannot transfer the producer's warranty to offset the informational asymmetry. This car will have to be sold at the average market price for one-year-old used cars, since there is a positive probability that it is a lemon. "The owner of a good machine must be locked in," as Akerlof puts it.

As a consequence, owners of a good used car do not have an interest in selling it because they cannot get a good price for it. Most used cars traded must be lemons. There is thus an analogy with Gresham's law, which says that "bad money drives out good money." Similarly, *the bad cars tend to drive out the good cars on the used-car market, on which the average quality must be low.*

To make his point, Akerlof constructs the following extreme numerical example, in which no market for used cars exists at all, although there are several qualities available. Assume that the demand for used cars depends on the price p of the car and on the average quality μ of used cars traded, whereas the supply depends on the price. In equilibrium, the supply must equal the demand for the given average quality, which depends in turn on the price.

To get algebraic results, specify the utility function of each of two groups of traders as follows. Group 1 has the utility function

$$U_1 = M + \sum_{i=1}^{n} q_i, \tag{3.7}$$

where M is the consumption of goods other than cars, q_i is the quality of the ith used car, and n is the number of qualities (or cars). Group 1 also has N used cars with uniformly distributed quality q, $0 \le q \le$

2. Group 2 has utility function

$$U_2 = M + \sum_{i=1}^{n} \frac{3}{2} q_i \qquad (3.8)$$

but no (used) cars at all. The linearity of these two utility functions is unrealistic (it does not take the risk aspect of uncertainty into account and implies that each additional car (quality) consumed adds the same amount of utility), but has the advantage of leading to corner solutions, which are typical for the case under analysis.

Consider group 1. Its budget constraint is

$$M + pn = Y_1, \qquad (3.9)$$

when the price of "other goods" M is set equal to 1 and Y_1 is the income (including that derived from the sale of used cars) of all type 1 traders.

The number of used cars demanded by group 1, that is, D_1, is obtained by maximizing the expectation of U_1 subject to condition (3.9) or by maximizing

$$E(U_1) = E\left(M + \sum_{i=1}^{n} q_i\right) = M + \sum_{i=1}^{n} E(q_i)$$

$$= M + \mu n = Y_1 + (\mu - p)n \qquad (3.10)$$

since the expectation $E(q_i)$ is equal to μ for all used cars. This expected utility is linear in n and therefore maximized if

$$D_1 = \frac{Y_1}{p} \qquad \text{when } \mu > p, \qquad (3.11a)$$

since Y_1/p is the largest possible value of n, that is, the corner solution, or

$$D_1 = 0 \qquad \text{when } \mu < p, \qquad (3.11b)$$

that is, the other corner solution (the smallest possible value of n). Then no market exists at all.

To find the supply of cars offered by type 1 traders, one can use the assumption that quality is distributed uniformly, as in Figure 3.6. In this figure, the shaded area represents the probability that q is between 0 and p. When $p = 2$, this area is equal to 1 by convention (all cars are supplied), so the vertical side of the rectangle, the uniform density, is equal to $\frac{1}{2}$. The supply of used cars by type 1 traders will thus be a

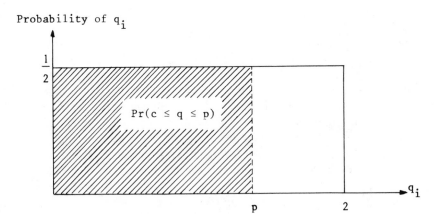

Probability of q_i

$$\frac{1}{2}$$

Pr($c \leq q \leq p$)

p 2 q_i

Figure 3.6. Distribution of quality between 0 and 2.

proportion of stock equal to

$$S_1 = \tfrac{1}{2}pN = p\,\frac{N}{2} \tag{3.12}$$

because they are ready to sell only if $p \geq q$, and the average quality μ will be $p/2$, because group 2 has no cars to offer.

The demand of type 2 traders is determined in an analogous way as

$$D_2 = \frac{Y_2}{p} \qquad \text{when } \frac{3\mu}{2} > p \tag{3.13a}$$

and

$$D_2 = 0 \qquad \text{when } \frac{3\mu}{2} < p. \tag{3.13b}$$

Total demand for used cars is thus

$$D(p, \mu) = \begin{cases} \dfrac{Y_1 + Y_2}{p} & \text{if } p < \mu, \\[2mm] \dfrac{Y_2}{p} & \text{if } \mu < p < \dfrac{3\mu}{2}, \\[2mm] 0 & \text{if } p > \dfrac{3\mu}{2}. \end{cases} \tag{3.14}$$

However, the average quality μ is equal to $p/2$, so the condition $p > 3\mu/2$ is always satisfied: *Average quality is too low compared to the price!*

3.3.1. *Adverse selection*

This example shows the importance of the relationship between the price and average quality. The demand of used cars by car owners vanishes, in the example, as soon as average quality drops below the price. With a uniform distribution of quality, those who did not own a car never wish to buy. Obviously, the example is extreme. It is meant to make the point that the presence of unidentifiable lemons makes it difficult to sell cars of better quality at a good price, with the implication that the average quality of *traded* used cars is lower than that of *non-traded* used cars. This has come to be known as the "lemons principle."

The more general phenomenon of asymmetric information coupled with a reduction of average quality of the goods and services traded in the market has received the name "adverse selection." A problem with adverse selection is thus a problem with asymmetric information and a concomitant reduced average quality of traded goods.

Adverse selection characterizes all markets in which one side of the market is less informed than the other about the properties of the goods and services being traded. These include markets of new as well as used durables, markets for professional and skilled services (doctors, lawyers), the labor market (in which the buyer – the employer – is less informed about the productivity of a potential employee), the credit market and the insurance market (in which the seller – the bank or the insurance company – cannot determine with certainty whether a potential customer is a high risk or a low risk).

By drawing the profession's attention to adverse selection, Akerlof opened a new line of research which led to many new insights. Starting from the market for lemons, these new developments proceeded by examining more closely the assumptions made explicitly or implicitly by Akerlof. It is of some importance, therefore, to take a closer look at these assumptions.

First of all, there is the assumption that, in equilibrium, a single price clears the market (cars of different quality are all traded at the same price). Where does this price come from – that is, by whom is this price fixed? by the sellers? by the buyers? How can it make total demand equal to total supply at equilibrium? And why should the equilibrium imply a single price rather than a distribution of prices? C. Wilson (1980) discusses these questions and finds that, indeed, when an adverse selection problem arises, trade may take place at different prices and part of the available supply may not be sold at equilibrium. To derive these results, Wilson takes a closer look at the utility-maximizing behavior of individual car owners and nonowners rather than postulating a utility function for each group.

Second, Akerlof and Wilson divide the agents in the market into buyers and sellers and thus overlook the ability of each agent to freely choose whether to be a seller or a buyer. In the used-car market, unlike other markets with adverse selection, such as the insurance market and the labor market, an agent can change its position from buyer to seller, or vice versa, with little or no transaction cost. If the price of used cars goes up, a used-car buyer may prefer to buy a new car and become a used-car seller.

Third, Akerlof (and Wilson) treat quality as exogenously given. Quality is a random variable distributed over some interval, and each car owner enjoys a particular quality drawn from the given distribution of qualities. In fact, the quality of a car depends on its owner through endogenous factors such as maintenance, driving habits, and so on. Kim (1985) introduces the effect of the maintenance level on quality and the ability to change from buyer to seller or vice versa, to find results that may contradict the lemons principle, in the sense that bad cars do not drive out good cars. The average quality of traded used cars may be higher than that of nontraded cars.

A counterexample to Akerlof's conclusions can thus be constructed, even without abandoning the assumption of a given asymmetry of information. Remember, indeed, that Akerlof (and Wilson) suppose that the less-informed part of the market has no way of getting information, with the implication that there are no costs and that the price is the only variable the agents may use to distinguish quality. In addition, the better-informed side of the market makes no effort to transmit relevant information to the other side. These assumptions are necessary to get at the core of the problem of adverse selection and may have descriptive value in some markets. However, in many markets, including the used car market, specialized third parties such as consumer unions and intermediaries (car dealers, credit agencies, insurance agencies, job agencies) make a living by providing the relevant information and selecting the better quality. In addition, both sides of the market do take steps to solve or reduce the adverse selection problem. Sellers of goods certify quality. Sellers of services display their diplomas and exclude unqualified people from professional practice. Job applicants signal their abilities by getting better educated.

Signaling is discussed in Chapter 5. The role of intermediaries in providing quality information is discussed in Section 3.6. The other questions raised are discussed in what follows, starting with Wilson's analysis of equilibrium in markets with adverse selection.

3.3.2. *Equilibrium and adverse selection*

How would the equilibrium, if it exists, of a used-car market look under perfect information? All quality differences would be reflected in the prices, and each quality of car would have a distinct price. These prices would be adjusted so that total supply is equal to total demand. And the equilibrium allocation would be such that the highest-quality cars are allocated to drivers with the highest marginal rates of substitution of quality for price. (We will discover, however, that some degree of informational asymmetry is needed for trade to take place in a used-car market!)

In a market with asymmetric quality information, the possible equilibria are different from the one just described, but may have some of its properties. Even if the uninformed cannot acquire information and the informed cannot use signals, trade must not take place at a single price that equates supply and demand, as assumed by Akerlof. There may be an equilibrium price dispersion, but this may in turn imply that some sellers of better-quality cars do not find a buyer and are thus "rationed" (excess supply).

To demonstrate this, C. Wilson[3] (1980) therefore supposes the absence of signaling and search and modifies Akerlof's model only to the extent that each agent is given an individual utility function. There still is a given set of cars with a random quality distributed over the interval $[q_0, q_1]$ with density $f(q)$. Each agent has the utility function

$$u = c + tq \tag{3.15}$$

where c is consumption of other goods, q is the quality of car it consumes, and t is a parameter that reflects its relative valuation of a car of quality q for consumption, and is thus equal to its marginal rate of substitution of car quality for consumption.

Initially a subset of the agents owns no car. They are the "nonowners" and are characterized by their positive utility index t, which is distributed over the interval $[t_0, t_1]$ with density $h(t)$. Since u is linear, they are risk neutral with respect to quality. Their expected utility depends only on the expected quality in the distribution of cars from which they may choose one. The higher t, the higher their reservation value for a given quality and the higher their marginal rate of substitution, so nonowners with a higher t will buy cars at least as expensive as those bought by nonowners with a lower t when higher prices imply a better average quality.

Figure 3.7, reproduced from Wilson (1980, p. 111), illustrates the

---

[3] C. Wilson (1979) gives a summary of his 1980 paper and some interesting afterthoughts on the scope of these results.

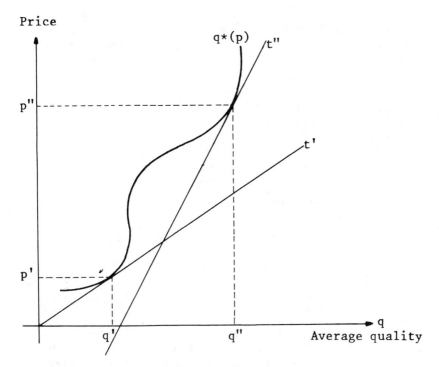

Figure 3.7. Buyers' quality valuations and prices.

argument. The curve $q^*(p)$ represents the average quality that corresponds to each price. Utility increases when q increases and p decreases. Therefore, with a valuation t' (an indifference curve with slope t') p' and q' maximize utility. However, at the price p', the nonowner is indifferent between buying a car of expected quality q' and not purchasing any car at all. There is a purchase if $p' < t'q'$. Similarly, a nonowner with valuation t'' buys if $p'' < t''q''$, and also if he or she were permitted only to purchase at price p'. The general implication is that, as the utility index rises to t'', the optimal price for buyer t'' must be at least as high as p'. In other words, *if buyer t' chooses to purchase at price p, then any buyer $t'' > t'$ will prefer (to buy at) a price at least as high as p.*

The other subset of agents owns a car. Each owner has the same utility index t, which lies somewhere between the highest and the lowest nonowner's valuation (suppose $t = 1$), to simplify the computations.

The question then arises whether there is a single equilibrium price that clears the market, as Akerlof assumes. To visualize this, Wilson uses the image of a price set by an auctioneer who has instructions to equate supply and demand (and calls this a "Walrasian equilibrium"). If this auctioneer were to compute aggregate supply and demand and average quality of the cars offered at the single price p, he would find the following.

The owner of a car of quality q sells at price p only if $p \geq q$, so more cars are supplied as the price rises. Total supply is equal to the number of cars for which $q \leq p$ or

$$S(p) = \begin{cases} \int_0^p f(q) \, dq & \text{for } p > q_0, \\ 0 & \text{otherwise.} \end{cases} \tag{3.16}$$

The average quality of the cars offered for sale at price p is then

$$q^a(p) = \begin{cases} \int_{q_0}^p qf(q) \, dq/S(p) & \text{for } p > q_0, \\ q_0 & \text{for } p = q_0. \end{cases} \tag{3.17}$$

A price increase must increase the average quality, because the marginal seller's car exceeds the quality of any other car offered for sale. Indeed, all sellers have the same utility function.

By assumption, the nonowners can observe only the average quality $q^a(p)$ sold at each price. Aggregate demand is therefore equal to the number of buyers with $t \geq p/q^a(p)$, on the assumption that buyers may purchase at most one car and are not permitted to resell a car in the same market, or

$$D(p) = \begin{cases} \int_{p/q^a(p)}^{t_1} h(t) \, dt & \text{for } p < t_1 q^a(p), \\ 0 & \text{otherwise.} \end{cases} \tag{3.18}$$

A positive equilibrium price p^e, such that $D(p^e) = S(p^e)$, always exists[4] if the owner's t ($=1$) is smaller than t_1 and $q_0 > 0$. Indeed, at price q_0, supply is zero and demand is positive. At $p = t_1 q_1$, supply is positive (since $t_1 > 1$ and $q_1 > q_0$) but demand is zero (since $q_1 > q^a(p)$, so $p > t_1 q^a(p)$). The existence of a positive equilibrium then follows from the continuity of S and D.

However, the equilibrium price may not be unique, therefore this model is not necessarily the appropriate one. Multiple equilibria may arise, because the aggregate demand curve may become upward slop-

---

[4] Akerlof got a zero-equilibrium price on the assumption that $q_0 = 0$ and that the distribution of q is uniform.

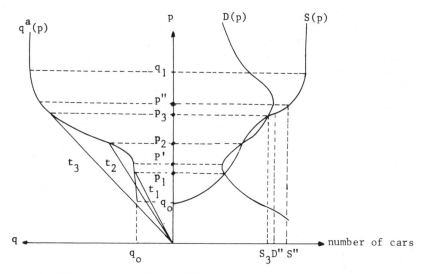

Figure 3.8. Multiple equilibria.

ing and flatter than the aggregate supply curve so that these curves intersect more than once.

That the demand curve need not be downward sloping follows directly from the fact that a utility-maximizing nonowner buys at price p if and only if $p < tq^a(p)$. If now the supply elasticity of the average quality is greater than 1, then the number of nonowners who choose to purchase increases with the price. And if this increase in numbers if sufficiently high, then the aggregate demand curve may even become flatter than the aggregate supply curve.

Figure 3.8 illustrates such a case. Aggregate supply is zero for all prices less than q_0, then rises continuously until all cars are supplied at $p = q_1$. With Akerlof's uniform distribution of q, S would be a straight line from $p = q_0$ to $p = q_1$. (Here the density $f(q)$ is not flat.) Aggregate demand comprises those nonowners whose indifference curves through the corresponding point on the average quality function (which reflects the shape of S; see equation (3.17)) intersect the price axis at or below the origin (recall our discussion of Figure 3.7). The slope of the ray from the origin to the point $(q^a(p), p)$ therefore represents the utility index of the marginal buyer.

From p' to p'' the average quality is supposed to increase faster than the price; hence the ratio of average quality to the price increases. As a result, the demand curve is upward sloping over this interval. If the number of nonowners with a utility index between $p''/q^a(p'')$ and

$p'/q^a(p')$ is sufficiently large, the demand curve can intersect the supply at three different prices (p_1, p_2, and p_3) as depicted.

Notice that both owners and nonowners prefer the higher of any two equilibrium prices between p' and p''. For the owners this is obvious, since the quality of their car does not depend on the price: Their welfare always increases with the equilibrium price. That the same can be true for nonowners is less obvious. Yet, we know that at p_2 the slope of any buyer's indifference curve is greater than or equal to t_2. When the price is increased to p_3, the indifference curve of the marginal buyer has become flatter. Consequently, any buyer who demands a car at p_2 reaches a higher utility at price p_3 and prefers p_3 to p_2.

What if a price increase leads to excess supply, as between p_3 and p''? Excess supply does not affect the welfare increase of the buyers, as long as the demand curve is upward sloping. But sellers face a trade-off between a reduction in the probability of selling a car and an increase in the price. This probability must not fall too rapidly as the price rises. Wilson shows that a sufficient condition for sellers to prefer p'' to p_3 is

$$\frac{S'' - D''}{S_3} < \frac{p'' - p_3}{p_3}.$$

This possibility that both sides of the market prefer a higher price suggests that competitive pressures do not necessarily force the price down toward a stable equilibrium.

3.4.*   Buyers' and sellers' equilibria

It is of some interest, therefore, to abandon the assumption of an auctioneer setting a single price and to consider what happens if either the individual buyers or the individual sellers set the price at which they will accept an offer to sell or to buy.

3.4.1.   Buyers set their price

The assumption that buyers are assigned the role of setting the prices is not unrealistic and has descriptive value in the labor market, where asymmetric information is often present and employers do announce the wage at which they wish to hire an employee with a particular qualification.

Under this price setting convention, sellers behave as before: They try to sell at the highest price possible and leave if they cannot find a price higher than the quality q of the car they own. Buyers announce a price that depends on (a) the average quality they expect to be offered at each price and (b) the likelihood that some seller will sell at the price announced. When can a buyer expect an offer? Assuming that sellers can search costlessly for the most favorable price (to simplify), a buyer *may expect an offer at price p only if there is an excess supply of cars at all prices higher than p.* (If all job applicants know all wages, an employer can expect to hire an applicant at the announced wage only if there is excess supply on the labor market at all higher wages.) This, I guess, is Wilson's basic insight.

It has important implications. In Wilson's (1980, p. 116) words:

> Therefore, I shall assume that buyers make a point estimate of a critical *cutoff price* $\underline{p}$. At prices at or above $\underline{p}$, their subjective probability of making a purchase is one; at prices below $\underline{p}$, the probability is zero. The average quality of car buyers expect to be forthcoming at each price may be summarized by an expected quality function, $q^e(\cdot)$, which I assume to be a continuous function of price. Both $\underline{p}$ and q^e are identical for all buyers. Given these assumptions, there is an optimal price announcement for each buyer.

Note that the assumption that the probability of making a purchase is positive is not really restrictive, because at equilibrium buyers will always be able to buy a car at the cutoff price. The same is true for the assumption that $\underline{p}$ and q^e are identical for all buyers, because it will also have to be satisfied in equilibrium.

The excess supply at price p given $\underline{p}$ and q^e, $E(p; \underline{p}, q^e)$ is equal to the number of sellers unable to sell their cars at higher prices. And there is a *buyers' equilibrium* if

$$q^e(p) = q^a(p) \qquad \text{for all } p > q_0, \tag{3.19a}$$

$$E(p; \underline{p}, q^e) = 0 \qquad \text{if and only if } p \le \underline{p}. \tag{3.19b}$$

That is, the buyers' expected quality is equal to the actual average quality function, so no one experiments by announcing a price either higher or lower than the equilibrium price. In addition, there is excess supply at all prices higher than the cutoff price.

This equilibrium takes two forms. Either it takes the form of a Walrasian equilibrium at which every buyer announces the *highest* price that equates demand and supply, or different buyers announce distinct prices resulting in a distribution around the highest Walrasian equilibrium price. (In a labor market with asymmetric information, there is either one equilibrium wage, the highest that equates demand and supply, or a distribution of wages around it.)

The first case arises if a buyer with the highest utility index, t_1, prefers to buy at a Walrasian equilibrium price p^* rather than at any higher price. Then all other buyers also prefer p^* to any higher price. If the cutoff price is equal to p^*, all will actually announce p^*, and since supply is equal to demand, this is a buyers' equilibrium: Excess supply is zero and $q^a(p^*) = q^e(p^*)$. So long as no buyer prefers to buy at a higher price, the buyers' equilibrium is no different from the one resulting when an auctioneer equates supply and demand.

The second case arises when some buyers do prefer to announce a price higher than a Walrasian equilibrium price p^*. Since they would also buy at p^*, the number of buyers who announce a price greater than or equal to p^* cannot exceed $D(p^*)$. However, those who announce a price greater than p^* would attract some sellers (who would not supply a car at p^*). Therefore, the owners who are ready to sell their car at p^* will not all find a buyer, and a positive excess supply arises at p^*. The same is true when all buyers who are willing to purchase at p^* also prefer to announce a higher price.

In this second case, the cutoff price must lie below p^*, because excess supply must be zero at the cutoff price. It is then possible to construct Figure 3.9, taken from Wilson (1980, p. 120). The unique Walrasian equilibrium at $p^* > \underline{p}$ illustrates the first case (p^* is the highest price that equates demand and supply). If buyer t_1 prefers p^* to any higher price, this is a buyers' equilibrium. But suppose buyer t_1 announces p_2, buyer t^1 is indifferent between p^1 and $\underline{p}$, and t^0 is the lowest buyer (and therefore announces the cutoff price). Then the buyers' equilibrium has the three equilibrium prices: $\underline{p}$, p_1, and p_2.

Note how the excess supply behaves. At prices at or above p^2, the E function and the S function are identical because demand is zero. From p^2 to p^1, additional buyers continuously enter. From $\underline{p}$ to p^1, there are no additional buyers. Therefore, the decline in E as $\underline{p}$ falls is proportional to S. At the cutoff price $\underline{p}$, there is a mass point of buyers who announce it; just enough buyers enter the market to eliminate the excess supply. Indeed, those buyers who would prefer to announce a lower price would have to revise it upward, because if they did announce lower prices, excess demand would have to appear over some range, thus forcing all buyers to raise their prices until all announce the cutoff price.

3.4.2. Sellers set their price

We now turn to the assumption, which is more appropriate for the used-car market and perhaps typical for the professions, that each seller announces a price. The situation is more complicated. The number of buyers who demand a car at each price depends on the quality

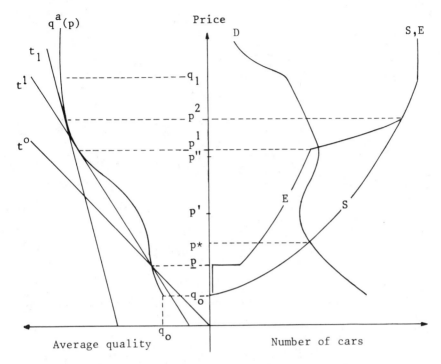

Figure 3.9. A buyers' equilibrium.

of cars they expect to be offered at each price; the quality of cars actually offered depends on the number of buyers sellers expect to demand a car at each price. Whether or not the expectations of one side of the market are confirmed therefore depends upon the expectations of the other side, and vice versa. Wilson is able to show that although there is always a pattern of expectations that are consistent with a Walrasian equilibrium, there is also always another pattern of expectations consistent with a continuous distribution of prices. Figure 3.10, taken from Wilson (1980, p. 126) illustrates a typical equilibrium of the latter type.

The ratio of the number of buyers to the number of sellers at each price defines the realized probability function, labeled π^*. It is a decreasing function of the price. The curves labeled v_0, v', and v_1 represent indifference curves for the owners of cars q_0, q', and q_1, respectively, each tangent to the π^* curve to illustrate the optimal price for each seller to choose. Note that the indifference curves of the owners of higher-quality cars are always flatter than those of the owners

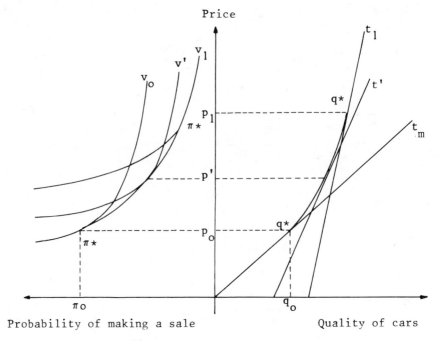

Figure 3.10. A sellers' equilibrium.

of lower-quality cars. Since π^* is less convex than any of the indifference curves, all points of tangency define the optimal prices to announce. The set of announced prices is therefore equal to $[p_0, p_1]$.

The resulting equilibrium quality function, q^*, is upward sloping, because the owners of higher-quality cars announce higher prices, and defined on $[p_0, p_1]$ only. Since $q^*(p_0) = q_0$, the lowest utility index of any active buyer is $t_m = p_0/q_0$; p_0 is the price at which the indifference curve of buyer t_m is tangent to q^*: and similarly for p' and p_1. These points of tangency are also maxima for the buyers. Thus (q^*, π^*) represents a sellers' equilibrium with a continuous distribution of prices.

3.5.*   The lemons principle reconsidered

In real life, a car owner does not have a car of a given quality. He can influence this quality by driving carefully, by having it serviced regularly, and so on. On the other hand, buyers are not necessarily non-owners and can become sellers when they decide to buy new cars and get rid of their old ones. To take these two features into account, Kim

(1985) constructs a two-period model, in which a car is new in the first period and used in the second. In each period, an agent can buy a new car, buy a used one, buy nothing, and keep or sell the car she bought in the first period. However, Kim maintains Akerlof's (and Wilson's) information structure, according to which potential buyers cannot acquire or transmit information about quality and can only observe the average quality of a used car.

Make quality q endogenous by making it a function of the level of maintenance, m, which represents the expenditure on a car for any preventive purpose, such as regular checkups. The quality of a new car, q_n, is a strictly concave function $q_n(m)$ increasing with m. Maintenance on a used car is assumed to have no effect on quality, so that the quality of a used car depends only on the level of maintenance in the previous period, m, or $q_u(m)$, which is also increasing and strictly concave. The quality of a new car is always higher than that of a used car, or $q_n(0) > q_u(\infty)$.

Each agent, whether it buys, sells, keeps the car, or decides not to have a car, is characterized by a real number t distributed on $T = [\underline{t}, \overline{t}]$ with density $w(t)$ and maximizes expected utility over two periods, with a one-period utility function

$$u = tq - e, \tag{3.20}$$

where e is the expenditure on a car. By Wilson's utility function (3.15) above, this amounts to putting the consumption of other goods, c, equal to $y - e$, where y is per-period income, and to assuming that $y = 0$, because each agent receives the same income so that it does not affect the optimal decisions. Finally, let p_u, p_n, and α be the price of used cars, the price of new cars, and the discount factor, respectively. Since p_u is "the" price of used cars, Kim stays within what Wilson called the "Walrasian" paradigm. The two other price-setting conventions (sellers or buyers set the price, respectively) are not studied.

Consider an agent who has no car at the beginning of the first period. A first option, option I, is to buy a new car, maintain it, and sell it in the second period. He or she end up having no car. Option 2 is to buy a new car, maintain, and keep it for both periods. In the two remaining options, the end situation is again to have no car. Option 3 is to buy a used car and sell it in the second period. Option 4 is not to buy a car.

If option 2 is taken, the corresponding two-period utility for an agent of type t is

$$U_2(t) = [tq_n(m_2(t)) - p_n - m_2] + \alpha t q_u(m_2(t)) \tag{3.21}$$

where $m_2(t)$ is the optimum maintenance.

Under the three other options, the agent goes back to the starting state of having no car. Therefore, if an option is optimal in the second period, it is also optimal in the first period. Only stationary policies leading to the same option in each period are to be considered. The corresponding two-period utilities are

$$U_1(t) = (1 + \alpha)[tq_n(m_1(t)) - p_n - m_1(t) + \alpha p_u],$$

$$U_3(t) = (1 + \alpha)[tq_u^e - p_u],$$

$$U_4(t) = 0, \tag{3.22}$$

where q_u^e is the expected average quality of used cars.

Using equations (3.21) and (3.22), we can define subsets T_i of agents who adopt a particular option because the corresponding U_i ($i = 1, 2, 3, 4$) is the highest two-period utility they can attain (if we assume for simplicity that two or more U_i never coincide over an interval of t and that, if some t belong to more than one subset, it is included in T_i with the smallest index). Agents in $T_1 = [t_1, \bar{t}]$ buy a new car *in each period* and sell it after one period, so T_1 is *a set of used car sellers*. Similarly, $T_2 = [t_2, t_1)$ is a *set of owners of a nontraded used car*, $T_3 = [t_4, t_2]$ is a set of used car buyers, and $T_4 = [\underline{t}, t_4]$ contains agents who *do not buy cars*.

How are the optimal maintenance levels m_1 and m_2 determined? From equation (3.22) we know that m_1 maximizes $tq_n(m) - m$, so it is the solution of $tq_n'(m) = 1$. Equation (3.21) tells us that m_2 maximizes $tq_n(m) + \alpha tq_n(m) - m$. Therefore m_2 is the solution of $tq_n'(m) + \alpha tq_n'(m) = 1$. On the other hand, the assumption of strict concavity implies $m_1'(t) > 0$, $m_2'(t) > 0$, and $m_2(t) > m_1(t)$ for all t. In other words, agents with higher preferences for car service (a higher t still means a higher marginal rate of substitution of car quality for consumption) select higher maintenance levels. Those who intend to keep their car in the second period select higher maintenance levels for new cars.

The average quality of traded used cars is simply

$$Eq_u(T_1) = \int_{T_1} q_u(m_1(t))w(t)dt/W(T_1), \tag{3.23}$$

where $W(T_1) = \int wT_1(t) \, dt$ is the total supply of used cars by agents in T_1. When $m_1(t)$ is replaced by $m_2(t)$, the average quality of nontraded used cars can be computed in the same way.

The used-car market is then in equilibrium if demand is equal to supply, or $W(T_3) = W(T_1)$, and the expectations about the average quality of traded used cars, q_u^e, are correct; that is, $q_u^e = Eq_u(T_1)$. Is this equilibrium unique? If so, are the traded cars of lower quality on average? Can there be an equilibrium dispersion of prices and qualities as in the Wilson approach? The answer is that the properties of the equilibrium depend upon the properties of the subsets of agents in terms of their U_i.

3.5.1. A counterexample to Akerlof's lemons principle

Let us take a closer look at the shape of U_1, U_2, U_3, and U_4 and therefore compute their first and second partial derivatives with respect to t. Kim finds

$$\frac{\partial U_1}{\partial t} = (1 + \alpha)q_n(m_1(t)) + (1 + \alpha)m_1'(t)[tq_n'(m_1(t)) - 1]$$

$$= (1 + \alpha)q_n(m_1(t)) > 0,$$

$$\frac{\partial U_2}{\partial t} = q_n(m_2(t)) + \alpha q_u(m_2(t)) > 0,$$

$$\frac{\partial U_3}{\partial t} = (1 + \alpha)q_u^e > 0,$$

$$\frac{\partial U_4}{\partial t} = 0,$$

$$\frac{\partial^2 U_1}{\partial t^2} = (1 + \alpha)q_n'(m_1(t))m_1'(t) > 0,$$

$$\frac{\partial^2 U_2}{\partial t^2} = [q_n'(m_2(t)) + \alpha q_u'(m_2(t))]m_2'(t) > 0,$$

$$\frac{\partial^2 U_3}{\partial t^2} = \frac{\partial^2 U_4}{\partial t^2} = 0,$$

$$\tag{3.24}$$

since $tq_n'(m_1) = 1$ and $tq_n'(m_2) + \alpha t q_u(m_2) = 1$. In words, all U_i's are increasing functions of t; U_1 and U_2 are increasing at increasing rates while U_3 increases linearly. And U_1 is always steeper than U_3, because $q_n(0) > q_u(\infty)$. But it is not obvious whether U_2 is steeper than U_1 and U_3.

Let us study the case[5] where U_2 is steeper than U_3 but flatter than

---

[5] When U_2 is steeper than U_1, $T_2 = [t_1, \bar{t}]$. The average quality of nontraded cars is definitely higher than that of traded cars. In addition, multiple equilibria may exist for the same reason given by Wilson. However, because buyers may become sellers cost-lessly, it is no longer possible to rank equilibria by the Pareto criterion in contrast with Wilson's argument. See Kim (1985, pp. 841–2).

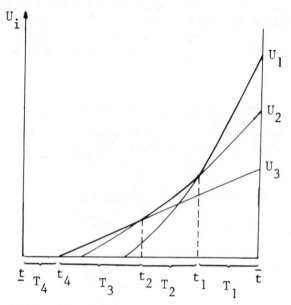

Figure 3.11. A counterexample to Akerlof's lemons principle.

U_1, as depicted in Figure 3.11. This case is interesting because it gives a counterexample to Akeriof's lemons principle and is also more likely to occur in practice than the other one.[6] Agents in T_1 and T_2 buy new cars. Agents in T_3 buy the used cars sold by the agents in T_1. If the total supply of used cars, $W(T_1)$, is equal to the total demand of used cars, $W(T_2)$, and the expectations about the average quality of traded used cars are correct, then the equilibrium implies that used cars of various qualities are traded in the market. The lemons principle is contradicted when the average quality of traded cars is higher than that of the used cars owned by the subset T_2.

The reader may object that $m_2(t) > m_1(t)$, so the quality of a used car in the hands of a member of group T_2 (the car keepers) is higher than the quality of a used car owned by a car seller, or $q_u(m_2(t)) > q_u(m_1(t))$. This is not a valid objection because these inequalities are defined for an agent of a given type t. Average quality of traded used cars depends upon the composition of group T_1 (the used car sellers)

---

[6] Kim (1985, p. 839) notes that if $q_n(\infty)$ is bounded from above and t is sufficiently large, U_1 must eventually be steeper than U_2, because as t grows, $q_n(m_2(t)) - q_n(m_1(t))$ becomes arbitrarily small while $q_n(m_1(t)) - q_u(m_2(t))$ is bounded away from some positive number. The same kind of reasoning shows that U_2 is steeper than U_3 for a sufficiently large t.

and the evolution of $q_u(m(t))$ as a function of t. The group T_1 consists of agents with higher t's selecting higher maintenance levels for a given option as discussed before. If $q_u(m_1(t))$ rises fast enough, then the average quality of traded cars will be higher than that of the nontraded cars.

Notice that, if an equilibrium exists, it is unique: There is a single equilibrium price of used cars! That is so because a rise of p_u extends T_1 to the left (supply increases) and reduces T_3 from the right and left sides (demand decreases), so the demand and supply functions have the usual shapes.

To see this, consider the marginal agents t_1, t_2, and t_4. Agent t_1 is indifferent between options 1 and 2 (and is not to be confused with Wilson's buyer with the highest utility index in Figure 3.9). Agents t_2 and t_4 are indifferent between options 2 and 3, and options 3 and 4, respectively. At equilibrium, we have therefore simultaneously

$$U_1(t_1) - U_2(t_1) = 0, \tag{3.25a}$$

$$U_2(t_2) - U_3(t_2) = 0, \tag{3.25b}$$

$$U_3(t_4) = 0, \tag{3.25c}$$

$$\int_{t_1}^{\bar{t}} w(t) \, dt = \int_{t_4}^{t_2} w(t) \, dt, \tag{3.25d}$$

$$\bar{t} > t_1 > t_2 > t_4 > \underline{t}. \tag{3.25e}$$

By totally differentiating (3.25a, b, c) with respect to p_u and then using the slope conditions (3.24) (which imply that U_1 increases and U_3 decreases when p_u rises), Kim is able to show that

$$\frac{\partial t_1}{\partial p_u} < 0, \quad \frac{\partial t_2}{\partial p_u} < 0, \quad \frac{\partial t_4}{\partial p_u} > 0. \tag{3.26}$$

He (1985, p. 841) concludes:

The reason why the demand and supply functions have the usual shape is the following. Suppose that the used car price goes up. This will make it more profitable than before to sell used cars, which will induce some agents who otherwise would be used car keepers to become used car sellers, lowering the average quality and increasing the supply of used cars. At the same time, an increase in the used car price and the resulting decrease in the average quality will depress the demand for used cars.

Before continuing, it seems worthwhile to investigate the structural difference between the present model and the Akerlof–Wilson model. In the Akerlof–Wilson model, sellers are identical except for the quality of cars they own. Then, given a used car price, owners of cars above some critical quality level do not want to offer their cars for sale in the market. So identical agents behave in different ways depending on the cars they own. By contrast, in this model, there are many different types of agents. All agents of the same type are assumed to behave in the same way, that is, take the same option so that the quality of a car is endogenously linked to the type of agent holding the car. The structural difference generates different outcomes in many ways. For example, in case of an increase in the used car price, the Akerlof–Wilson model predicts an opposite result that the quality will go up because owners of higher quality cars will be induced to sell.

Finally, note that if the agents are identical (or almost identical) so that buyers get perfect or almost perfect information about the quality of used cars ($t = \bar{t}$ or $\underline{t}$ and $\bar{t}$ close to each other), a used-car market cannot exist. Agents will keep their used cars because they cannot obtain gains from trade. In this sense, imperfect information makes the used-car market work!

3.6.   Resale price maintenance

To conclude this chapter, I wish to briefly discuss resale price maintenance. This may come as a surprise to the reader, who probably considers resale price maintenance as a device to prevent price competition. The traditional argument in the antitrust literature is, indeed, that producers use resale price maintenance to ease the difficulty of checking rivals for price shading (and thus to stabilize a producer cartel) or that retailers collectively put pressure on the producers to impose "fair trade" in order to limit price competition at the dealer level. Though this may be a correct explanation in some cases, it is probably of limited application. Resale price maintenance is often imposed by small producers, in the absence of collusion, or even by new entrants to competitive industries. And it is more popular for high-quality varieties than for low-quality varieties of the same good. The explanation offered in the more recent literature is that resale maintenance creates an incentive for retailers to provide valuable quality information.

In a seminal paper, Telser (1960) developed a "special service" free-rider argument as an alternative to price fixing. Telser draws attention to the fact that for many commodities retailers provide special services specific to the commodity and unrelated to the dealers' general business methods (such as providing a pleasant shopping atmosphere, delivery, credit, and the like). He argues that, by fixing the dealer's margin through resale price maintenance, the manufacturer hopes to induce retailers to single out his or her product for *special* presale treatment. A cogent example is presale demonstration of the product.

The free-rider argument runs as follows (Telser 1960, pp. 91–92):

Since the services provided are, by hypothesis, special, some retailers have good reason not to provide these special services and offer to sell the product at lower prices. They reduce their prices because they avoid the additional cost of the special services. If some retailers do provide these services and ask for a correspondingly higher price whereas others do not provide the services and offer to sell the product to consumers at a lower price then an unstable situation emerges. Sales are diverted from the retailers who do provide the special services at the higher price to the retailers who do not provide the special services and offer to sell the product at the lower price. The mechanism is simple. A customer, because of the special services provided by one retailer, is persuaded to buy the product. But he purchases the product from another paying the latter a lower price. In this way the retailers who do not provide the special services get a free ride at the expense of those who have convinced consumers to buy the product.

As a result few or none of the retailers offer the special services the manufacturer thinks necessary to sell his product. If the manufacturer is correct in his belief that point-of-purchase services increase the demand for his product then because less than the optimal amount of services are provided his sales decrease. He can prevent the diversion of sales from one kind of retailer to another if he removes the incentive to diversion. He accomplishes this by establishing a minimum retail price that guarantees a minimum gross mark-up. Therefore dealers are forced to compete by providing special services with the product and not by reducing the retail price.

The reader may think that there are several alternatives to this resale price maintenance policy. In fact, none of these will do. Couldn't the retailers charge a fee for demonstrating the product? Customers differ in the amount of special services they desire, and it would be very difficult to devise a method whereby each would pay a price equal to the services desired. Couldn't manufacturers charge retailers different prices according as they do or do not provide the special service? But how could they prevent transshipments from those who pay the low price to those who pay the higher price? A third alternative would be to pay retailers directly an amount equal to the cost of the special service they provide. But then the manufacturer has to check whether this service is provided. It is easier to police violations of minimum prices. A last alternative for the manufacturer is to refuse to sell her product to any retailer who does not provide the requisite services. But then she must arrange to remunerate those retailers she approves, and we are back in the third alternative and run into the same difficulty.

Since Telser's argument refers to the provision of a "special service," goods which require such services to sell well are natural candidates for price maintenance on this argument. New products, especially new durables such as video recorders or compact disks, clearly belong to this category. But well-known products may also require a special service if they are purchased infrequently by relatively few households. Here Telser cites sporting goods as an example, and drugs, because consumers rely heavily on the druggist's advice.

One wonders, though, whether Telser's argument could not be extended to a much broader class of commodities, that is, to all cases where the recommendation by a retailer is found useful and where the commodity can be purchased elsewhere. This extension was made by Marvel and McCafferty (1984), who emphasize that many, perhaps most, applications of resale price maintenance do not appear to involve tangible, product-specific, dealer-provided services. They argue that resale price maintenance guarantees the retailers a margin sufficient to cover the cost of *quality certification* or *style certification*. This argument applies to all branded goods, that is, to all cases where consumers rely on the brand label as a source of information about quality but are indifferent to the store from which the product is obtained.

Marvel and McCafferty (1984, p. 348) develop their point as follows:

By stocking a particular product on its shelves, the retailer attests that the quality and suitability of the item in question are consonant with the retailer's overall reputation. But this sort of dealer recommendation is subject to the same sort of free-riding as more tangible presale services. Consumers who are familiar with the reputation of a retailer as well as with the branded items that retailer offers for sale will find such information useful even if they purchase the goods elsewhere. So long as branding ensures consistent quality of the good across dealers, high-quality dealers will be unable to capture a premium price for the certification they provide.

The certification provided by retailers need not be limited to quality. For example, apparel deemed to be in style can command a premium over that considered merely utilitarian. In good part, apparel retailers act as the consumer's agent, expending resources on sophisticated buyers and other devices to sense fashion trends in the making. These resource expenditures are valuable only to the extent that consumers value the style information that is produced. A manufacturing firm will prefer to have its merchandise marketed at leading stores to benefit from this style certification, simply because style certification will shift out the demand schedule for its apparel items. If, however, the product is branded, and if consumers rely on the brand label as an indication of standardization, the consumer will be indifferent to the store from which his apparel item is obtained. Hence, the exclusive store will be unable to charge a premium price to cover the services of the buyers who certified the clothing as exclusive in the first place. The solution to the problem is either to refuse to sell to discounters or to guarantee the style-certifying retailer a margin sufficient to cover its costs through resale price maintenance.

CHAPTER 4

Auctions

This chapter is devoted to a new type of informational asymmetry. A monopolist is selling a unique object (an individual wants to sell a piece of art, say) or a monopsonist is buying a particular service (a government is contracting out the construction of a highway section). Because they do not know how much the potential buyers value the object or at what cost the potential contractors can produce the service, they choose to sell or buy by auction rather than posting a price. Indeed, posting a price is not optimal when there is a capacity constraint,[1] because such a price does not exploit the fact that some buyers (contractors) might be willing to pay more (ask less) before the monopolist (monopsonist) hits the capacity constraint. In the case considered, the capacity constraint is very severe. Organizing an auction is the best solution, because the participants in an auction *reveal* through the bidding mechanism, how much they value the object or at what cost they can produce the service.

Auctions in which buyers have independent private reservation values are studied first. Each buyer knows with precision how much the item is worth to him or her, but is ignorant about the others' private values. Each of these private values is independent of the reservation values of the others so that it conveys no information about any other buyer's value. Questions raised are: To what extent can such auctions be said to be demand-revealing mechanisms? Do such auctions lead to efficient allocations?

In a second section, another polar case is studied. There, the item to be auctioned has a single objective value, but no one knows it. Bidders have differing estimates based in part on private information and these estimates are not independent of those of the other bidders. The question is raised to what extent such "common value" auctions allow the seller to collect the common value.

Real-life auctions probably display an information structure that incorporates elements belonging to both the "private value" and the "common value" model, so the assumptions made appear to be ex-

---

[1] See Harris and Raviv (1981).

treme in each case. Much further work is needed to construct a theory capable of describing the operation of particular auctions (even if more general models become available recently). Yet, the analyses presented should be helpful in clarifying the basic issues involved.[2] A third section briefly discusses how, in the case of a procurement auction, the government can design a contract that shares the risk related to cost uncertainty in order to give bidders an incentive to reduce their bids. The final section is devoted to collusion and misinformation.

4.1.   Auctions with independent private values

Let us take the simple case in which one single product is auctioned, and in which there is a *single unique indivisible object* (this is a very strict capacity constraint indeed) to be sold to *one* of a number of potential purchasers. This is the problem studied by Vickrey in his pioneering 1961 article "Counterspeculation, Auctions, and Competitive Sealed Tenders." And let us postulate the particular information structure introduced by Vickrey: The seller is ignorant about the buyers' reservation values,[3] and each buyer is informed of his or her own reservation value only; in addition, this value is independent of the reservation values of other buyers, so it conveys no information about any other buyer's value.

For auctions of nondurable consumer goods, this information structure may be appropriate, because the satisfaction derived from such goods is largely a personal matter. The assumption that the bidder knows his or her own reservation value only, implies that if the object is a painting, this painting has no "prestige" value, that is, the fact of winning it does not provide prestige because other bidders admire it. The model thus does not apply to the work of famous painters, a Rembrandt say, which is admired by everybody. This assumption also implies that the authenticity of the painting is not in doubt. The independence assumption rules out the possibility that if I recognize a Rembrandt, others recognize it too.

This does not rule out the possibility that Vickrey's information structure may be appropriate for some durable items: A used Bösendorfer grand piano may be worth no more (or even less) than a cupboard

---

[2] Engelbrecht-Wiggans' 1980 survey presents a unifying framework for describing auctions and bidding models. Stark and Rothkopf (1979) provide a comprehensive bibliography. A penetrating survey of recent work in the area is given in McAfee and McMillan (1987).

[3] For clarity of exposition, buyers' reservation prices will be called reservation "values," and the seller's (minimum) reservation price will be called a "reserve price."

needed to fill an empty corner to the average bidder, but is surely worth a fortune to a pianist who happens to walk in by chance at the auction. Yet, even here there is a "prestige" value in owning a Bösendorfer, at least among pianists, and nonpianists may know this too.

For other goods, such as mineral rights on a tract of land or water, there definitely is a value that is common to all market participants if these are all oil companies. In most real-life situations, the truth probably lies in the middle, in that there is both a common value and differences from buyer to buyer, reflecting special tastes or special needs, plus some uncertainty about the private as well as the common values. Although extreme, the independence assumption certainly facilitates the analysis and is therefore a natural one to start with.

4.1.1. Four types of auctions

Vickrey discusses four types of auctions.[4] The first two – the usual English or progressive auction and the second-price sealed-bid auction – turn out to be isomorphic, in the sense that they have identical qualitative and quantitative characteristics. The last two – the first-price sealed-bid auction and the Dutch auction – are also isomorphic. In terms of their economic characteristics, the four types thus reduce to two.

Each type of auction is characterized by a particular decision rule. In the ordinary or progressive *English auction*, bids are freely made and announced publicly until no purchaser wishes to make any further bid. A utility-maximizing bidder participates if and only if he can win the auction with a bid that is less than his reservation value for the auctioned object and thus drops out only if the bid "on the floor" equals or exceeds his reservation value. Bids therefore do not depend on the bidder's risk preferences nor on his expectations about rival bids: They depend only on individual reservation values and observed bids on the floor. Individual utility-maximizing bids are thus "dominant" strategies and have the property that no individual can increase his expected utility by changing his strategy, given the strategies of his rivals. These strategies thus automatically satisfy the Nash equilibrium condition (see Section 1.3). The best thing to do is always to remain in the bidding competition as long as the bid on the floor does not exceed the bidder's reservation value and to drop out as soon as it exceeds that. The English auction is thus a demand-revealing mechanism. The result is that the bidding stops at a price approximately equal to the *second highest value*

---

[4] See also Cox, Roberson, and Smith (1982, pp. 1–13) for a more technical exposition.

among the values that the purchasers place on the object, because at
that price there will be only one interested bidder left. Notice also that
the winner is the bidder to whom it has the highest value. The English
auction thus leads to Pareto-efficient allocations, because total surplus
– the surplus to the seller (the bid) plus the surplus to the buyer (his
reservation value minus the bid) – is maximized.

The English auction is an "oral" or "open" procedure, because all
bids are made publicly so that any bidder can observe the bidding
behavior of his rivals. Given its interesting properties, Vickrey asked
himself whether there is some "sealed-bid" or "written-bid" auction
procedure, in which the behavior of rivals cannot be observed in the
absence of collusion, that would be isomorphic to it. He came up with
the following answer (Vickrey, 1961, pp. 20–21):

> It is easily shown that the required procedure is to ask for bids on the un-
> derstanding that the award will be made to the highest bidder, but on the basis
> of the price set by the second highest bidder. If this procedure is carried out,
> then the optimal strategy for each bidder (assuming, as is indeed necessary in
> the analysis of the progressive auction itself, the absence of collusion among
> bidders) will obviously be to make his bid equal to the full value of the article
> or contract to himself, i.e. to the highest amount he could afford to pay without
> incurring a net loss or to that price at which he would be on the margin of
> indifference as to whether he obtains the article or not. Bidding less than this
> full value could then only diminish his chances of winning at what would have
> been a profitable, or at least not unprofitable, price and could not, collusion
> aside, affect the price he would actually pay if he were the successful bidder.
> Bidding more than the full value, on the other hand, would increase his chances
> of winning, but only under circumstances that would involve him in an un-
> profitable transaction, the price to be paid being greater than this value.

Translated into today's terminology, this quotation says or implies
that (a) this "*second-price sealed-bid auction*" is a perfect demand-
revealing mechanism, because the expected utility-maximizing strategy
is to make one's bid equal to one's reservation value; (b) this strategy
is a dominant strategy, because it is independent of one's risk preferences or one's expectations about the rivals' strategies and is thus
the best thing to do whatever the rivals do; (c) the winner is the bidder
to whom the object or contract auctioned has the highest value, and
the allocation is Pareto-efficient. By construction, the winning bid is
equal to the largest of the reservation prices and the sales price equals
the second highest of these reservation prices.

Is anything wrong with the "*first-price sealed-bid auction*" in which
the highest bid (or the lowest, if it is a buyer who organizes the auction)
will be accepted and executed in accordance with its own terms? The
situation is drastically different. First of all, the expected utility-max-

imizing bidders must now take into account whatever information they have concerning the probable bids that might be made by others, so they have no incentive to make a bid equal to their reservation value: This auction is not a demand-revealing mechanism. In addition, the utility-maximizing strategy depends on each bidder's risk preference *and* on his or her expectations about the bids of the rivals: There is no dominant strategy. Finally, the highest bid is not necessarily submitted by the bidder with the highest reservation price, so that the allocation is not necessarily Pareto-efficient. It would be Pareto-efficient only if bids were an increasing function of the reservation values and if all bidders had the same risk preferences and the same expectations about their rivals' bids.

The same results hold for the *Dutch auction* in which ". . . the offer price starts at an amount believed to be higher than any bidder is willing to pay and is lowered by an auctioneer or a clock device until one of the bidders accepts the last price offer" (Cassady 1967, p. 67). "The first and only bid is the sales price in the Dutch auction." (Cox, Roberson, and Smith 1982, p. 1). This is how flowers are marketed in the Netherlands, how fish is sold every morning in the "fish mines" of Nieuwpoort and Zeebrugge in Belgium, and how fresh fruit is auctioned in many centralized fruit markets. Vickrey (1961, pp. 14–15) remarks:

> In the analysis of this form of auction, however, we find that we are faced with what is essentially a "game" in the technical sense. Each bidder, in attempting to determine at what point he should be prepared to make a bid so as to obtain the greatest expectation of gain, will need to take into account whatever information he has concerning the probable bids that might be made by others, and the bids made by others will in turn depend on their expectations concerning the behavior of the first bidder. To put in a bid as soon as the price has come down to the full value of the object to the bidder maximizes the probability of obtaining the object, but guarantees that the gain from securing it will be zero; as the announced price is progressively lowered, the possibility of a gain emerges, but as the gain thus sought increases with the lowering of the point at which a bid is to be made, the probability of securing this gain diminishes. Each bidder must thus attempt to balance these two factors in terms of whatever knowledge he has concerning the probable bids of the others.

4.1.2. Auctions as games with incomplete information

Auctions are games with "incomplete" information, technically speaking (see Section 1.4). In the "open" auctions, information is perfect in that the history of the game (i.e., the actual behavior of the bidders), is perfectly known by all: Bids are made publicly. In the sealed-bid auctions, information is perfect only for the seller. In all four types, information is incomplete in that the reservation values of the other bidders are not known (as long as there is no collusion).

In the English and second-price sealed-bid auctions, this incompleteness of the information does not create problems, because the individual expected-utility-maximizing strategy is a dominant strategy, and thus automatically has the Nash equilibrium property. In the two other auctions (the Dutch and the first-price sealed-bid auctions), the individual utility-maximizing strategies are not necessarily the equilibrium strategies. To find these, one has, in the absence of collusion, to find the noncooperative Nash equilibrium, that is a set of bid functions, one for each player, such that no player can increase his expected gain by changing his own equilibrium bid function, given that all other players make bids according to their equilibrium bid functions.

To be able to compute this equilibrium, we have to make some assumptions. First, most authors suppose that all bidders have the same risk preferences, to concentrate attention on the incomplete information aspect. Vickrey assumed all bidders to be risk neutral, so they all have the same linear utility or payoff function. The incomplete information is modeled as follows: Although each bidder does not know his rivals' bid functions, he can make informed guesses by supposing that the reservation values of all bidders are drawn from a probability distribution. Vickrey assumes this distribution to be the same for all players and to be rectangular (so that each value is equally likely). Any given player thus knows not only his own reservation value but also the (rectangular) distribution from which others consider his reservation value to be drawn. In addition, individual reservation values are supposed to be drawn on the same interval [0, 1] by a suitable choice of scale and origin. Finally,[5] buyers' values are independent: A buyer's reservation value conveys no information about any other buyer's reservation value. (If I draw a high value, that does not imply that others are likely also to draw a high value.) The situation is thus redefined as a game with complete information (on the probability functions from which each bidder draws his reservation value and on everybody's utility or payoff).

The Nash equilibrium strategies are now easy to find, because each player i simply has to maximize the expected payoff of the winning bid. This payoff is the difference between his reservation value v_i and the winning bid b_i (since his utility function is simply $(v_i - b_i)$ if he

---

wins, and zero otherwise), multiplied by the probability of making the winning bid. With a common rectangular distribution and independence, this probability[6] is nb_i^{n-1}, where n is the number of players. Each player thus maximizes

$$H_i = (v_i - b_i)nb_i^{n-1} \qquad (4.1)$$

with respect to b_i by putting

$$\frac{\partial H_i}{\partial b_i} = (v_i - b_i)n(n-1)b_i^{n-2} - nb_i^{n-1} \qquad (4.2)$$

equal to zero. This gives

$$(v_i - b_i)(n-1) - b_i = 0,$$

$$b_i + \frac{1}{n-1}b_i = v_i,$$

or

$$b_i = \frac{n-1}{n}v_i \qquad (i = 1, \ldots, n) \qquad (4.3)$$

as the unique Nash equilibrium strategy to be played by each player. It is thus a *common* equilibrium strategy: With two players, each should make a bid equal to one half of his reservation value in a Dutch or a first-price sealed-bid auction. In a Dutch auction, for example, each player should stop the clock as soon as the announced price is equal to one half of his reservation value under the assumptions made. Equilibrium bids get closer to reservation prices as n increases: The more bidders there are in a Dutch auction, the more likely it is that somebody else will stop the clock before you and the faster you should make a bid.[7] Notice that the equilibrium bid of player i is not a function of the value v_j of player j, as would be the case when a market has to be shared by several sellers, because of the independence of buyers' values. Notice also that with this particular information structure the person with the highest reservation value always makes the highest bid – and is thus the winner – so that this particular version of the Dutch and first-price sealed-bid auctions turns out to be Pareto-optimal.

[6] With a rectangular distribution $F(v) = v$, for $v \in [0, 1]$, and value independence, the probability that the first $n - 1$ players draw a value below b is b^{n-1}. This has to be multiplied by n, to allow for the possibility that any of the n players might have the top value.

[7] With $b_i = 0.5$, for example, $nb^{n-1} = 1$ when $n = 2$. But $nb^{n-1} = 0.75$ only, when $n = 3$, so your probability of winning goes down.

4.1.3.   Optimal auctions from the seller's point of view

Until now, we have been concerned with the optimal strategies of the
bidders. The next question is, given the types of auctions considered
by Vickrey, and under his assumptions of risk neutrality, value independence, and identically distributed reservation values, what type of
auction maximizes the seller's expected revenue?

Notice first that this question can be narrowed down to a comparison
between the second-price sealed-bid auction and the first-price sealed-
bid auction, because the first was shown to be isomorphic with the
English auction, and the second with the Dutch auction. Remember
also that, in a second-price auction, the optimal strategy of each player
is to submit his reservation value, without bothering about the other's
strategies. In a first-price auction, this is no longer true. Nevertheless,
there is a common equilibrium strategy, such as the one in equation
(4.3), in which each buyer's bid is the same strictly increasing function
of his reservation value. Whatever the auction rule, there is thus always
a common equilibrium strategy of the type $b_i = b(v_i)$ for all i, with
$b(v_i) = v_i$ in the second-price auction.

The answer is that all four types of auctions are equally good from
the seller's point of view. Indeed, his expected revenue (the expected
price, in fact) was shown by Vickrey to be *the same* in all four types
of auction. In a Dutch (or first-price sealed bid) auction, the expected
price is the expected value

$$\int_0^1 \left[\frac{n-1}{n} v \right] nv^{n-1} \, dv = \int_0^1 (n-1)v^n \, dv$$

$$= \left[(n-1) \frac{v^{n+1}}{n+1} \right]_0^1 = \frac{n-1}{n+1}.$$

Since v is normalized between 0 and 1, you should not be surprised to
find a number smaller than 1. With eight players, the expected price
is thus $\frac{7}{9}$ or 0.77. In an English (or second-price sealed-bid) auction,
the optimal bid is equal to the value, but the expected price is the
second highest value expected or

$$\int_0^1 v[n(n-1)v^{n-2}(1-v)] \, dv = n(n-1) \int_0^1 (v^{n-1} - v^n) \, dv$$

$$= n(n-1) \left[\frac{v^n}{n} - \frac{v^{n+1}}{n+1} \right]_0^1$$

$$= n(n-1) \frac{n+1-n}{(n+1)n} = \frac{n-1}{n+1},$$

because $n(n - 1)v^{n-2}(1 - v)$ is the probability of the second highest value. Vickrey also shows that the *variance* of the prices is higher in a second-price auction than in a first-price auction.

Knowing all this, one might wonder whether the seller could not, in some way, manage to increase the common expected price. The answer is yes.

Expected seller revenue is maximized using *either* of these auction rules, *if the seller announces that he will not accept bids below some minimum reserve price* b_0 to be chosen appropriately. (This reminds us that Vickrey supposed a zero reserve price, because such a minimum never showed up in his reasoning.)

Riley and Samuelson (1981) prove this in three steps.[8] In a first step, it is shown that, for any of these auctions, the expected revenue of the seller can be determined if one can determine the lowest reservation value, v_*, for which it is worthwhile bidding, *without explicit reference to the bidding strategy*. In a second step, the degree to which a bidder will "shade" his bid below his reservation value in the first-price auction is determined, and it is shown that $v_* = b_0$ in either auction. The implication is that expected seller revenue is the same (from step one) in all four types of auctions (as already shown above). In step three, all four types of auctions are shown to be optimal for the seller if he chooses v_* (and thus b_0) well, *whatever the number of buyers.*

Because the proofs are rather technical, I shall simply note that the final step determines the optimal v_* as

$$v_* = v_0 + \frac{1 - F(v_*)}{F'(v_*)} \tag{4.4}$$

where $F(x)$ is the probability that a competing bidder draws a reservation value less than x, and v_0 is the seller's personal valuation of the object that is being auctioned. Equation (4.4) thus says that the seller should always announce a reserve price strictly greater than his personal valuation, because $b_0 = v_*$. The second step determines the equilibrium bidding strategy of a typical buyer with reservation value $v \geq b_0$ as

$$b(v) = v - \int_{b_0}^{v} F^{n-1}(x) \, dx / F^{n-1}(v). \tag{4.5}$$

This bidding function is strictly increasing in v.

To illustrate, Riley and Samuelson suppose that the reservation values are uniformly distributed on the unit interval, so $F(v) = v$ for $v \in$

[8] See also Milgrom and Weber (1982).

[0, 1], as did Vickrey. They also assume that the object has no value to the seller, so $v_0 = 0$. Then the seller should design the auction so that only those with reservation values exceeding $v_* = 0 + 1 - v_*$ or $v_* = \frac{1}{2}$ find it worthwhile bidding, and therefore he should announce a reserve price $b_0 = \frac{1}{2}$. For buyer i, with reservation value $v_i \geq \frac{1}{2}$, the equilibrium bid is, according to equation (4.5),

$$b(v_i) = v_i - \frac{[v^n/n]_{1/2}^{v_i}}{v_i^{n-1}}.$$

If there are only two buyers, $n = 2$ and

$$b(v_i) = v_i - \frac{\frac{1}{2}v_i^2 - \frac{1}{2}(\frac{1}{2})^2}{v_i} = \frac{v_i}{2} + \frac{1}{8v_i}.$$

In the case analyzed by Vickrey, the seller has no reserve price so that $b_0 = 0$, and the equilibrium bid reduces to

$$b(v_i) = v_i - \frac{\frac{1}{2}v_i^2}{v_i} = v_i - \frac{v_i}{2} = \frac{v_i}{2}$$

as found in equation (4.3). The seller's expected revenue is $(n - 1)/(n + 1) = \frac{1}{3}$ or $\frac{4}{12}$ in the Vickrey case (with $b_0 = 0$) and[9] $\frac{5}{12}$ when $b_0 = \frac{1}{2}$. By announcing a reserve price $b_0 = \frac{1}{2}$, the seller increases expected revenue by 25%!

The intuition behind this result, and behind equation (4.4), is the following. Take an English auction. The reserve price announced by the seller is equal to the winner's bid if the second-to-last bidder drops out before this price is reached and if the remaining bidder's reservation value exceeds it. The winner then pays more than he would have paid in the absence of the reserve price. That is why equation (4.4) says that the seller should add to his personal valuation (v_0) a positive number $1 - v_x$ equal to the probability that some bidder has a reservation value higher than the announced reserve price. Needless to say, the seller runs the risk that the remaining bidder's reservation value lies below the announced reserve price, in which case the seller loses the sale, although this bidder might have been willing to pay more than v_0.

---

[9] Riley and Samuelson show that the seller's expected revenue is, in general, $n\int_{b_0}^{\bar{v}}(vF'(v) + F(v) - 1)F^{n-1}(v)\,dv$. With $n = 2$, $F(v) = v$, $F'(v) = 1$, and $\bar{v} = 1$, this implies an expected revenue, when $b_0 = 0$, of $2\int_0^1(2v^2 - v)\,dv$ or $2\left[\frac{8}{12}v^3 - \frac{v^2}{2}\right]_0^1$

$= 2(\frac{8}{12} - \frac{1}{2}) = \frac{4}{12} = \frac{1}{3}.$

4.1.4. *Experimental results*

The theoretical results obtained have been checked with the help of experimental auctions. Smith's 1964 pioneering experiment was followed by a series of similar experiments of increasing complexity designed by Frahm and Schrader (1970), Coppinger, Smith, and Titus (1980), and Cox et al. (1982), among others. The work by Coppinger et al. concentrates on Vickrey's seminal results and was replicated by Schmets (1985), whose findings are reported here.

The experimental design is very simple. Eight students are asked to act as bidders in a classroom auction of a single (undefined) object. Each student is given a reservation value that is unknown to the others, but the student is told inside which range these values were chosen randomly. Communication among the bidders is not allowed. The seller is silent: He or she does not announce a minimum reserve price (below which bids are not accepted), to stick to Vickrey's implicit assumption.

Consider first the English and Dutch auctions. Vickrey's results are reformulated as hypotheses to be tested experimentally. Let p_e be the price at which the object is sold in an English auction, let p_d be the price at which the object is sold in a Dutch auction, and let p_0 designate the second highest reservation value. Then the hypothesis of Pareto optimality is written as

$$H_0: E(p_e - p_0) = 0 = E(p_d - p_0).$$

The seller's expected revenue (i.e., the expected price) should be the same in both types of auctions. This is written as

$$H_1: E(p_e) = \frac{n - 1}{n + 1} = E(p_d).$$

Third, the variance of the price in an English auction should be larger than the variance of the price in a Dutch auction, or

$$H_2: V_e > V_d.$$

Vickrey's results are not contradicted if it turns out that (a) H_0 is accepted for English auctions; (b) H_0 is accepted or rejected for Dutch auctions (because they are not necessarily Pareto-optimal); (c) H_1 is accepted, and (d) H_2 is accepted.

The experiment consists of several sessions, with twelve auctions of the same type (either English or Dutch) in each session. (Because one auction takes only a few minutes to carry out, a session lasts less

$p(t)-p_0(t)$

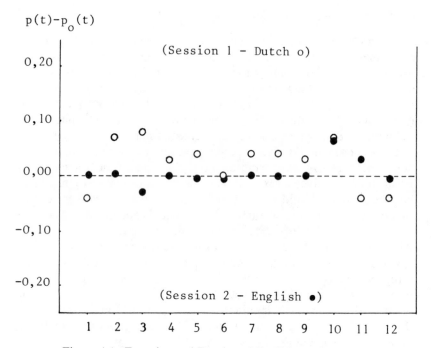

Figure 4.1. Experimental Dutch and English auctions.

than an hour.) In the Dutch auctions a microcomputer displayed the announced price, which was lowered every 7 s.

Figures 4.1 and 4.2 represent the differences between the realized prices and p_0. These differences are close to zero for the English auctions: H_0 turns out to be accepted. They are generally positive, however, for the Dutch auctions: Here H_0 is often rejected. This rejection is not surprising and does not contradict Vickrey's theory. What is surprising is that the differences are mostly positive (they are mostly negative in the Coppinger–Smith–Titus experiment). Rather than waiting too long before stopping the clock (the microcomputer), the players often stopped it *before* p_0 was reached. One possible explanation is that in the Schmets experiments players were not paid out their gains (whereas they were in the American experiment), so they played safe (i.e., were not risk neutral). They preferred to be awarded the object with a small (theoretical) profit rather than to realize the largest possible profit.

As for the hypothesis on the seller's expected revenue (H_1), this revenue is equal to $\frac{7}{9}$ or 0.778 with $n = 8$. Hypothesis H_1 is accepted

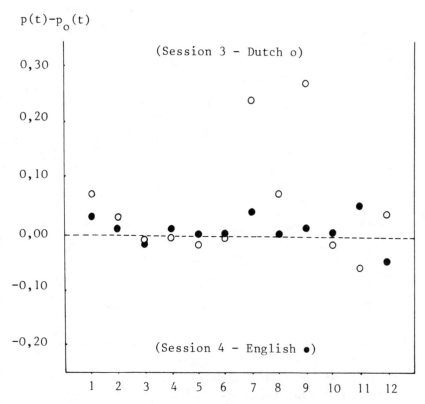

Figure 4.2. Experimental Dutch and English auctions.

in both types of auctions. (The average price is 0.7759 in the English auctions and 0.817 in the Dutch auctions.)

Finally, H_2 is also accepted for both types of auction.

We now turn to the first-price and second-price sealed-bid auctions. The hypotheses are reformulated as

$$H'_0: E(p_1 - p_0) = 0 = E(p_2 - p_0),$$

where p_1 is the price realized in a first-price sealed-bid auction and p_2 is the price realized in a second-price auction,

$$H'_1: E(p_1) = \frac{n-1}{n+1} = E(p_2),$$

and

$$H'_2: V_2 > V_1.$$

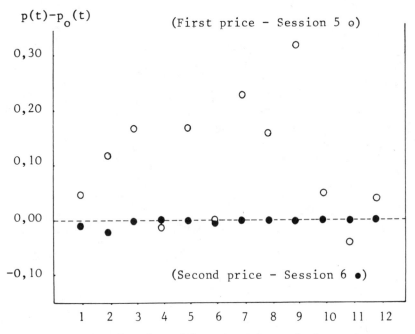

Figure 4.3. Experimental first-price and second-price auctions.

If the Dutch and the first-price auctions are isomorphic, on the one hand, and the English and second-price auctions are isomorphic, on the other hand, then H'_0, H'_1, and H'_2 should be verified in the same way as H_0, H_1, and H_2.

The experimental results are displayed in Figure 4.3. The prices obtained in the second-price auctions are remarkably close to the second highest reservation value: Preferences are (almost) perfectly revealed. But for the first-price auctions this is not the case (as with the Dutch auctions).

H'_1 is accepted for the second-price auctions, but not for the first-price auctions, in which the realized price is much higher than the expected price of 0.778 (the difference turns out to be statistically significant according to a t-test). Apparently, the isomorphism between the Dutch and the first-price auctions is thus contradicted (although less strongly than in the Coppinger–Smith–Titus experiment, because here both prices are too high on average). In fact, risk aversion may be the explanation (in accordance with Riley and Samuelson 1981, p. 388).

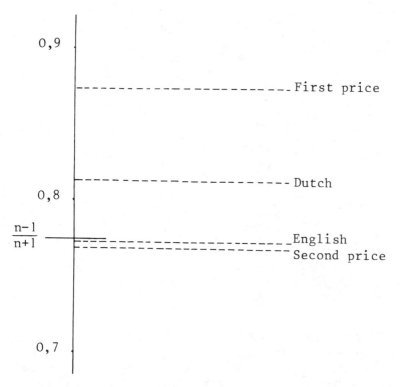

Figure 4.4. Average experimental results.

Finally, H_2' is accepted again for both types of auction. Figure 4.4 displays the average price realized in the four types of auction.

After this replication of the Coppinger–Smith–Titus experiment, Schmets (1985) goes on to test the properties of auctions in which the seller announces a minimum price below which bids are not accepted. We noticed above that this simple fact increases the expected price, whatever the type of auction. In the experiment, the seller was given no information about the true reservation values (a realistic assumption) and was left free to announce the minimum price (between 0 and 1) he thought appropriate (instead of being given the optimal $b_0 = v_* = 0.5$). As a result, it was not possible to test the equality of the seller's average revenue and the theoretical expected price, because the latter is a function of v_* while the former is a function of the actually chosen minimum price. The seller in fact announced much higher min-

Table 4.1. *Dutch auctions with announced minimum price*

Auction[a]	Realized price	p_0	Minimum price
1	0.90	0.87	0.6
2	0.88	0.77	0.675
3	0.735	0.62	0.70
4	0.85	0.77	0.70
5	0.81	0.86	0.72
6	0.78	0.86	0.72
7	0.845	0.66	0.71
8	0.735	0.70	0.70
9	0.855	0.63	0.75
10	0.84	0.87	0.73
11	0.87	0.93	0.80
12	—	0.69	0.80
13	0.84	0.87	0.78

[a] All auctions except 12 were successful.

imum prices (between 0.6 and 0.8, prices so high that no bids could be made in some auctions).

The experiment shows that the average realized prices are significantly higher than those obtained without announced minimum price, in both a series of Dutch and a series of English auctions. Tables 4.1 and 4.2 reproduce the detailed results. Notice, in Table 4.2, how the seller managed in several English auctions to push the price above the second highest reservation value (p_0). But remember also that the seller's expected revenue would have been higher with a minimum price pegged at the optimal value of 0.5 than with no minimum price. (Again, this theoretical result could not be verified given the setup of the experiment.)

Notice, finally, that the announcement of a minimum price can be combined, in an English auction, with a mechanism that further reduces the time needed to reach these higher prices. The mechanism consists in giving a percentage of the increase to any potential buyer who bids up the price, whether the buyer is awarded the object or not.[10] In the Schmets experiments, the average number of bids necessary for a sale went down from 16.5 for ordinary English auctions to 7.3 for auctions

[10] Riley and Samuelson (1981) call these "Santa Claus auctions." In Flanders, where they are in common use for real estate sales, they are called "verkoop met recht van verdieren."

Table 4.2. *English auctions with announced minimum price*

Auction[a]	Realized price	p_0	Minimum price
1	0.78	0.60	0.775
2	—	0.77	0.80
3	0.775	0.62	0.76
4	0.771	0.77	0.77
5	0.81	0.86	0.77
6	0.83	0.78	0.775
7	0.781	0.66	0.78
8	0.79	0.70	0.78
9	0.785	0.63	0.785
10	0.80	0.87	0.785
11	0.93	0.93	0.785
12	—	0.69	0.80
13	0.901	0.87	0.80
14	—	0.70	0.80
15	0.80	0.69	0.80

[a] All auctions except 2, 12, and 14 were successful.

with a minimum price and to 2.5 for auctions where such a percentage is given.

4.2. Auctions with a common value

The results discussed so far are based on the extreme assumption that the bidders know their private reservation values, that these values are independent, and that each bidder knows his or her own reservation price only. Individually speaking, there was no uncertainty about the true (private) value. But these private values had nothing in common. Models with this information structure capture the essential features of auctions for nondurable goods and some durable goods, but are clearly inappropriate for the analysis of auctions of, say, offshore oil leases. For these, it is more appropriate to go to the other extreme and to suppose that the values of these leases are the same for all bidders, but that bidders may have differing estimates of the common value. These estimates will depend on the general information about the presence of oil available to all and on the private information some oil companies may have. For this common value model, the equilibrium of the first-price sealed-bid auction has been studied extensively (see

Milgrom 1979a,b; Milgrom and Weber 1982; Reece 1978; R. Wilson 1977; and Kagel and Levin 1986).

Oil leases for the outer continental shelf (OCS) are indeed sold by the U.S. government[11] by first-price sealed-bid auctions. Hendricks, Porter, and Boudreau (1987) describe the mechanism as follows. After making a certain area available for exploration, the government invites nominations from the oil companies as to which tracts should be offered for sale. A tract typically consists of 5000 or 5760 acres. The companies are not allowed to drill any on-site wells. To gather information, all they can do is to use seismic surveys and off-site drilling.

Wildcat sales consist of tracts whose geology is not well known, and only seismic exploration precedes these sales. Drainage sales consist of tracts which are adjacent to tracts on which a deposit has been discovered.

Companies submit a separate bid on each tract (on the list of nominated tracts) that it is interested in. A bid is a dollar figure, called a "bonus," which a company promises to pay to the government at the time of the sale if it is awarded the tract. The bids on all tracts and the identities of the bidders and the winners are announced at a public meeting.

The winner has five years to explore the tract, otherwise the government may auction it off again. If the winner begins production, the lease is automatically renewed for as long as it takes to extract the oil. A fixed fraction of the revenues, called the "royalty," is paid annually to the government.

During the auction, the government may announce a reserve price. It may reject the winner's bid on a tract if it believes the bid is too low.

4.2.1. The winner's curse

How can we derive the bidding strategy of an oil company? It is natural to suppose that each company makes an independent estimate of the common value, V, by drawing from a single underlying distribution parameterized by V, and determines its bid b_i by maximizing

$$(V_i - b_i)F(b_i) \tag{4.6}$$

with respect to b_i, where V_i is the estimated value and $F(b_i)$ is the probability of making the winning bid, as in the earlier independent private value model (compare with equation (4.1)).

---

[11] For the North Sea, oil licenses were only sporadically sold by auction and most often by discretionary allocation. A comparative study can be found in Dam (1965, 1974).

In fact, this formalization is not correct. It ignores the fact that "winning the auction is itself an informative event" (Wilson, 1977, p. 512). The bidder with the largest estimate will make the highest bid, so the winner must conclude (from the fact that he is the winner) that all other participants obtained lower estimates which induced them to enter lower bids. He must conclude that he must revise his estimate of the value of the rights he has won. This phenomenon is known as the *winner's curse* and must be incorporated in the information structure. (In auctions with private values this is not the case, because there is no "true" common value.)

The difference is important. When it is ignored, so that the player is supposed to determine V_i solely on the basis of the probability of V (conditional on the available information on the presence of oil), his expected value might be computed as

$$\int Vf\left(\frac{V}{s}\right) dV \tag{4.7}$$

where $f(V/s)$ is the conditional probability density function of common value V, given information s. Once a player knows that he has won, he must use this information and revise his expectation of the true value as

$$\frac{\int VF(b_i, V)f(V/s) \, dV}{\int F(b_i, V)f(V/s) \, dV}. \tag{4.8}$$

The numerator in equation (4.8) is the expected value when the winning bid is submitted. The denominator is the probability of winning the auction when the information received is s. Bidding strategies based on (4.8) are different from strategies based on (4.7). Their analytic derivation is difficult, often impossible, so numerical methods have to be used.

4.2.2. *Division of rent*

Economic rent of a tract is the difference between its common value and the cost of determining whether this tract will yield commercial quantities of oil. When the winning bid is equal to the common value, the seller (here the government) captures the entire rent. The greater is the difference between V and the winning bid, the larger is the rent captured by industry. It is of great interest, therefore, to know how the fraction captured by industry depends upon the number of bidders

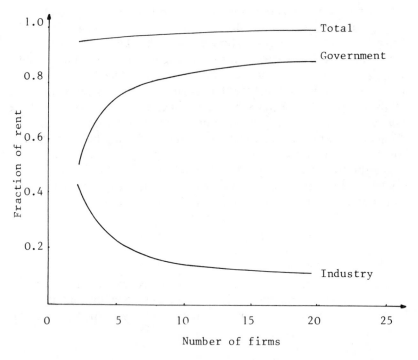

Figure 4.5. Division of rent from oil leases, low uncertainty.

and the degree of uncertainty. Reece (1978) simulates a game with identical firms, which receive an estimate of the common value drawn from a lognormal distribution. [The lognormal distribution is used because (a) bids submitted for a particular tract are often approximately lognormally distributed, and optimal bids are roughly proportional to estimated values, and (b) the value of an oil lease is thought to depend on a number of independent multiplicative random factors, and the central limit theorem suggests that their product (the estimated value) approaches a lognormal distribution.] The resulting division of rent, for cases of low and high uncertainty, as a function of the number of firms is represented in Figures 4.5 and 4.6. Uncertainty is measured by the variance of the signal, that is, the variance of the estimated value.

According to this model, the oil industry could, by adopting optimal bidding strategies, capture a large fraction of the economic rent. For a given number of firms, the industry's share increases with the degree of uncertainty about the common value of the tract (compare Figures

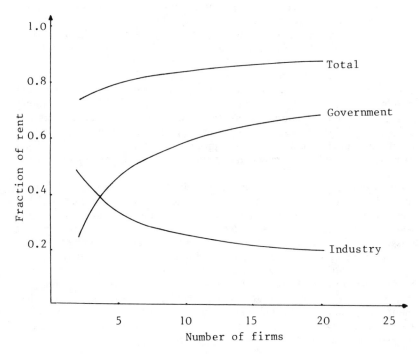

Figure 4.6. Division of rent from oil leases, high uncertainty.

4.5 and 4.6). Its share also increases when the number of firms gets smaller, and may become larger than 50% when uncertainty is high. Notice that the total economic rent recovered by society (government plus industry, labeled "total") increases as uncertainty decreases. The reason is that better-informed firms are better able to locate economic tracts and avoid uneconomic ones. Notice also that total rent recovery is an increasing function of the number of participants. Since the winning bid is the maximum among all the estimates, it conveys an upper bound on all the losers' estimates. The more bidders there are, the more information is thus aggregated and the closer is the winning bid to the common value.

Reece (1978, pp. 380–1) derives the following policy implications:

The government generally benefits from a decrease in uncertainty and should therefore favor policies which place as much information as possible in the public domain prior to lease sales. However, it appears that current regulations do not always lead to maximal generation and dissemination of presale information in at least two instances.

First in undeveloped or "wildcat" regions, the exploration techniques which firms may use prior to lease sales cannot establish with certainty the presence or absence of oil. This determination can be made only when a site is actually drilled. The government allows presale test drilling only occasionally, and the tests are limited to shallow holes in areas where oil is unlikely to be discovered. It appears likely that the drilling of a few exploratory wells in potentially productive regions could significantly reduce presale uncertainty.

A second policy issue concerns the information generated by firms during developments of tract they have under lease. This body of geological knowledge may be of considerable use in estimating the value of nearby tracts subsequently offered for lease. Under current policies this information is, at least for a substantial period of time, the proprietary property of the developing firm. Thus, an OCS lease may confer rights to information monopolies as well as oil.

One would expect to observe an increase in the perceived value, and therefore the bids, for a lease which is likely to confer monopoly information rights. Correspondingly, a decrease in competition, and therefore in the bids, for a lease is to be expected when the owner of a nearby tract is thought to be in possession of monopoly information. In effect, then, an information monopoly is a claim on a portion of the economic rent associated with nearby tracts.

Unfortunately, these claims are likely to be sold with tracts in undeveloped areas, characterized by high presale uncertainty and low government rent capture. The government might do better to require disclosure of tract development data, eliminate the information monopoly rights, and later lease the nearby tracts in an environment of lower uncertainty and higher expected government rent capture.

Reece also notices that, at present, the winning bid has to be paid in cash before the drilling starts. Competition may be promoted if this "bonus" system were replaced by auctions based on a royalty on the oil actually extracted or on a profit-share fraction, so as to remove what may be a barrier to entry.

4.2.3. *Information pooling through joint bidding*

In the preceding discussion it was implicitly assumed that there are as many bids as participating oil companies. What if several companies make a joint bid as is often the case in practice? Joint bidding has been objected to (and restricted since 1976) on the ground that it reduces the number of competitors and therefore reduces the total rent and the government's share of it. On the other hand, the oil industry has argued that joint bidding serves as a vehicle for entry of small firms (that would otherwise be excluded from the auctions) and favors diversification of risk.

DeBrock and Smith (1983) have developed an argument in favor of joint bidding that is independent of the diversification of risk and entry arguments. It is based on the pooling of information. By pooling their private information on the unknown value of a tract, joint bidders have more accurate estimates. This change in their information structure allows them to more accurately identify tracts for which the market value of reserves exceeds the cost of recovery. This increases the total rent. In addition, because joint bidders are more knowledgeable regarding tract value, they tend to bid more aggressively, which tends to offset the anticompetitive effect of a reduced number of bidders. As a result, the percentage of the common value captured by the government is not significantly reduced.

To make their point, DeBrock and Smith use the Reece model and simulate the Nash equilibrium bids under the assumption that joint bidding occurs. Bidders are supposed to be risk neutral, so the results do not depend on the diversification of risk. The number of bidders, n, is fixed, so there is no entry of new firms. The results thus depend only on the pooling of information and its effect on the joint estimate of the common value.

Let m be the number of members in *each* joint venture, so the degree of joint bidding is uniform throughout the industry. Then the number of independent bidding entities is simply $N = n/m$. In the simulation, the number of bidders is fixed at $n = 20$. The number of firms permitted to enter into a single joint venture (m) varies over 1, 2, 4, 5, and 10. When m is equal to 1, there is no joint bidding and the number of independent bidding entities is equal to 20. When m is equal to 10, there are two independent bidding entities. The prevailing value of m is known by all participants.

The Nash equilibrium bids and the resulting division of rent are computed under different degrees of uncertainty. The most striking result is that the total rent increases directly with m, whatever the degree of uncertainty. The increase is the more pronounced the larger is the uncertainty, because of the greater benefits of pooling information. Surprisingly, the share of government also increases in all cases when m moves from 1 to 2, despite the fact that the number of bidders is thus reduced from 20 to 10. When m moves to 4 and 5, the share of government only slightly decreases. It is only when the process of joint bidding is carried even further that the government's share significantly declines. (When $m = 10$, there is a duopsony of bidders.) Figure 4.7 represents the division of rent under high uncertainty.

Compare Figures 4.7 and 4.6. The results are opposite in terms of the number of bidders. Reece found that decreasing the number of bidders causes the industry's share to rise sharply, the government's share to drop sharply, and the total rent captured by society to fall more and more. 'Although increasing the degree of joint bidding reduces

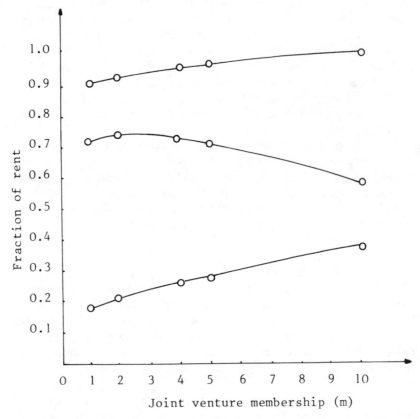

Figure 4.7. Effect of joint bidding on division of rent, high uncertainty.

the number of bidders accordingly, it raises the industry's share moderately, regularly increases the total rent captured by society, and only reduces the government's share when carried too far. These opposite effects are explained by the fact that the anticompetitive effect, captured by Reece, is more than offset by the fact that the bidders, although fewer in number, are better informed and act more aggressively.[12]

4.2.4.   A general model

Milgrom and Weber (1982) developed a general auction model for risk-neutral bidders which includes as special cases the independent private

---

[12] Econometric results that point in the same direction can be found in Rockwood (1983).

value model and the common value model. It can also handle intermediate cases, such as the auction of a painting. In all cases, the basic
assumption is that a high value of one bidder's estimate makes high
values of the others' estimates more likely. In this sense, the bidders'
valuations are said to be "affiliated." (This is true for the independent
private values as well as for the estimated common values.)

The model yields several interesting results. Milgrom and Weber
(1982, p. 1095) summarize these as follows:

First, the Dutch and first-price auctions are strategically equivalent in the
general model, just as they were in the private values model. Second, when
bidders are uncertain about their value estimates, the English and second-price
auctions are not equivalent: the English auction generally leads to larger expected prices. One explanation of this inequality is that when bidders are uncertain about their valuations, they can acquire useful information by scruti-
nizing the bidding behavior of their competitors during the course of an English
auction. That extra information weakens the winner's curse and leads to more
aggressive bidding in the English auction, which accounts for the higher expected price.
A third prediction of the model is that when the bidders' value estimates
are statistically dependent, the second-price auction generates a higher average
price than does the first-price auction. Thus, the common auctions forms can
be ranked by the expected price they generate. The English auction generates
the highest prices followed by the second-price auction and, finally, the Dutch
and first-price auctions. This may explain the observation that "an estimated
75 per cent, or even more, of all auctions in the world are conducted on an
ascending-bid basis" (Cassady [1967, p. 66]).

When the seller has access to private sources of information – as
may the case when the U.S. government sells offshore oil leases –
honesty is shown to be the best policy: It maximizes the expected price
in the first-price, second-price sealed-bid, and English auctions. It is
better for the seller always to report all information completely than
to never report any information, to add noise to the data before reporting, and even to report only the most favorable information.

4.2.5. Further problems

In the highly abstract models we have discussed, many important features of real-life auctions have been (deliberately) ignored to make the
analysis feasible. Future research will have to try to incorporate these.
Let me pinpoint a few of the most obvious complexities, following
Milgrom and Weber (1982, pp. 1117–8).

In many auctions, the bidders realize that the contract price will later
be subject to profitable renegotiation. This is typical for sophisticated

weapons systems, whose specifications will inevitably be changed later on. How does this knowledge affect actual bidding behavior?

The existing theory of auctions is cast in terms of one single auction, seen in isolation. What if hundreds of tracts are offered for sale simultaneously, as is the case when the U.S. Department of the Interior auctions drilling rights for oil? How many tracts should a bidder try to win?

One basic assumption made throughout is that of a noncooperative game. When the bidders know each other well, as is inevitable in a small country such as Belgium or in a highly specialized trade, this assumption must be very unrealistic indeed. It is particularly unrealistic when the same bidders compete with each other over successive auctions. Collusion typically consists in agreeing on which bidder is allowed to win any particular auction and reauctioning the item afterward among the "ring" (cartel) members. (On this, see Graham and Marshall 1984, 1985.) However, successive auctions also provide opportunities for systematic misinformation of the other side of the market. These are explored in Section 4.4.

Finally, new issues arise when what is auctioned is not a single object but a bundle of objects. Bundling of products or services is a well-understood discriminatory device when the seller has complete and perfect information.[13] Under incomplete and asymmetric information, the seller may again improve profits by bundling several goods into a single lot and selling the lot in an auction, as shown by Palfrey (1983).

4.3.   Incentive procurement contracts

Our discussion of auction theory has been entirely in terms of a seller who wants to sell an object to a number of potential buyers. What if the auction is organized by a buyer, as is often the case when a governmental agency uses sealed bid auctions to acquire supplies or to hire the services of a firm to build a road or run a public service such as a cable TV network? In principle, all that was said before carries through, except that now it is the lowest (or second lowest) bid that is the winning bid. Instead of maximizing utility, the bidder is maximizing his or her profit function and the bidder's production costs play the role of the reservation values. In fact, several specific problems arise when the services needed for a tailor-made job are auctioned.[14]

One important issue is whether it is better to provide the service

---

[13] See Phlips (1983, chap. 11).

[14] The bidding for government contracts is analyzed as a principal-agent problem in McAfee and McMillan (1986).

through a private firm selected through a sealed-bid auction rather than through a regulated public enterprise. This question is thoroughly discussed by Williamson (1976), who stresses the difficulty of defining the service to be offered with sufficient precision for the auction to be an efficient allocation mechanism.

A related issue, which is to be briefly discussed here, hinges on the uncertainty about the actual costs that will be incurred, once the works are carried out. At the time bids are made, the bidders (entrepreneurs of public works) only have estimates of the costs involved. What if, once the works are finished, ex post costs are higher than expected? If there is such a risk, how will this affect the bids made? Couldn't one devise a contract, offered to the bidders, such that the risks related to this uncertainty be shared between the government and the winning firm, so the bidders will have an incentive to reduce the bids? And such that the government would not have to pay all the extra costs into which the winning firm might run and for which it will claim extra payment (threatening to go bankrupt before the works are finished)?

One possibility, discussed by Scherer (1964), is to offer a contract according to which the winning firm will receive its bid plus a proportion β of the difference between this bid and the ex post costs c that are effectively incurred, or

$$b + \beta(b - c) \tag{4.9}$$

where $0 \le \beta \le 1$. If it turns out that $b > c$, the winning firm gets an additional bonus. If, however, $c > b$ so that $b - c$ is negative, then the winning firm will have to support only the proportion β while the government supports $(1 - \beta)(b - c)$ of the loss. Hopefully, such a contract would create an incentive for risk-averse bidders to reduce their bids (because part of the possible loss, if b turns out to be too low, will be borne by the government) and for the winning firm to reduce its costs (because it will make an additional profit if $c < b$).

To make sure that the cost uncertainty doesn't raise the bids, one could go one step further and offer, in addition, a guaranteed profit, as discussed by McCall (1970) and Baron (1972). The winning firm is now offered

$$\alpha b + \beta(b - c) + c \tag{4.10}$$

where $0 \le \alpha \le 1$ and $0 \le \beta \le 1$. Its profit is thus $\alpha b + \beta(b - c)$. When $\alpha = 0$ and $\beta = 1$, we have the usual fixed-price contract in which the winning firm bears the full risk and gets a profit (or loss) equal to the difference between its bid price and the ex post production cost.

The parameter α is the "guaranteed profit rate," and the parameter β is the "sharing rate."

When the contract is awarded to the lowest bidder, we have a first-price sealed-bid situation, in which the Nash equilibrium has to be computed in order to know the optimal bids. In other words, one has to analyze the bidding decisions of all bidders simultaneously. Holt (1979, 1980) has derived a symmetric equilibrium bidding strategy on the assumption that all bidders have the same utility function and are equally efficient in the sense that the probability distribution of the procurement cost c is the same for each firm. The bidding strategy is specified as a relationship between the bid price, the expected cost, *and* the alternative profit a bidder can make in an alternative private-sector operation.

Not unexpectedly, Holt is able to show that an increase in the guaranteed profit rate α will decrease equilibrium bids (and increase the probability of cost overruns) without affecting the expected procurement cost. On the other hand, an increase in the sharing rate β will not only increase equilibrium bids for all bidders but also the expected procurement cost. The implication is that the government could reduce its expected procurement cost by reducing β and in the limit accepting all risk ($\beta = 0$). However, a higher β induces firms to keep costs down once the contract is awarded. When this efficiency effect is taken into account, the need arises to compare it with the risk effect: On balance, β should be the lower, the higher is the cost uncertainty. For the initial production of special projects, this risk element dominates, so β should be set very low. As experience with this type of activities increases, β can be increased to induce cost reductions. It should be the highest for the continued production of standard equipment, where the risk element is the smallest.

4.4.*   Misinformation in auction markets

A government procurement agency regularly buys office equipment, furniture, military clothing, and so on, and does this through first-price sealed-bid auctions at regular time intervals. Or it frequently holds such auctions to award projects (government buildings to be constructed, miles of highways, etc.). Typically, it is badly informed about production costs and about the market structure (the number of available bidders in any period).

Goods purchased, or projects awarded, in adjacent periods are substitutes for one another, so the agency has an incentive to buy more or less today, depending upon whether the current price is lower or higher than tomorrow's expected price. The agency has to form expectations about the price tomorrow and therefore needs to acquire information about the evolution of production costs (the bidder's valuation of their unit cost), the dispersion of these costs among the bidders, and the number of bidders. Indeed, we saw that all bids (including the winning lowest) are functions of the bidder's private values (their estimated production costs), the distribution from which these are drawn, and the number of bidders. To hold auctions frequently is a way to acquire such information.

Given this information, the purchasing agency can maximize intertemporal profits by making the appropriate substitution. If tomorrow's price will be higher than today's, forward substitution is profitable: It is profitable to buy more today and less tomorrow.

Feinstein, Block, and Nold (1985) have shown that bidders, once they become aware of this, will have an incentive to collude in order to misinform the agency, thus skewing its intertemporal allocation to their advantage. To show this, Feinstein et al. first describe how the agency uses past data to improve its forecasts. They then show by which means a cartel can manipulate these forecasts to its advantage, and finally they derive the optimal short-run and long-run cartel policy such that the cartel's presence will remain undetected. It is possible for a cartel to follow a policy that takes the profit of intertemporal demand allocation away from the agency and yet confirms its belief that it faces a competitive market! The following pages give a simplified and nontechnical presentation of the different steps leading to this fascinating conclusion.

4.4.1. The purchaser's expectations

The information structure is as follows. The costs of production fluctuate randomly around a fixed value $\bar{c}$. Bidders' individual costs are independently drawn from a common distribution f which is normal (not rectangular). They are thus equal to

$$c_t^i = \bar{c} + z_t^i \tag{4.11}$$

where $z_t^i \sim N(0, \sigma_c^2)$. The mean $\bar{c}$ is identical across periods and bidders, to simplify the problem. Both the agency and the bidders know that the c_t^i's follow a normal distribution, but are ignorant of the true mean $\bar{c}$ and the true variance of the costs σ_c^2.

The agency has to forecast, at time t, the winning bid expected at $t + 1$, e_{t+1}, after the period t bids have been submitted. How does it do this updating of its estimate of next period's winning bid? To begin with, the agency approximates the cost distribution f by a subjective cost distribution $g_t \sim N(\theta_t, \sigma_t^2)$. In other words, θ_t is its best estimate of the mean $\bar{c}$ in any period t and σ_t^2 is its best estimate of the true variance σ_c^2 in any period t.

Then the agency computes its Bayesian estimate of g_{t+1}, using the observed bids (and corresponding costs) in t, g_t, and the knowledge that f is normal. This gives θ_{t+1} and σ_{t+1}^2, the agency's new estimates of $\bar{c}$ and σ_c^2, as functions of the mean m_t and variance s_t^2 of the costs in t. To estimate the density of the expected lowest cost in period $t + 1$, the agency combines the revised cost density g_{t+1} with the estimate of the number of bidders in period $t + 1$, $\hat{N}_{t+1}$. The latter obeys

$$\hat{N}_{t+1} = n(\hat{Q}_{t+1}, \hat{R}_{t+1}) \tag{4.12}$$

where $\hat{Q}_{t+1}$ is demand in period $t + 1$ and $\hat{R}_{t+1}$ is the expected pool of bidders, which is composed of the R_t suppliers already in the bidders pool and potential entrants. The larger is demand in $t + 1$, the more suppliers will be expected to actually bid in $t + 1$ (i.e., $\partial \hat{N}_{t+1}/\partial \hat{Q}_{t+1} > 0$). Similarly, the larger is the expected pool, the more suppliers will be expected to take part in the bidding in $t + 1$.

Finally, the expected winning bid in period $t + 1$ is obtained using equation (4.5), because it is a Nash equilibrium strategy, after taking the expectation of the lowest cost. The expected lowest cost is thus transformed into the expected winning bid e_{t+1} (i.e., the expected price at the next auction).

4.4.2. Manipulation of the expected price

It was necessary to indicate by which steps the purchaser constructs his forecasts, to see how a bidders cartel can manipulate it. Since the purchaser's perception of next period's winning bid depends on today's bids, which depend in turn on the corresponding costs of production and the number of bidders, the cartel can affect the agency's forecasts if it can affect either m_t, the mean of the costs of production in the current period, their variance s_t^2, or the number of bidders in the pool R_t.

Feinstein et al. (1985) show that the cartel can, for example, inflate the agency's estimate of e_{t+1} by any of the following strategies:

(a) Reducing the number of market suppliers R_t, that is, $\partial e_{t+1}/\partial R_t < 0$.

(b) Increasing the mean cost of production m_t, or $\partial e_{t+1}/\partial m_t > 0$.

(c) Decreasing the variance of the costs s_t^2, or $\partial e_{t+1}/\partial s_t^2 < 0$.

The cartel can manipulate the purchaser's e_{t+1} by any of these three tactics or any combination of them. Is it in the cartel's interest to inflate e_{t+1} in successive auctions? Yes!

4.4.3. The cartel's short-run policy

The cartel's problem is to maximize

$$\Pi_t = Q_t(b_t^1, e_{t+1}; Q_{t-1})(b_t^1 - c_t^1) + J(b_t^1, e_{t+1}) \qquad (4.13)$$

with respect to b_t^1, the lowest bid to be submitted in the current auction, and the price e_{t+1} expected for the next auction by the government agency but "chosen" for it by the cartel. The function $J(b_t^1, e_{t+1})$ is the discounted value of future profits.

Notice that if intertemporal substitution is not possible, so demand depends only on today's price, or $\partial Q_t/\partial e_{t+1} = 0$, the cartel's problem is simply to maximize

$$\Pi_t = Q_t(b_t^1)(b_t^1 - c_t^1) \qquad (4.14)$$

with respect to b_t^1, so the winning bid will be set equal to the standard monopoly price.

The cartel will not only set b_t^1 at the monopoly level but will inflate e_{t+1} above b_t^1, that is, fool the purchaser into believing that period t's winning bid is lower than period $(t + 1)$'s winning bid will be, *thus inducing the purchaser to substitute future demand forward* into period t. In period $t + 1$, the cartel will again inflate e_{t+2} above b_{t+1}^1, washing out the negative substitution from period $t + 2$, again misleading the purchaser, and so on. Fooling the purchaser in this way is a source of additional profits because

$$\frac{\partial \Pi_t}{\partial e_{t+1}} = \frac{\partial Q_t}{\partial e_{t+1}} (b_t^1 - c_t^1) + \frac{\partial J}{\partial e_{t+1}}, \qquad (4.15)$$

and the first (positive) expression on the right side is larger in absolute value than the (negative) expression $\partial J/\partial e_{t+1}$, since the latter is discounted and the decrease in Q_{t+1} implied in ∂J cannot be larger in absolute value than the increase in Q_t.

What would be the best moment to set up such a cartel? Since its policy amounts to convincing the government agency that a jump in costs occurred, it will pick a situation in which the agency has little past data that is relevant to the current auction:

For example, we would expect cartels to pick situations where there is 1) technological innovation which sharply reduces real costs; 2) a large shift in demand, such as a state decision to embark on a major road-building campaign; 3) new product, such as the shift in road building to interstates; or 4) a substantial and sustained inflation. (Feinstein et al., 1985, p. 448, note 11)

4.4.4.   *The cartel's long-run policy*

The short-run policy just described cannot continue forever. After some time, the government agency will discover that its forecasts are incorrect and will stop updating its estimates of θ_{t+1}, σ^2_{t+1}, and R_{t+1}. Yet, the cartel must make sure that its presence is not discovered. In other words, it must preserve the agency's faith in its own forecasts. This is possible if the purchaser's estimates are made "consistent" in the technical sense of the word – that is, if they are made to eventually converge to constant values (when $\bar{c}$ is constant) and if these values are compatible with market demand and the actual number of bidders. The long-run average $\bar{e}$ must equal the long-run average lowest bid $\bar{b}$. Then the agency's long-run demand is $Q(\bar{b}, \bar{b})$, and the cartel will pick $\bar{b}$ such that the profit $Q(\bar{b}, \bar{b}) (\bar{b} - \bar{c})$ is maximized. The cartel's presence will remain undetected under these conditions: The cartel is able to hide itself in the long run! If $\bar{c}$ is not constant but increasing (there is cost-push inflation), then the cartel will let the government's estimates rise rapidly first and then level off.

4.4.5.   *An example*

The Belgian small and middle-sized firms that supply the government through first-price sealed-bid auctions have an association called "office de cotation des marchés publics." This office has a data bank in which past bids are stored. These data are used to compute an average price PM, a maximum price PM', and a lower limit LM.

The price PM is called "the market price" and is defined as "the price with the smallest error from a technical point of view and taking economic conditions into account." This average price is used to compute PM', the maximum value a corrected bid may take: It is the value below which the "correct bid" is located with a 95% probability. The limit LM is the lower limit below which there is a very high probability that a bidder will make losses. A bid below LM cannot be considered as "statistically normal."

The members of the association have their proposed bids checked and receive the following information. Either they are told that their proposed bid is below LM or above PM', without indication about the size of the deviation, or they are told that their proposed bid is between

LM and PM', in which case they are given the maximum authorized (positive) correction or the minimum mandatory (positive) correction. The value of LM and PM' is never revealed (?). Only those participants whose bids are located between LM and PM' are allowed to correct their bids. Corrections that make bids equal to PM' are not allowed, because such corrections would make all bids equal. In addition, the ranking of the initial proposed bids must be preserved.

All participants must make a bid equal to the one that results from this "error correcting mechanism." Only those whose proposed bid is below LM are allowed to drop out of the auction to which their proposed bid refers.

Since PM is an average price based on past bids, including those that were not the winning ones, it must be above the equilibrium price. Since only positive "error corrections" are made and only the lowest bids may be dropped, the mean of the bids must increase as a result of the procedure. Since bids above PM' and below LM are eliminated, the variance is reduced. And because participants with bids below LM are encouraged to drop out, the number of actual suppliers is reduced. Clearly, this is an illustration of how a cartel can misinform the government and thus manipulate the latter's expectations. My guess is that the procedure incorporates a long-run consistency condition that confirms the government in its belief that costs are due to rise in the future.

CHAPTER 5

Signaling equilibria

Auctions generate information about values whether private or common. "Signaling" generates information about attributes of individuals (their intellectual abilities, for example, or their attitude towards risk or their creditworthiness). The purpose of this chapter is to explain how and when such signaling can be used as a "self-selection mechanism" that generates information "endogenously." Let us illustrate each of these rather esoteric concepts before embarking on a more detailed analysis.

Examples of signals abound. Producers signal through advertising; job applicants invest in education in order to be able to show diplomas; careful drivers signal their low accident probability by accepting a large "deductible" when they take out automobile insurance; borrowers signal their low risk by refusing to pay high interest rates or by accepting a high collateral requirement.

In each of these examples, the signal conveys the appropriate message, even if it is not informative as such: Even if the advertising campaign gives no real information about the product, the fact that the advertising is made shows that the product *is* worth promoting, because advertising is not advantageous for low-quality goods (especially when the product is bought repeatedly, as argued by Nelson 1974, 1975). Even if the diploma says nothing about the quality and the content of the teaching, it shows at least that the bearer was sufficiently well organized and worked sufficiently hard to obtain it. An additional implication is that the marginal cost (in terms of money and time) of education must have been lower for those who get a degree than for those who don't. The willingness to accept a large deductible reveals nothing directly about driving habits, but conveys relevant information on the probability of serious accidents. Indeed, "the higher the probability of loss, the higher is the marginal loss in utility associated with accepting less than full coverage. Thus the marginal cost of accepting a large 'deductible' is greater for low-quality risks (those with high loss probabilities)" (Hirschleifer and Riley 1979, p. 1406). Therefore, people with high loss probabilities will not accept high deductibles. A person who accepts a high deductible is likely to be a good driver. The willingness to pay high interest rates is not directly informative about the borrowers' financial situation, but reveals at least that they expect to make large profits, and large profits are in general associated with risky undertakings. In this sense, the signal is a selection mechanism.

The endogenous nature of this self-selection mechanism results from the circumstances that the other side of the market (which receives the signal) uses this mechanism to its own advantage in order to select the high-quality product, the more productive employee, the low-risk driver or the low-risk borrower. If both sides of the market are satisfied with the working of the mechanism, some kind of equilibrium emerges.

Consider the labor market. Employers gladly use the educational signals to *screen* the job applicants. To this effect, they link their wage offers to the level of education (among other things, such as sex, race, age, etc., which are not signals, since nothing can be done to change, hide, or improve these!) and offer a wage schedule which increases stepwise with the level of education. One may think that this behavior reflects their belief that a more educated employee is more productive and thus deserves being paid more. The explanation offered here is very different: the wage schedule is meant to encourage the job applicants to select themselves, hoping that more productive applicants (for whom the cost of education is low) will turn up with more or better diplomas and thus reveal themselves. If these hopes are confirmed, there is no reason to change the wage schedule: The schedule turns out to have done its screening job. It is in this sense that information is said to be generated endogenously by the self-selection mechanism.

5.1. Job signaling

The analysis of signaling in the hiring process in the labor market was initiated by Spence's pathbreaking book on *Market Signaling* (1974), on which most of this presentation is based.

5.1.1. Signals, indices, and abilities

Spence first defines signals as manipulable attributes or activities which convey information. For job applicants, for example, signals are personal appearance, diplomas, previous work experience, and so on, which the employer has to interpret. To some extent, applicants can manipulate these signals: They can buy suitable clothing before going to an interview, they can accumulate diplomas (intellectual abilities permitting), and so on. Second, there are some attributes that cannot be altered, such as race or sex. These are not signals, strictly speaking, and may be called "indices." "The perspiration on the forehead of the nervous job applicant is an index" (Spence 1974, p. 11).

Third, individuals have different "abilities," which are innate: Some people simply are more gifted than others, more intelligent, more business oriented, or whatever. The basic assumption is that applicants know their abilities and use signals to inform employers about this in a credible way. It should therefore be stressed that education is not treated here as a way of improving one's productivity and one's suitability for a particular job, but rather as a self-selection device that will reveal innate abilities in a convincing way. This is not to say that better-educated people are not more productive. The signaling approach simply tries to take account of the common observation that people with a general education in the "humanities" end up doing highly specialized jobs or that people with a very specialized training (such as engineers) tend to become general managers. This observation probably indicates that their diplomas were used as signals of their innate capabilities of adjusting to new situations or of working hard and fast, which are largely innate. Firms are said to care not too much about the precise type of degree acquired, which suggests that they treat the degree as a test of basic abilities.

In the modeling of the job signaling problem, one thus has to find a simple way of representing differences in abilities. The particularities of the signal (such as the particular features of the courses followed) can be ignored, and the reasoning can be in terms of more or less "education," the content of which is left unspecified.

5.1.2. A simple model without signaling

Spence starts with a very simple model that captures the essential features of the problem. Suppose an employer faces a collection of people whom it will ultimately hire in a competitive labor market. In fact, there are two types of individuals: Group I has a marginal product of 1, and group II has a marginal product of 2, because of differences in innate abilities. If these values were known, the employer would pay each person his or her marginal product. However, in the absence of signaling, the employer is unable to distinguish between the two groups and will thus pay everybody the expected marginal product.

To determine this expected product, the employer knows (from past experience) the proportion of people who have a marginal product of 1, say q, so that the remainder $(1 - q)$ have a marginal product of 2. The equilibrium wage is the same for all and is equal to

$$\overline{w} = q \cdot 1 + (1 - q) \cdot 2 = 2 - q.$$

Table 5.1. *Data of the signaling problem*

Group	Marginal product	Proportion of population	Cost of education
I	1	q	y
II	2	$1 - q$	$y/2$

But then, the members of group I receive a wage that is larger than their marginal product ($\overline{w} > 1$), and the more gifted members of group II are hurt. The gain to the former is $1 - q$ and increases as their proportion in the population falls. The loss to the latter is q and increases as their proportion in the population increases. The more gifted thus have an interest to convince the employer that they deserve to earn more. However, this information is not convincing, because the less gifted could also pretend to belong to group II and the employer would have no way of checking this.

5.1.3. Education as a signal

The message from the high-productivity types would be convincing if it were translated into their having a better education (and a better performance in education) as compared with the low-productivity types. And the employer would pay attention to such a signal, because it allows him to compete for talented people and simultaneously avoid the costs associated with training, selecting, and firing people once they are hired, the more so because these are sunk costs which cannot be recovered if the hired person has to be fired.

To model this situation, Spence assumes greater abilities imply lower costs of education. And "education" is measured by a composite index of years and performance in education, denoted by y. In Table 5.1, the cost of education for members of group I is supposed to be y, and the cost of obtaining an educational level y is $y/2$ for a person in group II. It is because education is costly and because this cost is negatively correlated with capability that education becomes a signal of capability.

Faced with this situation, the employer will associate an expected productivity to each education level and offer a corresponding wage. In other words, the employer will offer a wage *schedule*, denoted by $W(y)$. This is a step function, associating higher wages with higher education levels (see Figure 5.2). Each wage is equal to the expected marginal productivity determined by the employer, using its conditional probabilities over productivity given educational levels.

How will potential employees react to the announcement of such a wage schedule? And how will employers react to these reactions? The story goes as follows, in Spence's words (1974, pp. 16–17):

> The potential employee, looking forward to his working life, faces the schedule $W(y)$. This schedule tells him the payoff to be had from each choice of education level. There are also costs of education. Given the costs, and the payoffs, the individual will select a level of education which maximizes the difference between payoffs and costs. In other words, he maximizes the return net of signaling costs by choosing y appropriately.
>
> If this were where the story ended, it would not be very interesting. But it does not end here. Applicants, having invested in education, go onto the market and are hired at the rates determined by the employer's current conditional probabilistic beliefs. In the period subsequent to hiring, the employer will learn about the actual productive capabilities of the people he has hired. He also knows the education levels they brought to the market. Putting these two types of information together, he can and will test his probabilistic beliefs concerning the relationship between productivity and education. In general, this newly acquired experience will cause him to alter his former beliefs. When this happens, the wages offered to people with various levels of education will change when the game starts again. This, in turn, will alter the investment behavior of individuals, and the new market data will cause further revisions in the employer's beliefs (Fig. 5.1).
>
> To study situations that are not transitory, one looks for places at which the circular ebb and flow of the feedback mechanism settles down. Such places are referred to as equilibria. They will occur when the employer's beliefs feed back upon themselves in the form of market data which do not cause him to revise his beliefs any further. Beliefs having this property will be described as self-confirming.

To illustrate, suppose that an employer who faces the two groups described in Table 5.1 believes that if $y < \bar{y}$, then productivity is 1 with probability 1, and that if $y \geq \bar{y}$, then productivity is 2 with probability 1, where $\bar{y}$ is just some number. The wage schedule offered $W(y)$ is as in Figure 5.2, with wages $w_1 = 1$ for $y < \bar{y}$ and $w_2 = 2$ for $y \geq \bar{y}$, if the market is competitive. We let $C_I = y$ be the cost-of-education function of group I; $C_{II} = y/2$ is the cost-of-education function of group II.

Will this wage schedule, given C_I and C_{II}, provide an incentive for the members of group II to acquire at least education $\bar{y}$, and for members of group I to be satisfied with an education smaller than $\bar{y}$, so that the two groups are thus effectively separated and innate capabilities are correctly revealed? To answer this question, we must analyze the choice of education by both groups.

The optimal choice of education for any potential employee is to choose that value of y for which the difference between the wage of-

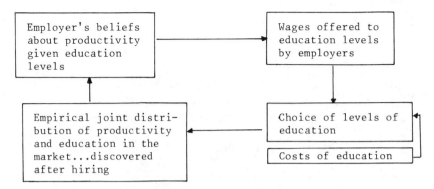

Figure 5.1. The flow of interrelationships in the signaling model.

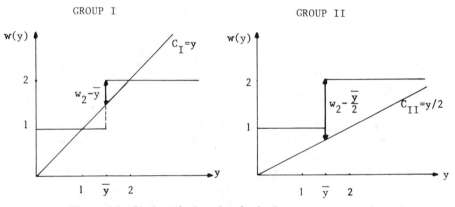

Figure 5.2. Choice of education for both groups.

fered $w(y)$ and the cost of education is maximum. For members of group I, the optimal choices are either to choose no education at all, or $y = 0$, or to choose exactly $\bar{y}$. Indeed, $y = 0$ gives the maximum difference $w(y) - y = w_1$, when $y < \bar{y}$. For $y \geq \bar{y}$, the maximum difference is $w(y) - y = w_2 - \bar{y}$. Their decision rule is thus as follows:

> Choose $y = 0$ if $w_1 > w_2 - \bar{y}$.
> Choose $y = \bar{y}$ if $w_1 < w_2 - \bar{y}$.
> Be indifferent between $y = 0$ and $y = \bar{y}$ if $w_1 = w_2 - \bar{y}$.

The numbers in Figure 5.2 are chosen in such a way that group I decides not to be educated at all.

The members of group II maximize $w(y) - y/2$ with respect to y. They

Choose $y = 0$ if $w_1 > w_2 - \bar{y}/2$.
Choose $y = \bar{y}$ if $w_1 < w_2 - \bar{y}/2$.
Are indifferent between $y = 0$ and $y = \bar{y}$ if $w_1 = w_2 - \bar{y}/2$.

In Figure 5.1, $w_1 < w_2 - \bar{y}/2$, so group II gets education $\bar{y}$.

Putting the two decision rules together, we see that both groups choose $y = 0$ as long as $w_1 > w_2 - \bar{y}/2$. The groups are separated, and each group chooses the appropriate education or signal if

$$w_2 - \frac{\bar{y}}{2} > w_1 \geq w_2 - \bar{y},$$

or, with the numbers chosen, if

$$2 - \frac{\bar{y}}{2} > 1 \geq 2 - \bar{y},$$

or

$$2 > \bar{y} \geq 1,$$

on the assumption that group I chooses $y = 0$ when $w_1 = w_2 - \bar{y}$. Because $\bar{y}$ satisfies this condition in Figure 5.2, it depicts a signaling equilibrium: The employer's beliefs are confirmed by market experience. If the employer had put $\bar{y}$ above 2, group I would have continued to prefer $y = 0$ (because $w_2 - \bar{y} < 0$), but group II would also have decided not to become educated at all (because $w_1 > w_2 - \bar{y}/2$). If the employer had put $\bar{y}$ below 1, the two groups would have chosen $\bar{y}$. In both cases, education would not have done its signaling job of separating the more capable from the less capable: We would have had "pooling" or "nonseparating" equilibria. By choosing a critical education level in the correct range, the entrepreneur depicted in Figure 5.2 has realized a signaling equilibrium, because the reactions of the potential employees confirm the entrepreneur's beliefs. The end result is that wages increase with education, but this does *not* result from nor imply a positive influence of education on productivity. It is a property of the screening or signaling mechanism.

5.1.4. Signaling equilibria

Taking a closer look at the signaling equilibrium, we first notice that there are an infinite number of possible equilibrium values for $\bar{y}$, because any value between 1 and 2 will do in the example just discussed.

Indeed, any of these values will allow the employer to perfectly separate the two groups of potential employees.

Second, these equilibria are not equivalent from a welfare point of view. An increase in $\bar{y}$ obliges members of group II to invest more in education, without affecting the other group (whose members stay at $y = 0$). And everybody may be worse off with signaling than without signaling, because the wage $\bar{w}$ (without signaling) may be higher than the net return to group II. (For example, if $q = 0.5$, $\bar{w} = 1.5$ while $w_2 - \bar{y}/2$ may be smaller.) In general, a signaling equilibrium with a lower $\bar{y}$ Pareto dominates equilibria with a higher $\bar{y}$, because it implies spending less on education. This property results from the fact that $\bar{y}$ is considered only as a screening device.

Third, these equilibria are "weak," in the sense that they do not exclude the possibility that it might be in the employer's interest to deviate from them by offering another wage schedule. In other words, the competitive interplay between competing employers is not fully taken into account. Still in other words, these signaling equilibria are not Nash equilibria in general.

One could strengthen their definition and impose the additional condition that no other wage schedule would give the employer who offers it a positive profit. (Implicit is the condition that at a signaling equilibrium wages are equal to productivities, so employers make no profit.) We would then have a Nash equilibrium (also called a "strong" signaling equilibrium).

With the data of Table 5.1, such a strong equilibrium would occur if $\bar{y}$ is put equal to one (its lowest possible value) *and* $q > 0.5$. With $q < 0.5$, no such equilibrium exists. Indeed, suppose the existing equilibrium has $\bar{y} = 1$. It can be seen, from Figure 5.2, that the net return to group II is then the highest one compatible with a signaling equilibrium and equal to 1.5. No member of group II would accept to be hired away by another employer, because this would imply higher education costs if this other employer had a two-step wage function. And if he offered a unique wage to both groups, that wage would be smaller than 1.5 when $q > 0.5$, because it would be at most $\bar{w} = 2 - q$ (a higher wage leads to losses for the employer). When the proportion of group I in total population is smaller than 0.5, however, it is always possible for a deviant to offer a unique wage that attracts members of both groups (because it is higher than the net returns to both groups) and gives a positive profit. A common wage of $\bar{w} = 2 - q - \frac{1}{2}(\frac{1}{2} - q) = 1.75 - \frac{1}{2}q$ will do, because it is larger than the net return (equal to 1.5) of group II and the net return to group I (equal to 1) and because it is smaller than the average productivity $(2 - q)$. The members of group

II will then gladly accept a lower wage, because it gives a higher net return, and prefer not to be separated from members of group I.

5.1.5. Reactive equilibria

Since Nash equilibria do not exist in general for wage-education schedules, one might infer that competition on the labor market could lead to instability and chaos. This may be the reason why wage–education schedules are determined in some European countries by nationwide, industrywide negotiations and imposed by long-term contracts between associations of employers and trade unions. Alternatively, one might argue that these long-term contracts freeze a more sophisticated type of noncollusion equilibrium that would have emerged spontaneously in the relevant (possibly regional) labor markets. C. Wilson (1977) and Riley (1979) initiated research toward defining such more refined equilibria, the former for the insurance market, the latter for the labor market. They propose the concept of a "reactive equilibrium" in which, still in the absence of collusion, *each firm takes reactions by other firms to changes in its own list of offers into account, and concludes that it therefore is not profitable to deviate.* Such an equilibrium requires that (a) a first deviation leads to loss once another firm reacts with a profitable counter offer, and (b) the reaction of the other firm is always profitable (even if there are further reactions).

Figure 5.3, adapted from Hirschleifer and Riley (1979), illustrates this reasoning. The assumptions are the same as in the Spence model. There are two groups of workers: low-productivity workers with marginal productivity 1, and high-productivity workers with marginal productivity 2. With perfect information on each worker's productivity, each group would receive a wage equal to its productivity, or $w_1 = 1$ and $w_2 = 2$. If employers were unable to distinguish the two groups, they would have to hire members of the two groups in the proportion $q/(1 - q)$, where q is the (known) proportion of workers in the low-productivity group. All workers would be paid the same wage $\overline{w} = q \cdot 1 + (1 - q) \cdot 2 = 2 - q$, because $2 - q$ is the average (known) productivity.

Now the high-productivity workers feel that they are underpaid and wish to signal their greater ability by investing in education, because their cost of education is low. This lower cost leads to indifference curves between wage and education (u_2) with a slope that is smaller than the slope of the indifference curves of the less able workers (u_1): For any wage offer, the more able are capable of getting more education. The employers realize this.

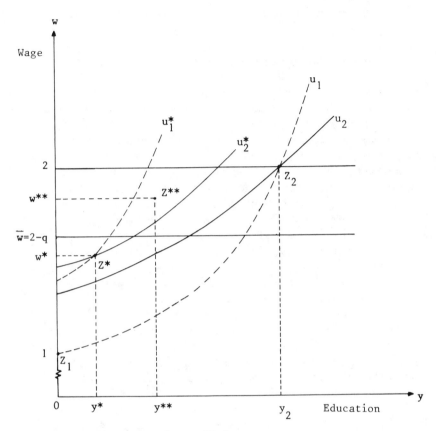

Figure 5.3. A reactive equilibrium.

If the employers were to offer a single wage-education pair Z^*, implying a wage w^* smaller than $\bar{w}$, they would make larger profits and get better-educated workers[1] on average, because all workers would make sure to obtain an education y^*. However, this cannot be an equilibrium, because some firm will realize that it can offer Z^{**}, attract only high-quality workers (because Z^{**} is below u_1^* and above u_2^*), and still make a profit (because $w^{**} < 2$).

It is likely that the firms will make it possible for the workers to select themselves by offering a wage schedule with two wages, one for each group, and a minimum education level associated with each wage. Suppose they find a schedule that satisfies both groups and yields zero

---

[1] Better-educated workers might also be more productive, but this is ignored here, because productivities are supposed to remain unchanged at levels 1 and 2, respectively.

profits, for example the pair (Z_1, Z_2). The lower-quality workers accept Z_1 and totally abstain from investing in education; the higher-quality workers invest y_2 in education. (In Figure 5.3, one among many possible wage–education pairs is picked out for easy reference.) The pair (Z_1, Z_2) is thus a signaling equilibrium. It is even an efficient equilibrium: Locating Z_1 above 2 would produce losses; locating Z_2 more to the left, with $Z_1 = 1$, would induce the low-quality workers to invest in education to obtain the same high wage as the other group, so the two groups would not be separated; locating Z_2 more to the right-hand side reduces the utility of the high-quality workers but keeps them separate from the low-quality workers. The latter would also get less utility if they invested more than y_2 in education rather than staying at Z_1. All in all, all pairs other than (Z_1, Z_2) that yield zero profit and lead to self-selection provide lower utility to the high-quality workers.

This signaling equilibrium is not a Nash equilibrium. Given that its competitors offer (Z_1, Z_2), any firm can make a profit by deviating, for example by offering Z^* (a unique wage w^* smaller than average productivity and thus a source of profit), which will in turn be deviated from by some other firm, as we saw, and so on. However, (Z_1, Z_2) is a reactive equilibrium!

The first requirement is that a first deviation leads to loss once another firm reacts with a profitable counter offer. This requirement is satisfied since a first deviation to Z^* would be followed by the counter offer Z^{**} which attracts high-quality workers only. This counter offer would reduce the average productivity of the workers staying with the initial defector until Z^* generates losses. The second requirement of a reactive equilibrium is that a counter offer is always profitable. This is the case here, because Z^{**} is always profitable. Consequently, the initial potential defector (the firm that considers offering Z^*) realizes that such a deviation would eventually lead to losses. It is deterred from making the offer Z^*.

The same reasoning can be applied to Spence's Figure 5.2, where cost of education functions are used instead of indifference curves and workers maximize net returns. We know that the particular signaling equilibrium with $\bar{y} = 1$ is a Nash equilibrium if the proportion of low-ability workers q is larger than 0.5. Can we also locate a reactive equilibrium? Yes. In fact, the signaling equilibrium with $\bar{y} = 1$ is also a reactive equilibrium, whatever the value of q. (Whatever the distribution of abilities in the population, a wage schedule that separates the two groups and gives the highest possible net return to education is a reactive equilibrium.) Indeed, when $q > 0.5$, no deviation (alternative wage schedule) could attract workers away, as we already discovered.

We also know that, when $q < 0.5$, a first deviation could consist of an offer of some common wage larger than 1.5 (attractive to both groups) and smaller than $2 - q$. However, a profitable counter offer could always take the group II workers away from the first deviant. It would suffice to offer them $w_2 = 2 - q + \epsilon$. This is always profitable because w_2 is smaller than the productivity of group II. And the potential first deviant would make a loss, because it would end up paying a wage that is larger than the productivity of the members of group I who stay with it. The two requirements of a reactive equilibrium are satisfied, and the potential first deviant wisely decides *not* to deviate.

5.1.6. *Signaling games and stable equilibria*

The concept of a reactive equilibrium was used to reduce a plethora of equilibria to a unique signaling equilibrium (with $w = 1$, $w = 2$, and $\bar{y} = 1$). I now wish to note briefly that the same result can be obtained through an alternative approach, which uses the concept[2] of a "sequential" equilibrium introduced by Kreps and Wilson (1982b). This concept requires that every decision of the players be optimal for the remainder of the game and be based on an assessment of the probabilities of all uncertain events, including any preceding but unobservable choices made by the other players. How this applies to our signaling problems was made clear by Cho and Kreps[3] (1987). The general reasoning goes as follows. Redefine Spence's signaling model as a sequential game between job applicants of group I and group II, on the one hand, and two employers, on the other hand. At the start of the game, the job applicants learn their true type, but the two employers remain uninformed. Then the job applicants choose an education level y, which is the signal observed by the two employers. Employers then engage in bidding competition for the applicants' services and end up offering the same wage schedule, defined by a value of w_1, a value of w_2, and a value of $\bar{y}$. Given this schedule, no job applicant can increase his or her net return by choosing a level of education other than either $y = 0$ or $y = \bar{y}$ (see Figure 5.2), whatever the value of $\bar{y}$. In this game, all equilibria, whether separating or pooling, therefore appear as Nash equilibria. Instead of too few, we now have too many Nash equilibria! And now the question is, how can this immense number be reduced?

---

[2] Or the even more refined concept of a "strategically stable" equilibrium proposed by Kohlberg and Mertens (1986).

[3] Hellwig (1987) makes a similar application to the credit market of the sequential equilibrium approach and shows that the type of equilibrium depends upon who (the informed or the uninformed) moves first.

This reduction is obtained by requiring that the two employers assess the probability that a job applicant belonging to group I should show up with a diploma corresponding to education $\bar{y}$, that a job applicant belonging to group II should not go to school or invest in an education of $y > 1$ when the highest wage he or she can get is $w_2 = 2$, and so on. Given the data of Table 5.1, and competition between the two employers, they should offer wages not lower than $w = 1$ and not higher that $w = 2$. Group I applicants then know that getting no education ($y = 0$) gives them the highest net return, whatever is the value of $\bar{y}$. Employers should therefore attach a high probability to the hypothesis that an applicant with an education $y = \bar{y}$ belongs in fact to group II. They should also attach a high probability to the possibility that members of group II, given $w_2 = 2$, would invest in an education higher than $y = 1$ to separate themselves from members of group I. If all players maximize expected returns, their final conclusion (after a careful assessment of the probability that other players make any particular choice) will be that the unique separating equilibrium implies $w_1 = 1$, $w_2 = 2$, and $\bar{y} = 1$ (the reactive equilibrium obtained earlier). The detailed argument is too sophisticated to be reproduced here.

5.2.   The insurance market

Just as employers cannot observe the capabilities of potential employers during the hiring process, insurance companies have no way of observing the accident probability of a particular customer at the time the insurance contract is signed.[4] On the other hand, they have to define with precision both the price and the extent of the risk to be covered, that is, the premium and the amount of insurance that the customer can buy at that price. This is a difficult problem. Indeed, a higher premium makes the pool of insurance applicants more risky, because people with small risks will drop out: There is *adverse selection*.[5] On the other hand, a higher insured value creates an incentive for the subscriber to increase risk (by driving more dangerously, say, or leaving the front door unlocked, or keeping gasoline in the garage): There is *moral hazard*.[6] Insurance companies thus have to find the optimal combination of the premium and the extent of risk covered. Will they offer one type of contract to all customers? or try to insure all types

---

[4] In most countries drivers buy insurance with the same insurer for many years. Such multiperiod contracts give the insurance company the opportunity to observe the driver's behavior, to evaluate its riskiness, and to adjust the premium. On this, see Dionne and Lasserre (1987).

[5] For a discussion of this concept in relation to the lemons principle, see Section 3.3.

[6] See the discussion of moral hazard and warranties in Section 3.1.

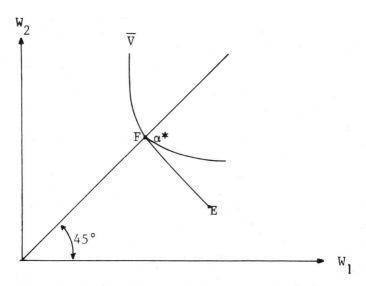

Figure 5.4. Competitive insurance market with identical customers.

of risk, high as well as low, at different premiums? possibly refuse to cover high risks? or the reverse? The answer is not what you might expect: Different contracts will be offered and high-risk customers will receive full coverage, but low-risk customers will get only partial coverage, or no coverage at all.

Consider the simple case described by Rothschild and Stiglitz (1976). An individual has an income of W if he is lucky enough to avoid accident. If an accident occurs, his income is only $W - d$. The individual can insure himself by paying to an insurance company a premium α_1, in return for which he will be paid $\hat{\alpha}_2$ if an accident occurs. If he does so, his income is $W_1 = W - \alpha_1$ if no accident occurs. If he is unlucky, his income is $W_2 = W - d + \alpha_2$, where $\alpha_2 = \hat{\alpha}_2 - \alpha_1$.

In a competitive insurance market with identical customers, equilibrium would occur, in Figure 5.4, at point α^* which represents the equilibrium insurance policy $\alpha^* = (\alpha_1^*, \hat{\alpha}_2^*)$, that is, a policy with premium α_1^* and payment $\hat{\alpha}_2^*$. Indeed, start from point E, which represents the typical customer's uninsured state ($\alpha_1 = 0$, $\alpha_2 = 0$). The curve $\overline{V}$ is the indifference curve in terms of expected utility[7] of W_1 and W_2, the same for all customers. Purchasing an insurance policy moves the

---

[7] $V = (1 - p)U(W_1) + pU(W_2)$. Customers are supposed to be risk averse, so $U'' < 0$ and the indifference curve is convex to the origin.

customers away from E to the northwest: W_1 is decreased by α_1, and W_2 is increased by α_2. In perfect competition with free entry, expected profits are zero, so $\alpha_1(1 - p) + \alpha_2 p = 0$, where p is the probability of incurring an accident. The set of all insurance policies that break even is given by the "fair odds" line EF, with a slope $(1 - p)/p$. The policy α^* is the one that will be chosen in equilibrium, because it is on the EF line (zero profit) and locates the customers at the tangency of their indifference curve with EF, and thus provides the highest expected utility. Notice that along the 45° line, $W_2 = W_1$ or $W - d + \alpha_2 = W - \alpha_1$ or $d = \hat{\alpha}_2$, so the payment just covers the damage in the event an accident occurs. The line EF cannot cross the 45° line: Moral hazard makes it impossible for the payment to be larger than the damage. The equilibrium policy α^* lies on the 45° line, because the marginal rate of substitution[8] between W_1 and W_2 is $(1 - p)/p$ when $W_2 = W_1$.

The other points on the EF line represent a partial coverage of loss. Insurance markets offer several possibilities for retaining some part of the risk. Insurance companies limit the dollar amounts of recovery by including clauses such as deductibles, franchises, coinsurance arrangements, and dollar limits of insurer's liability. These special clauses seem to be very popular in the United States, but they are not in fashion on the Old Continent. For example, it is very common to stipulate that a definite dollar amount will be borne by the insured before the insurer becomes liable (clause of deductible or franchise). This case is very common in automobile insurance, where deductibles of $50, $100, or $200 are proposed to the insured. More recently, deductibles have been used in fire insurance. It is to the insured's advantage that such clauses be available because they allow considerable saving in the insurance cost. For example, in automobile insurance the saving in the annual premium by the use of a $100 deductible for collision claims rather than a $50 deductible might amount to $35.

It is usually said that the purpose of these deductibles is to eliminate small claims. Small losses are expensive to pay, sometimes causing more administrative expense than the actual amount of the payment. We will see that there is another explanation for this behavior.

Consider a competitive market in which customers *are* different and the insurance companies do not know their characteristics (accident probabilities). These companies will try to find ways to force customers to make choices in such a way that they both reveal their characteristics and make the choices the companies would have wanted them to make had their characteristics been known.

---

[8] Namely $-dW_2/dW_1 = U'(W_1)(1 - p)/U'(W_2)p$.

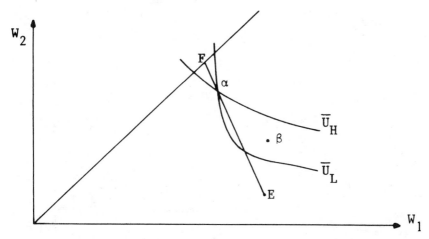

Figure 5.5 Competitive insurance market with different customers.

Suppose, then, there are only two kinds of customers: low-risk individuals with accident probability p^L, and high-risk individuals with accident probability $p^H > p^L$. Could it be that both groups will be offered the same contract, as was the case in Figure 5.4? No. Competitive equilibrium now implies that different types purchase different contracts.

If they were offered the same contract, it would have an average accident probability $\bar{p} = \lambda^H p + (1 - \lambda)p^L$, where λ is the faction of high-risk customers. Such a contract could be represented by point α in Figure 5.5. It is located on the zero-profit line EF, which now has a slope of $(1 - \bar{p})/\bar{p}$. This line EF is called the "market odds" line. At that point the indifference curve for high-risk customers $\bar{U}_H$ crosses the low-risk indifference curve from below.[9] However, there is a contract, β, near α, which low-risk types prefer to α. (The high-risk customers prefer α to β.) It is also profitable for the insurance companies to have (only) the less risky buy β. Indeed, these β contracts would then give almost the same profit as if the α contracts were offered to the less risky only. And the latter contracts would, by definition, be more profitable than if they were offered to all customers. The policy α cannot be an equilibrium: If there is an equilibrium, each type of customer must purchase a separate contract.

The nature of these two contracts is illustrated in Figure 5.6. First of all, we need two "fair odds" lines, say EH and EL. The contract

---

[9] Marginal utilities of income are the same: Only the accident probabilities differ between the two groups. Hence, $MRS^H/MRS^L = p^L/(1 - p^L)\cdot(1 - p^H)/p^H$.

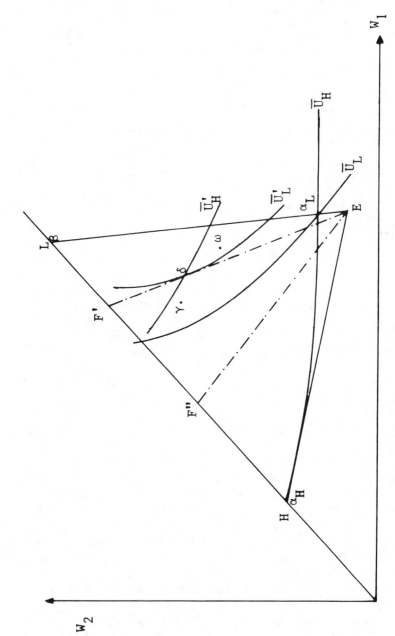

Figure 5.6. Equilibrium contracts for high-risk and low-risk customers.

on EH most preferred by high-risk customers is α_H and gives complete insurance. Of all contracts on EL, low-risk types would prefer β. However, β cannot be part of the equilibrium! Although it gives complete insurance, it also gives more income than α_H, so high-risk types will prefer it to α_H. If both β and α_H are offered – and because insurance companies cannot distinguish the two sets of customers, although it would be profitable to do so – all will demand β and must be sold β. Profits will be negative, because β gives zero profits for *low*-risk customers only. In other words, the set (α_H, β) is not an equilibrium.

The fact that high-risk individuals will switch to β implies that low-risk types must be offered a less attractive contract, such that the high-risk customers are indifferent to it. The contract α_L, on the intersection of the two indifference curves, has this property and is also the one that low-risk types most prefer. We conclude that the set (α_H, α_L) is the only possible equilibrium for a market with low- and high-risk customers, if ít *is* an equilibrium.

To see whether (α_H, α_L) is an equilibrium, we must analyze two different cases. In the first case, the proportion of high-risk agents is low, and the market odds is EF', say. If a contract γ were offered by a new firm, all customers would prefer it, and it is a profitable one. This implies that the set of contracts (α_H, α_L) disappears from the market.

But if the proportion of high-risk agents is higher and the market-odds line is EF'', there is no other contract that will be attractive for all customers and profitable. In consequence, (α_H, α_L) is a competitive equilibrium. High-risk customers are fully insured, and low-risk individuals will take a deductible with a reduced premium. Intuitively, high-risk customers don't choose the deductible because the saving in premium is not large enough to compensate the risk they take in retaining a part of the probable loss.

Rothschild and Stiglitz conclude that in some circumstances, there is no competitive signaling equilibrium. If there exists one, the presence of high-risk individuals exerts a negative externality on the low-risk types: Even under competition, low-risk types will have incomplete coverage.

Since a signaling equilibrium may not exist, it is necessary to suppose that each insurance company takes into account the reaction by other companies when contemplating a defection from the initial set of contracts. Those "quasi-dynamic" considerations lead to the concept of Riley's reactive equilibria.[10] These equilibria depend on how we define

[10] See Section 5.1.

the reactions of the companies to a defection. As a special case, Charles Wilson (1977) proposes an equilibrium defined as follows: The defector who wants to introduce a new contract computes her profit as if other companies will respond by dropping all contracts that are not profitable. According to this anticipated behavior, the defector calculates her new profit: If it is positive, she proposes the new contract; if not, it is not proposed.

With this definition, it has been proved that there exists a stable set of contracts, that is, a set for which there is no possible defection that is profitable after reaction of the existing companies. To analyze this reactive equilibrium, let us look at Figure 5.5 again. In the first case, where there is a low proportion of high-risk customers and where there is no signaling equilibrium, the reactive equilibrium is illustrated by contract δ. This is a nonseparating contract with a compulsory deductible. Indeed, this contract is preferred to (α_H, α_L) by all customers. In addition, we can see that δ is stable. If a defector were to propose contract w for example, all low-risk individuals would buy it, and δ would become unprofitable. As hypothesized before, companies would react by dropping all contracts δ. Then, all high-risk agents would buy contract w too. In consequence, w would be unprofitable – it will not be proposed!

For a high proportion of high-risk insureds, it is easy to verify that the reactive equilibrium corresponds precisely to the Rothschild and Stiglitz equilibrium, that is, to (α_H, α_L). Every point on the market-odds line EF is destroyed by a defector who proposes (α_H, α_L).

What has been argued is that the potential instability of the insurance market is not, after all, so devastating. Stability is achieved by building into the equilibrium concept a recognition of possible reactions by other agents.

It is rather unrealistic to suppose the insurance market to be perfectly competitive and the insurance companies to make zero profit. Consider then a market with profit-maximizing insurance companies that are able to discriminate. Under the assumptions made, they will offer a menu of contracts: With two groups of customers, they will offer a full coverage contract to the high-risk type, and partial insurance or no insurance at all to low-risk types. This is what Stiglitz (1977) established in the following way.

The negative externality implies that a monopolistic seller must sell high-risk individuals a contract which they prefer to the contract purchased by the low-risk group, say α^L. Given α^L, it should thus be located in the shaded area in Figure 5.7. The line EF^H is not a zero-

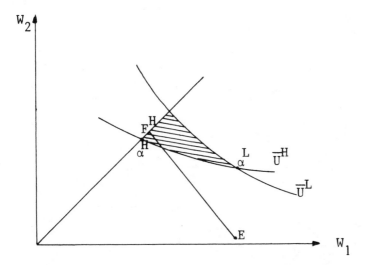

Figure 5.7. Discriminating monopolistic insurance companies, α^L given.

profit line, but corresponds to a given positive profit on contracts offered to the high-risk group. A higher profit leads to another parallel isoprofit line, located to the left of EF^H, because moving to the left implies a higher premium (or smaller W_1) and a lower payment (smaller W_2). The profit-maximizing contract for the high-risk group must be located at the point where the slope of $\overline{U}^H$ is equal to the slope of an isoprofit line, and therefore on the 45° line. It must be α^H, at the intersection of the 45° line and the high-risk individuals' indifference curve through α^L. Each type of individual prefers his or her contract to the other contract, and profit is maximized.

Now assume the contract α^H is given (Figure 5.8). It must lie along the 45° line. Draw the high-risk indifference curve through it. Also draw the low-risk indifference curve through E (the no-insurance point). The set of contracts a monopolistic seller can choose and which separate the groups are the points *below* the indifference curve $\overline{U}^H$ (through α^H) and *above* the curve $\overline{U}^L$ through E. The fact that the indifference curves are flatter than the isoprofit lines implies that profits are maximized at the point located most to the left, that is, at α^L. This establishes that the low-risk individual's utility is very close to what it would have been had the individual not purchased any insurance. He or she might as well decide to stay at E, that is, to remain uninsured.

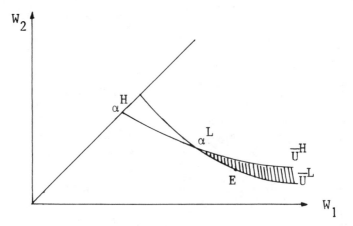

Figure 5.8. Discriminating monopolistic insurance companies, α^H given.

All this implies that high-risk and low-risk individuals will never be offered the same contract.[11] If they were, and the common contract involved incomplete insurance, then it would always be profitable to introduce an additional policy offering complete insurance (moving to the left in the figures above). If the common contract involved complete insurance, it would always be profitable to introduce an additional policy involving incomplete insurance.

5.3.* Credit rationing

When you apply for a bank loan, you typically obtain only a limited amount at the going rate of interest. Generally, credit is "rationed" in the sense that you cannot buy as much credit as you want at the given market price. This is in sharp contrast with goods markets, where one can buy as much as one desires.

The traditional argument, that rationing results from the rigidity of the fixed price, is not applicable here, because interest rates are rather flexible (they change over time and differ between types of borrowers). One also observes that banks try to expand their credits, not by offering more credit to a particular applicant, but by trying to attract more borrowers (while rationing each individual applicant).

The explanation offered here is analogous to the one offered for the

---

[11] The efficiency effects of this discrimination by types are studied in Crocker and Snow (1986).

limited risk coverage in the insurance market, in that the phenomenon is linked with the asymmetry in the information structure. When a bank gives a loan, all it obtains in return is a promise of reimbursement from the borrower. But it has no way of evaluating the quality of this promise with certainty. If the lender is a gambler or risk lover, the promise is not worth much. If the lender is dishonest, the promise may be worthless. The nature of the contract is such that a rise of the price (the loan rate) or a differentiation of the loan rates will do nothing to solve the problem: A dishonest lender will gladly sign contracts with higher interest rates! The traditional argument in favor of higher prices under uncertainty does not hold.

In fact, asking higher interest rates would have perverse effects of the same nature as the effects observed in the insurance market. Again, there is *adverse selection*: The pool of loan applicants becomes riskier as interest rates rise. This effect may be due to the (generally) positive relationship between risk and return on investments. One possibility is that less risk-averse applicants represent a larger proportion as more risk-averse applicants drop out of the market. Another possibility is that higher interest rates increase the proportion of dishonest borrowers in the market for consumption loans, because not to repay becomes more tempting (in a sense to be defined shortly).

As in the insurance market, there is also a *moral hazard* effect, independently of the information problem. As interest rates rise, borrowers have an incentive to use borrowed funds in ways that increase their return but are not in the interest of the bank. The bank is only interested in the probability of repayment, because it does not benefit from the returns on the investment in excess of the principal and interest.

However, a reduction of the amount of individual loans might increase the overall quality of the contracts for a bank, because it is not worthwhile for a borrower to go bankrupt for a small loan. Individual credit rationing may thus be seen as a means to reduce the number of dishonest borrowers. If successful, it may ultimately lead to lower interest rates, so both banks and honest borrowers would benefit from it. This is the point made by Jaffee and Russell (1976) for the case of consumption loans.

5.3.1. *Honesty versus dishonesty*

Suppose loans are for consumption only, and let all consumers have the same intertemporal two-period utility function

$$u(c_1) + \gamma u(c_2) \tag{5.1}$$

where c_1 and c_2 are the expenditures on consumption in periods 1 and 2, respectively, and γ is a subjective discount factor. If the corresponding incomes are y_1 and y_2, and such that they wish to consume more than y_1 in period 1, these consumers will take a loan L in period 1 and consume $c_1 = y_1 + L$, with the implication that they will have to repay $L(1 + r)$ in period 2 (r being the interest rate) and will be able to consume only $c_2 = y_2 - L(1 + r)$.

However, if the cost[12] of default, Z, were smaller than $L(1 + r)$, it would be in their interest to default. Indeed, replacing c_2 by $(y_2 - Z)$ in equation (5.1) would then give a higher utility than if c_2 were equal to $y_2 - L(1 + r)$. Dishonest borrowers will then actually default. But if $Z > L(1 + r)$, even dishonest borrowers will prefer to repay the loan.

It is now a simple matter to characterize the demand for credit of honest and dishonest borrowers.

Honest borrowers will maximize

$$u(y_1 + L) + \gamma u[y_2 - L(1 + r)] \tag{5.2}$$

with respect to L, and their demand for credit satisfies

$$u'(y_1 + L) - \gamma(1 + r)u'[y_2 - L(1 + r)] = 0 \tag{5.3}$$

because the second-order condition is satisfied on the assumption that the second derivative of u is negative. Total differentiation of equation (5.3) shows that their demand for credit is a decreasing function of the rate of interest (see Figure 5.9).

Dishonest borrowers, on the contrary, compare

$$u(y_1 + L) + \gamma u[y_2 - Z] \tag{5.4}$$

with the utility (5.2) they would have if they behaved honestly. If $Z > L(1 + r)$, they will prefer to repay, as noticed before. But what if $Z < L(1 + r)$? Now they should maximize equation (5.4): Since L appears only in the first-period utility, utility maximization implies that L should be as large as possible! Their demand for credit becomes infinitely large. Of course, it would be unwise to ask a bank for unlimited credit, because this would immediately reveal that one belongs to the group of dishonest borrowers. One should rather mimic the honest behavior described by equation (5.3) and act as if one's demand were a decreasing function of the rate of interest.

Considering the entire market, it is thus clear that, with a given cost

---

[12] It will be argued later that this cost could be interpreted as the amount of collateral required.

Z, the proportion of borrowers who repay their debts, say λ, decreases when r or L increase, because Z is to be compared with $L(1 + r)$.

5.3.2.   The supply of credit to a particular borrower

What consumption loan contract will the banks offer to their customers, when they know that these behave in the way just described, so they are unable to recognize dishonest borrowers? With a given rate of interest, this question boils down to the determination of the amount L, to be offered to any potential customer, that is optimal from the banks' point of view.

Since a bank knows the function $\lambda(r, L)$, it can compute the expected revenue of a loan, which is $\lambda(r, L)L(1 + r)$. (Indeed, when there is no repayment, the revenue is zero.) Its cost is $L(1 + i)$, where i is the rate at which the bank itself borrows on the capital market. Its expected profit is therefore

$$\Pi = \lambda(r, L)L(1 + r) - L(1 + i). \tag{5.5}$$

Each bank will want to maximize Π if it is risk neutral. Notice that this expected profit could easily be negative (when r is close to i), in which case no bank would be willing to offer any credit. On the other hand, as soon as Π is positive, anybody will be willing to lend money. The conclusion is that expected profit must be zero in equilibrium, or

$$\lambda(r, L) = \frac{1 + i}{1 + r}, \tag{5.6}$$

from which the supply of credit (to individual lenders) can be derived (because λ is a function of L). When $i = r$, λ must be equal to 1: All loans must be 100% sure, which implies that L must be such that $Z \geq L(1 + r)$ or $L \leq Z/(1 + i)$. When $i < r$, λ decreases as r increases. As a result, the amount of the loan offered, L, might either increase or decrease, depending on the speed with which λ decreases. If the proportion of honest borrowers decreases fast enough, it might be necessary to offer *smaller* loans at higher interest rates: The supply of credit curve may be backward bending, as in Figure 5.9.

All this does not imply credit rationing, yet. Comparing the supply and demand curves in Figure 5.9, one discovers an equilibrium amount of L equal to L^*, at which there is no rationing because borrowers are on their demand curve. At L^* corresponds a rate r^* which is larger than the marginal cost of funds i, in order to compensate the banks for the fact that a proportion $(1 - \lambda)$ of the contracts defined by point S are not honored.

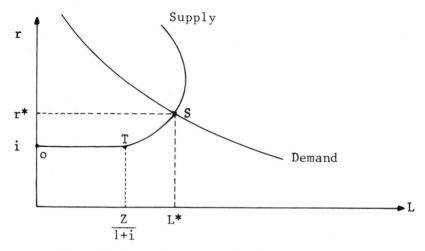

Figure 5.9. Demand and supply of credit.

5.3.3. Equilibrium with rationing

However, the equilibrium contract (r^*, L^*) without rationing is not likely to occur in the credit market. Indeed, both the borrowers who are honest at point S and the banks have an interest in choosing a contract that lies to the left of point S, on the curve TS, and thus implies a lower interest rate *and* a smaller loan, so credit rationing occurs.

Consider how a reduction of r and L would affect the utility of the borrowers who are honest at point S. According to equation (5.2), their utility is

$$U^H = u(y_1 + L^*) + \gamma u[y_2 - L^*(1 + r^*)].$$

Total differentiation of this expression gives

$$dU^H = -\gamma L^* u'[y_2 - L^*(1 + r^*)]\,dr$$
$$+ \{u'(y_1 + L^*) - \gamma(1 + r^*)u'[y_2 - L^*(1 + r^*)]\}\,dL$$
$$= -\gamma L^* u'[y_2 - L^*(1 + r^*)]\,dr$$

because the second expression on the right side is zero according to the first-order condition (5.3). A reduction of r $(dr < 0)$ thus implies an increase in utility $(dU^H > 0)$.

Total differentiation of the banks' expected profit (5.5) similarly shows that a reduction of L below L^* can be profitable. Since L^* is the amount of credit asked for, credit rationing occurs.

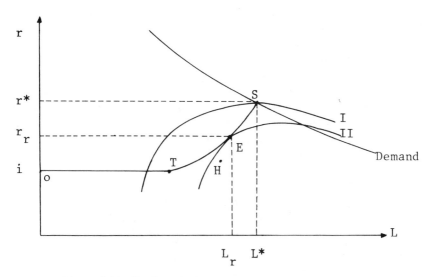

Figure 5.10. Credit rationing.

The reasoning just made can be illustrated graphically, as in Figure 5.10, in which an indifference curve through S is drawn. This curve gives all the contracts (r, L) that produce the same utility as the contract (r^*, L^*) and has zero slope at point S (see Jaffee and Russell). Among the indifference curves giving a higher utility, there must be one such as curve II that is tangent to the supply curve, say at E, so that the corresponding contract (r_r, L_r) with rationing is preferred by the honest customers.

Is contract E an equilibrium with free entry? At first sight, E certainly is an equilibrium with free entry. Contracts above the supply curve (OTS) make positive profits so that there will be excess supply of these; contracts below the supply curve imply losses and will thus not be offered; contract E implies zero profits, and there will be as many offered of these as requested by the borrowers.

On a second thought, one might object that, although contract E was obtained by considering what is in the honest borrowers' interest, dishonest borrowers will mimic their behavior and also sign E. At E, the pool of any banks' customers will still contain a proportion of dishonest borrowers ($\lambda < 1$) who will not repay. A bank, possibly a new entrant, could therefore deviate from E, offer a contract, such as H, that lies *below* the supply curve and yet make a profit. Contract H gives a higher utility than curve II and would thus be preferred to E by the honest borrowers – while the dishonest would stick to E, because it gives a higher loan – and would be profitable, because it implies $r > i$ and attracts honest borrowers only. [Notice that, given this possibility of making a profit by deviating from E, contract E cannot be a Nash (or "strong") equilibrium.]

However, if H were offered, E would itself disappear, because banks sticking to E would attract dishonest customers only and go bankrupt. And once E is no longer offered, the dishonest would have to sign contract H, which would then cease to be profitable. It is thus evident that, in contrast to the insurance market, an equilibrium with two contracts – one for the honest and a different one for the dishonest – is impossible.

In the long run, when the full impact of the possible entry of H on E and the eventual lack of profitability of H itself is acknowledged, E appears as the only possible equilibrium with free entry. At E, credit rationing is bound to appear and subsist; E is also a nonseparating or pooling equilibrium: There can be no separation between honest and dishonest borrowers.

5.3.4. Collateralization

The preceding analysis suggests that credit rationing arises to the extent that a separating equilibrium cannot be achieved. The equilibrium with rationing was a pooling equilibrium because it is never profitable to have dishonest borrowers select themselves for the purpose of being offered a separate contract (which would by definition imply a loss for the bank) and because it was supposed that banks have no way of separating them.

The arguments used to obtain a pooling equilibrium were crude and narrow in scope. First, one would like to replace the rather pathological distinction between honest and dishonest borrowers, which is useful for the analysis of consumption loans only, by a distinction between borrowers of different types. In particular, these types could correspond to (investment) projects with different returns and different probabilities of default. And banks could be allowed to try to influence their clients' choice of project by introducing collateral requirements. If, as will be argued, a higher degree of collateralization induces investment in safer projects, then collateral is an *incentive device* which the banks can use as a response to the moral hazard problem.

Second, one would like to drop the brutal assumption that lenders have no way of ascertaining the "honesty" of a borrower or the riskiness of his project. Everybody knows that banks use quantitative methods of "credit scoring" to screen applicants for consumption loans. What is less obvious is that collateralization can also be used as a *signaling device* to separate the high-risk from the low-risk types: Low-risk types accept higher collateral requirements and thus reveal themselves. In this sense, collateralization is a response to the banks' adverse selection problem.

Third, once the usefulness of introducing collateral into the analysis is recognized, one would like to give the banks the opportunity of using this variable simultaneously with the rate of interest and the amount of credit in their struggle with adverse selection and moral hazard. Stiglitz and Weiss (1981) have shown that credit rationing may be a solution to the adverse selection problem rather than an increase in the collateral, for a given rate of interest, or an increase of the rate of interest, for a given collateral. Bester (1987) used the three variables simultaneously. (In his 1985 article, Bester was the first to analyze collateral requirements as a signaling device.)

5.3.5. Collateral as a signaling device

Bester's model has the following features. There are n types of entrepreneurs. Each type is characterized by a probability p_i that its investment project will be a success and yield a positive return X_i, and a probability $1 - p_i$ that it will fail and yield a zero return. An essential feature of the model is that $1 > p_1 > p_2 > \cdots > p_n > 0$ and $L < X_1 < X_2 < \cdots < X_n$, where L is now the fixed amount of investment to be financed by a bank loan. Each entrepreneur has an initial wealth W insufficient to cover the cost of the project ($W < L$). A credit contract specifies the gross interest payment $R = L(1 + r)$ to be repaid if the project is successful and the collateral C which the entrepreneur loses if the project fails.

In the consumption loan model, the borrower had an incentive for dishonesty when the "cost of default" (Z) is smaller than R. That cost can now be interpreted as the amount of collateral required (C). Here it is supposed that the law precludes dishonesty, based on C being smaller than R. In other words, it is no longer necessary to have $C > R$ to enforce repayment. Bester therefore supposes $C < R$. Under this assumption, collateral becomes a signaling device. The reasoning goes as follows.

Suppose, to begin with, that banks are able to identify the type of entrepreneur to which a particular borrower belongs. In that sense, there is perfect information. Then there is no need for banks to require any collateral from their borrowers. And a zero-profit equilibrium implies that low-risk borrowers are charged lower-interest payments because they are more likely to repay. Indeed, on loans to firms of type i, the banks' profit is $p_i R_i - L(1 + i)$. Putting this equal to zero gives

$$R_i = \frac{L(1 + i)}{p_1} .$$

Similarly, on loans to firms of type $i + 1$ the zero-profit condition implies

$$R_{i+1} = \frac{L(1 + i)}{p_{i+1}} .$$

Since the probability of success $p_i > p_{i+1}$, R_i must be smaller than R_{i+1}.

If, on the contrary, banks only know the probability distribution of the returns on the investment projects but do not know which probability p_i and which return X_i is applicable to a particular borrower, then they will wish to identify these characteristics. Indeed, less risky customers are more profitable because they are more likely to meet their repayment obligations (their p_i is higher). This identification is possible only if the contracts offered act as a self-selection mechanism, that is, induce individual borrowers to correctly reveal their types by signing a contract that corresponds to their true type. In other words, no borrower should have an incentive to misrepresent his or her type. Technically speaking, the contract chosen by borrowers of a particular type should be such that no other contract gives them a higher expected utility. (Such contracts are said to be "incentive compatible.")

The analogy with the job signaling problem should be clear. There, employers face job applicants who belong to different types defined by different innate abilities and do not know to which type a particular applicant belongs. They have to induce the applicants to freely choose an education level that correctly reveals their abilities. The device used for this purpose is to offer a wage schedule linking different wages to different levels of education.

The device used by banks is to offer credit contracts with different combinations of collateral requirements and interest rates. *Less risky entrepreneurs will accept a higher increase in collateral for a given reduction in interest payments and thus reveal themselves.* This is so, because entrepreneurs with a higher probability of success exhibit a higher marginal rate of substitution between R and C. An entrepreneur of type i has expected utility V_i given by

$$V_i = p_i U(X_i - R + W) + (1 - p_i)U(W - C), \tag{5.7}$$

where U is a utility function with[13] $U' > 0$ and $U'' < 0$. The type i marginal rate of substitution dR/dC is therefore

$$- \frac{(1 - p_i)U'(W - C)}{p_i U'(X_i - R + W)} \tag{5.8}$$

and $p_i > p_{i+1}$ implies that type i has a larger marginal rate of substitution than type $i + 1$. Being less likely to lose their collateral, type i entrepreneurs prefer contracts with higher collateral and smaller interest payments.

If, therefore, borrowers can provide enough collateral, that is, if their initial wealth is high enough, each type of borrower will receive a distinct contract in equilibrium. There is no pooling and no rationing (every potential borrower receives a loan). Rationing can occur only to the extent that a separating equilibrium cannot be achieved. And separation is impossible only to the extent that some borrower's initial wealth restricts the use of collateral as a signal. (The formal proofs of this are in Bester 1987.) Interestingly, the zero-profit equilibrium implies that no collateral is required from the most risky type of entrepreneurs (type n). Being the most risky, there is no need to distinguish it from riskier types! Only the most risky type therefore receives the same contract under imperfect as under perfect information.

5.3.6.   Collateral as an incentive device

Under perfect information, there is no moral hazard problem: Banks could impose the condition that a borrower of type i who receives a credit contract of type i characterized by R_i and C_i (call it $\gamma_i = (R_i, C_i)$) actually invests the loan in a project of type i (characterized by p_i and X_i) and not in a riskier project. Under imperfect information, the inability of banks to monitor the use of the loan, once it is awarded, creates the moral hazard problem. Once they have obtained their loans, borrowers could use the money in riskier projects. As suggested above, the choice of an appropriate combination of R and C can prevent this, in giving the borrowers an incentive to use a project of type i when they got a contract γ_i.

In a discussion of collateral as a signaling device, it was shown that borrowers with a given lower probability of success will prefer a lower collateral and a higher interest payment. We now have to show that

---

[13] U is therefore a so-called von Neumann–Morgenstern utility function. Its concavity implies risk aversion.

borrowers with a given lower collateral and a higher interest payment, as stipulated in their contract, will prefer a project with a lower probability of success, so that the contract is self-enforcing. (Such a contract is again said to be incentive compatible.)

Suppose there are two different contractors $\gamma_i = (R_i, C_i)$ and $\gamma_j = (R_j, C_j)$. Contract γ_i is signed by entrepreneurs of type i, and contract j is signed by entrepreneurs of type j. Contract γ_i is incentive compatible if it has a higher expected utility for type i than for type j, that is, if

$$V_i(\gamma_i) \geq V_j(\gamma_i). \tag{5.9}$$

Similarly, contract γ_j is incentive compatible if it has a higher expected utility for type j than for type i, that is, if

$$V_j(\gamma_j) \geq V_i(\gamma_j). \tag{5.10}$$

Equations (5.10) and (5.11) imply that

$$V_j(\gamma_j) - V_j(\gamma_i) \geq V_i(\gamma_j) - V_i(\gamma_i). \tag{5.11}$$

This in turn implies that, if $R_i \geq R_j$ and $C_i \leq C_j$, the borrowers who signed the contract γ_i (with the higher interest payment and the lower collateral) will prefer the project with the lower probability of success. In other words, it must be that $p_i \leq p_j$.

To see this, rewrite equation (5.11) making use of the expected utility defined in equation (5.7). You obtain

$$p_j[U(X_j - R_j + W) - U(X_j - R_i + W)$$

$$- U(W - C_j) + U(W - C_i)] \geq p_i[U(X_i - R_j + W)$$

$$- U(X_i - R_i + W) - U(W - C_j) + U(W - C_i)]. \tag{5.12}$$

If $p_j < p_i$, then inequality (5.12) would imply

$$U(X_j - R_j + W) - U(X_j - R_i + W)$$

$$> U(X_i - R_j + W) - U(X_i - R_i + W). \tag{5.13}$$

However, by assumption, $X_j > X_i$ and $R_i \geq R_j$, so U would be convex instead of concave. This shows that the whole analysis of collateral as an incentive device hinges on the concavity of U, that is, on the condition that riskier projects are not preferred per se and that entrepreneurs are not indifferent to risk.

PART II

Dynamics

CHAPTER 6

Oligopoly and collusion

A number of interesting new developments on the oligopoly front can be traced back to Stigler's 1964 seminal article "A Theory of Oligopoly," which examines the relationship between collusion and the information structure of an oligopolistic market. The basic hypothesis is that oligopolists wish to collude to maximize joint profits, whether explicitly (through cartel agreements) or tacitly, when explicit collusion is illegal (through the adoption of practices or rules of behavior that facilitate coordination). The problem is not so much joint profit maximization as such (on this problem, see Roberts 1985), but rather that of policing a collusive agreement, that is, the factors governing the feasibility of collusion. This turns out to be a problem in the theory of information, because secret price cutting (or shipment in excess of production quotas) must be detectable for retaliation to be possible, or for a threat of retaliation to be credible. Stigler discusses different ways for partners of a collusive agreement to detect "cheating," starting from the principle that the basic method of detection must be the fact that a cheater is getting business he or she would otherwise not obtain.

Given this framework, subsequent research has tried to clarify a number of questions which have tended to become more and more precise as the (game theoretic) techniques used to answer them have become more sophisticated. These developments have reached such a degree of technicality that some "decoding" might be useful. We shall try to formulate each question in the "old" antitrust terminology, and then translate it into the "modern" jargon of game theory. Three sets of problems emerge.

First, how much information (among rivals) is needed for collusion to be possible? This may be translated as: Is "complete" and/or "perfect" information needed to solve the prisoner's dilemma (if it can be solved)?

Second, does less information (among rivals) promote "active competition" or "price wars"? To the extent that active competition can be interpreted as a move from the profit frontier to a noncooperative Nash equilibrium, this question can be reformulated as: Does a noncooperative Nash equilibrium require perfect information? If not, related questions are these: (a) Do duopolists, taken individually, wish to acquire more information in a noncooperative equilibrium? (b) Do they wish to share information in such an equilibrium? If the answer to (b) is negative, then the suspicion with which antitrust policy treats information sharing may have more solid theoretical foundations than would appear at first sight, because information sharing would indicate collusion. If the answer to (a) is positive, then the search for more information by oligopolistic sellers does not indicate per se that they wish to collude.

Third, the plausibility of oligopoly theory would be enhanced if price wars or active competition could be shown not to be the result of a myopic pursuit of self-interest (and therefore of a lack of (intertemporal) rationality on the part of oligopolistic competitors leading to disequilibria), but to be properties, together with collusion, of rational behavior. In game theoretic terms, this raises the question whether one can define a noncooperative equilibrium that includes both episodic price wars as well as periods of effective collusion. If imperfect information turns out to be a prerequisite for price wars to actually occur (in such a superequilibrium), then imperfect information could certainly be said to promote active competition.

6.1. Explicit collusion

The aim of explicit collusion is to maximize the *joint profit* of the colluding firms, that is, the sum of their profits. When joint profit is maximized, it is not possible to increase the profit of one firm without reducing the profit of some other firm. (Indeed, away from the maximum, joint profit is smaller. If nevertheless one firm gets more, some other firm must get less.) The maximum joint profit must therefore be a point on the profit frontier, such as point M in Figure 6.1, which represents the profits of two firms.

All points on the profit frontier[1] are, by definition, such that it is impossible to strictly increase the profits of all firms. In that (restricted) sense, these points are said to be Pareto-optimal. Point M in addition is assumed to have the property that the joint profit is maximized. The other points on the profit frontier therefore are below the straight line DC, which represents the profit combinations that give the same joint profit as M. (To find DC, given point M, add OA to OB to find point C, and add OB to OA to find point D, so that $OC = OD = OA + OB$.) Obviously, the same maximum joint profit can be allocated very dif-

---

[1] The profit frontier is postulated to be concave. See Friedman (1972).

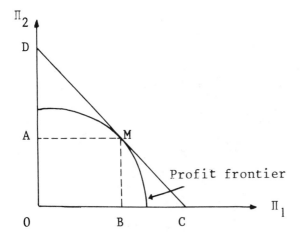

Figure 6.1. Joint profit maximization.

ferently among the colluding firms. An agreement to collude in order
to reach point M does not imply that there is agreement about the
allocation of the joint profit among the colluders. They may have to
pool all profits and have these redistributed in order to reach some
other point along DC. The feasibility of these interfirm compensations
is studied in detail in Fellner (1960) and will not be analyzed here. We
want to concentrate attention on the conditions under which point M
can be reached and enforced and highlight the underlying informational
requirements, following the pathbreaking analysis by Osborne (1976).

Firms that wish to maximize joint profits face (at least) four problems. First, although it is in their common interest to do so (i.e., to
reach point M), each of these has an individual interest to cheat (i.e.,
to deviate from point M in the direction that increases its individual
profit). This is the well-known "prisoner's dilemma." Second, a way
must be found to deter cheating. Third, the information necessary to
find point M is generally not available. Fourth, the implementation of
a deterring mechanism requires information about the actual behavior
of the colluding firms. The conclusion will be that perfect information
on the actual behavior of the partners is a *conditio sine qua non* for
the agreement to be operational. We consider each problem in turn.

6.1.1. A prisoner's dilemma

Consider an agreement to maximize joint profits at M. All members
of the agreement could increase their individual profit by deviating from

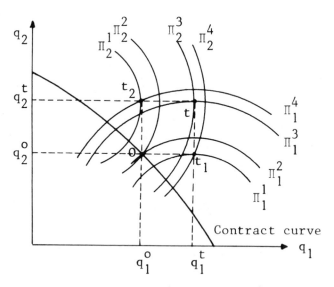

Figure 6.2. A prisoner's dilemma.

it (moving away from it along the profit frontier). However, if all were to do so, they would end up at a point below the profit frontier, so that all would make smaller profits! This is clearly a situation that can be described as a prisoner's dilemma. Shubik (1982, p. 254) formulates its usual verbal scenario as follows:

> Two prisoners who are suspected of having committed a crime are interrogated separately by the police. If both maintain silence, at most they can be booked on a minor charge. Each is encouraged to incriminate the other with a promise of leniency if he is not himself incriminated. If they double-cross each other, they are both in trouble.

Osborne (1976) illustrates the dilemma as follows (in the quantity domain). Instead of measuring profits on the axes, let us use the quantities produced and let q_i^0 ($i = 1, 2$) be the production quotas agreed on, so that they correspond to a point O on the contract curve in Figure 6.2. This point implies tangency of two isoprofit curves and may or may not maximize joint profits. (It is clear, though, that the corresponding profits must be on the profit frontier.)

Notice that the profit realized by firm i is higher along the isoprofit curve Π_i^1 than along the curve Π_i^2, along the curve Π_i^2 than along Π_i^3, and so on. Let $F_i(q_1^0, q_2^0)$ be the profit of firm i at point O.

Clearly,

$$\frac{\partial F_i(q_1^0, q_2^0)}{\partial q_i} > 0. \tag{6.1}$$

Each firm can increase its profit by producing more than its quota q_i^0.

Second, a comparison of points[2] t_1 and t_2 with point O shows that

$$F_1(q_1^t, q_2^0) > F_1(q_1^0, q_2^0) \tag{6.2}$$

for firm 1, because t_1 is on Π_1^1 and O is on Π_1^2, and

$$F_2(q_1^0, q_2^t) > F_2(q_1^0, q_2^0) \tag{6.3}$$

for firm 2, because t_2 is on Π_2^1 while O is on Π_2^2. In words: If firm i expects its competitor to stick to its quota q_j^0, firm i can increase its profit by producing q_i^t instead of q_i^0. It is profitable to cheat, if one expects the other not to cheat.

Third, compare point t with point O. This amounts to considering that each competitor expects the other to observe the quota they agreed on, so both end up cheating. Then

$$F_1(q_1^0, q_2^0) > F_1(q_1^t, q_2^t) \tag{6.4}$$

and

$$F_2(q_1^0, q_2^0) > F_2(q_1^t, q_2^t). \tag{6.5}$$

Both make less profits when they both cheat than if they had both refrained from cheating.

Nevertheless, if the other cheats, it is better for each firm also to cheat than to observe the quota! On comparing point t with point t_2, one finds that, for firm 1,

$$F_1(q_1^t, q_2^t) > F_1(q_1^0, q_2^t). \tag{6.6}$$

Similarly, a comparison of points t and t_1 gives, for firm 2,

$$F_2(q_1^t, q_2^t) > F_2(q_1^t, q_2^0), \tag{6.7}$$

because t is on Π_2^3 and t_1 is on Π_2^4. The conclusion is that, whether the other cheats or not, cheating dominates observing the quota for any particular firm.

The situation can also be described as a game in which each of, say, two players has two strategies (observe the agreement or cheat) and the profits are the payoffs. The following payoff matrix, with conveniently chosen numbers (representing each firm's profit for a given pair of strategies), illustrates points O, t_2, t_1, and t numerically. The profits of firm 1 are in the upper left corners. The profits of firm 2 are in the lower right corners.

---

[2] Point t_1 gives the highest profit if firm 1 deviates from point 0, because it is located on the isoprofit curve with the highest profit. Similarly for t_2.

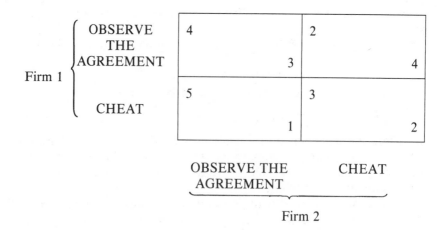

Whether member 2 cheats or not, member 1 prefers to cheat, because cheating gives the highest profit (5 or 3). Whether member 1 cheats or not, member 2 prefers to cheat, because that strategy gives the highest profit (4 or 2). When both cheat, both lose (they get only 3 and 2, respectively), while they would have made 4 and 3, respectively, if they had both observed the agreement. The strategy pair (cheat, cheat) is off the profit frontier, because both profits could be increased by shifting to another strategy pair. In this sense, it is said to be Pareto-dominated. The other three strategy pairs are on the profit frontier (or Pareto-optimal), because one profit cannot be increased without de-creasing the other firm's profit. Since the pair (cheat, cheat) is inside the profit frontier, it could be a Cournot–Nash equilibrium (see Section 6.2). In the three Pareto-optimal pairs, at least one firm refrains from using a more profitable strategy (cheating).

6.1.2.   How to deter cheating?

Is there a way out of the dilemma? A dilemma is a dilemma, and cannot have a solution. Yet, in real life, collusive agreements sometimes are successful, in the sense that they are not only signed but also enforced during several years. Firms thus seem to find a way out.

Pooling of revenues in order to make interfirm compensations may be one of those ways. This amounts to redistributing the joint profit $4 + 3 = 7$ obtained in the payoff matrix when both observe the agree-ment. Perhaps member 2 would refrain from cheating (cheating gives an additional profit of $4 - 3 = 1$ or $2 - 1 = 1$) if he or she were offered a 50-50 redistribution (each would get 3,5) or some analogous split of the joint profit. And similarly for member 1, for whom cheating also brings in an additional $5 - 4 = 1$ or $3 - 2 = 1$. However, member 1 is somehow capable of making more profits (probably has a larger market share) than member 2, so 50-50 may not be acceptable, and so on.

This kind of profit-sharing agreement, on top of an agreement on production quotas, was long thought to be the only means by which cartels could survive.[3] Since it is difficult to negotiate, cartels should not have a long life. Yet, Osborne observed that the OPEC cartel of oil-producing countries was created in October 1973 and was still very powerful three years later. In 1983 OPEC saw its share of the world oil market reduced drastically and internal disagreements were more and more frequent (cheating occurs more and more frequently). Yet, it still very much existed and continued to have a strong stabilizing[4] influence on the world oil price.

Osborne then goes on to show that the dilemma can be "solved" or overcome without pooling of revenues if each firm is assigned an operating rule incorporating a deterrant to cheating which keeps all firms at the joint profit maximizing point. This "best reply" rule to cheating is for the loyal firms to increase output in the same proportion as the cheaters increase theirs.

To understand this, one has to know how to find the vector (q_1^0, q_2^0) that maximizes joint profit. Osborne (1976) shows that it corresponds to that tangency point of two isoprofit curves (on the contract curve) at which the tangent $L(q^0)$ to these two curves passes through the origin. (This is generally not a 45° line, of course.) Along this line, market shares are constant because q_2/q_1 is constant (see Figure 6.3).

The idea is then to make sure that each firm is kept on the tangent $L(q^0)$ and has an incentive to stay at point (q_1^0, q_2^0). Let

$$s_i^0 = \frac{q_i^0}{\sum\limits_{j=1}^{n} q_j^0}$$

be the market share of firm i at that point, when there are n cartel members. Then it suffices for the cartel to assign to each of its member the rule

$$\max \left\{ q_i^0, \; q_i^0 + \frac{s_i^0}{s_j^0} \Delta q_j \right\} \qquad (6.8)$$

[3] See Patinkin (1947).
[4] Why and in what sense OPEC tries to stabilize the world oil price can be explained with reference to a model proposed by Hotelling. See Phlips (1983, chap. 7).

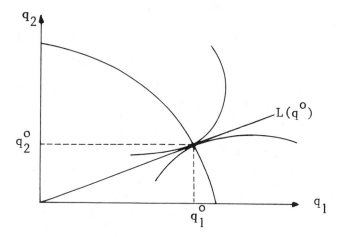

Figure 6.3. The joint profit-maximizing quantities.

when the production of member j deviates from his quota q_j^0 by Δq_j. Then the vector of productions moves in such a way that each member keeps his or her market share.

This is a deterrent to cheating, because member j will not cheat when he knows that the others will follow this rule. Indeed, cheating would then put him on a point above (q_1^0, q_2^0) where his profit is smaller (remember, from Figure 6.2, how the isoprofit curves are positioned). And it is a credible deterrent, because with n of these rules operating simultaneously, nobody can normally[5] win by deviating unilaterally from these rules. For example, if member i were to stay at q_i^0 when j moves to $q_j^0 + \Delta q_j$, she would lose more, according to equations (6.6) and (6.7), than if she applied the rule. When these rules are interpreted as strategies, we thus see that the vector of n strategies defined by equation (6.8) turns (q_1^0, q_2^0) into a noncooperative Nash equilibrium. In other words, the threat that cheating by one member will lead to cheating by *all* others gives everybody an incentive not to cheat.

The reader who is not convinced that the production vector chosen must be the one that maximizes joint profit is requested to consider a vector (on the contract curve) that is not on a ray through the origin but on, say, $L(q')$.

---

[5] Holahan (1978) has shown that following rule (6.8) may leave loyal members worse off if sufficiently large differences exist between the profit functions of loyalists and cheaters. R. Rothschild (1981) identifies conditions under which loyal firms are worse off than they would have been if they had stood pat, even when all firms have identical profit functions.

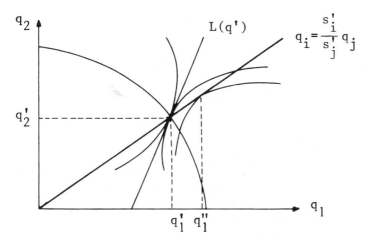

Figure 6.4. Another quantity vector.

Then the n strategies would be to

$$\max \left\{ q_i', q_i' + \frac{s_i'}{s_j'} \Delta q_j \right\}. \tag{6.9}$$

Suppose the cartel members produce (q_1', q_2'). Then (see Figure 6.4) firm 1 could make a larger profit by pushing its production to q_1'' where the ray through q' touches a better isoprofit curve and would therefore win by cheating. At least one member would be tempted to cheat. And he would win, even if he were certain to be caught, because retaliating would not be credible. Indeed, retaliation according to (6.9) would move the other firms along $L(q')$, and then some are bound to lose market share (because market shares are constant only along a ray). Those standing to lose would have a less credible threat. The threat to apply (6.9) is not a credible deterrent to cheating. And the set of strategies (6.9) is not a Nash equilibrium.

Before considering the amount of information involved in all this, it is important to ask in what sense Osborne's rule is a solution to the prisoner's dilemma as defined earlier. Because that dilemma occurs in a one-period game by definition, while Osborne's rule implies the passage of time, with some cheaters increasing their output first and loyal firms reacting subsequently, it should be clear that Osborne's rule is not theoretically satisfactory. A rigorous theoretical treatment should consider it as a set of strategies in a game that is played over several time periods. Section 6.3 will try to show how this can be done for an alternative set of strategies (according to which, if one cheats, all will jump to a Cournot–Nash equilibrium). May it suffice to stress the dynamic nature of the problem for the time being. Going through Osborne's analysis had the advantage of clarifying the economics involved and provides a better understanding of the solution of a truly dynamic game.

6.1.3. Joint profit maximization and incomplete information

Firms wish to collude and to find the combination of profits (point M in Figure 6.1) and therefore of productions (point (q_1^0, q_2^0) in Figure 6.3) that maximizes the joint profit. Under what kind of information structure will they succeed in locating these points? This is a question about the "completeness" of the information, because it refers to knowledge about the rules of the game, that is, about the players' information on the payoff matrix (what are the possible strategies and the corresponding payoffs?) or on the contract curve (how are the isoprofit curves located and where are they tangent to each other?). Collecting this type of information is not a trivial business.

First, a cartel does not necessarily include all firms in the industry. The nonmembers are "free-riders" and receive higher profits than the members. Nevertheless, it is always possible to form a stable cartel (see d'Aspremont et al. 1983). Variations in the total output of the nonmembers affect the profits of the members with the result that the contract curve is shifted. These variations depend in turn on the production of the cartel, so that the contract curve is itself a function of the total cartel production when there is a competitive fringe.

Second, members may disagree among themselves about the location of the contract curve, and this may prevent the formation of cartels. There often are differences of opinion about the availability of substitutes, different expectations about the future evolution of the market, and differences in the factor used to discount future profits. A member with a larger time horizon will use a smaller discount factor. For her, the contract curve is higher than for the others, so that she will be tempted to cheat even if the others stick to rule (6.8) and retaliate accordingly.

These difficulties in locating the contract curve should be kept in mind when setting up dynamic games, as in Section 6.3. To overcome these difficulties, it is generally necessary to have perfect information about the actual behavior of the cartel members and the nonmembers. Such information is also necessary to be able to deter cheating so that perfect information appears as a *conditio sine qua non* of joint profit maximization.

6.1.4. *Cheating and imperfect information*

An implicit assumption in the discussion of Osborne's rule (6.8) should now be made explicit: This rule works only if cheating is detected. Only under that condition can the rule be said to deter cheating. For if cheating goes undetected, the n strategies (6.8) cease to be a Nash equilibrium, because the threat that others will also cheat ceases to be credible.

Stigler (1964) discusses different ways by which a cartel member can detect price cutting by other members, the basic method of detection being the fact that the cheater is getting business he or she would otherwise not obtain. One method is to check whether one is losing more old customers than is statistically probable. Another method is to verify whether the suspected cheater is not keeping more customers than is statistically justified. A third method is to watch the number of new customers attracted by a competitor. Though interesting, these methods are not directly relevant in the present context. First, we have been considering Cournot strategies, that is, firms determining their rates of production while the price is determined by the market. Second, Stigler's methods do not reveal the identity of the cheater with certainty.

Osborne therefore discusses the information structure in terms of individual quantities produced. The information structure required for his operating rule to be effective is one of perfect information about the production rates of each cartel member. It is only with such perfect information that any deviation is detected and that his rule will effectively deter cheating.

In real life situation, information is often less perfect. Consider the realistic case where the cartel knows the total production of its members, taken together, but has no way of knowing the output of individual members. A second-best solution, that will have some deterrent effect, is then to suppose that the cheater has the average quota share $1/n$ and to tell the cartel member to

$$\max \left\{ q_1^0, q_i^0 + \frac{s_i}{1/n} \Delta q \right\} = \max \left\{ q_i^0, q_i^0 + n s_i \Delta q \right\} \qquad (6.10)$$

where Δq is the deviation of total output from $\sum_{i=1}^{n} q_i^0$ (total output under joint profit maximization). This rule will deter cheating on the average, because it keeps the *expected* output vector on $L(q^0)$. A drawback is that it will not deter cheating by a member with a particularly small quota who could increase its market share enough to overmatch the price depressing effect of the greater cartel output. Clearly, the more market shares are equal, the better rule (6.10) will work. But it cannot be more than a second-best solution.

Even worse, from the cartel point of view, is a third situation where it knows total industry output only, not the total output of the cartel. A fourth case is when it does not even know total industry output. In both cases explicit collusion is doomed to failure. Such situations can arise in the case of international agreements such as OPEC, which appears to be in the third situation.

In 1976, Osborne (pp. 842–3) wrote down the following scenario, describing what might happen to OPEC. Today (in 1985) that prediction appears as a very realistic description of what is actually happening to oil prices:

> With only the shortest of lags, world shipments of crude oil are known by all interested parties. The information is collected and reported by trade journals and various national and international agencies, and could in any case be inferred from a number of sources (for example, tanker charterings). All producers know their current market shares to a high degree of accuracy, and can thus learn if someone is cheating; they cannot so easily learn *who* is cheating. The members are sovereign states; they can attempt to keep their sales statistics secret if they wish. And some important producers (for example, Mexico) remain outside the cartel. OPEC thus finds itself in the third of the four positions. The likely consequences are a matter for speculation, but the following events are possible.
>
> An increase in world shipments reduces the market shares of the loyal members who, however, cannot detect its source. If they assume the source to be external and remain at $\underline{x}_i^0$ [i.e., q_i^0], they will, in effect, demonstrate the profitability of cheating; those loyal to the cartel will then secretly increase their output. On the other hand, if the loyal members assume the source to be internal and obey their quota rules (however modified), they will risk a needless increase in cartel output. With either choice the additional cartel output, added to the original increase from the unknown source, reduces prices. Distrust grows. Discipline weakens generally, and can be expected ultimately to disappear. Each member must look out for himself. Plenty of business can be done at a dollar under the cartel price; but it must be done quickly, for the buyers are daily demanding better terms. There is a general scurry for orders, and long-term commitments are made at $1, then $2, then $5 and $6 under the cartel price. The cartel has collapsed.

The antitrust implications are clear. Public policy must place firms in a situation where they don't know each other's output and refrain from publishing individual output statistics. In a similar vein, consuming nations facing an international cartel such as OPEC should refrain from establishing a central purchasing agency (through which all orders are funneled) in order to present a "united front." Such an agency would strengthen the cartel, since sellers will be identified and unde-tected cheating would become impossible.

6.2.   Cournot–Nash equilibrium

Suppose information is incomplete and sufficiently imperfect for the players to be off the profit frontier. Is a noncollusive equilibrium pos-sible under these conditions? For a collusive agreement to be workable, complete and perfect information was seen to be a necessary condition (without it, the prisoner's dilemma cannot be solved). Here, the answer is the opposite: A noncooperative Nash equilibrium[6] is a possibility which does not require complete or perfect information. (This is not too surprising, because without collusion the prisoner's dilemma does not arise.)

For noncooperative games, it has become clear (mainly through the work of Harsanyi 1967–68) that the equilibrium of a game with *incom-plete* information can be found when the game is redefined as a game with complete information. An example was given in Section 4.1, where auctions were analyzed as games with incomplete information. Some type of auctions had dominant strategies (the English and the second-price sealed-bid auctions) such that the optimal bidding strategies are determined without any information about the other bidders' payoffs. The Nash equilibrium of the other type of auctions (the Dutch and the first-price auctions) was found by supposing that all bidders draw their private reservation values from a known distribution. By this trick, information becomes complete again: Knowing the distribution means that all possibilities and all associated probabilities are known. An anal-ogous trick will be used below to find the noncooperative Cournot–Nash equilibrium under complete information.

As for *imperfect* information, this should be no problem. The pos-sibility of writing a noncooperative game in extensive form solves the problem of imperfect information analytically (through the use of "in-formation sets," which[7] describe the lack of information at each stage of the game for each player). And once a Nash equilibrium is found, the problem of detecting cheating does not arise, because the equilib-rium has the property that one always makes more profit if one does not cheat than if one cheats, even without being detected, so detection does not matter.

---

[6] The noncooperative Nash equilibrium is defined in Section 1.3.
[7] See Luce and Raiffa (1957, pp. 42–43).

6.2.1. *Experimental results*

A series of experiments have suggested much the same answer.[8] Experimental games conducted by Hoggatt (1959 and 1967), Fouraker and Siegel (1963), Friedman (1963, 1969, 1970), Dolbear et al. (1968), and Sauermann and Selten (1967) show that when information about competitors is limited, and in the absence of communication between players, (posted) prices actually tend to a competitive equilibrium when Bertrand price strategies are played, even with very few players. With quantity decisions, the outcome is most often a noncooperative Cournot–Nash equilibrium.[9] The accuracy of the joint maximization model was found to decrease with a reduction of information about other agents' actions. But joint profit maximization was the outcome under perfect information with experienced players (Stoecker 1980 and Friedman and Hoggatt 1980). Notice that under imperfect information

the number of sellers becomes a very important treatment variable in that an increase in the number destroys the accuracy of the joint maximum model. In the duopoly markets, significant (but less than perfect) cooperation occurs, but, with an increase in the number of firms, it vanishes almost completely and the Cournot model is very accurate by comparison (Plott 1982, pp. 1516–7).

6.2.2. *Incomplete information*

Let us start by showing how a Cournot–Nash equilibrium under incomplete information can be worked out and let us follow Novshek and Sonnenschein (1982). Imagine that duopolists do not know each others' profit functions because they are uncertain about the position of their industry's inverse demand function,[10] which is specified as

$$p = \alpha - q = \alpha - (q_1 + q_2) \tag{6.11}$$

by a suitable choice of units. The uncertainty is about the numerical value of the random intercept α, about which each duopolist receives a signal s^i ($i = 1, 2$) in each period.

---

[8] Excellent reviews of experiments in this field can be found in Selten (1979) and Plott (1982).

[9] The distinction between Bertrand price strategies and Cournot quantity strategies appears as less fundamental once it is realized that the Cournot outcome is also a perfect equilibrium in a two-stage game in which the players choose their capacity in the first stage and compete in prices in the second stage, as shown by Kreps and Scheinkman (1983). See also MacLeod (1984).

[10] Uncertainty about firm-specific costs is studied by Okada (1982), Fried (1984), Shapiro (1986), and Seidmann (1987). Ponssard already showed in 1979 that firms prefer not to share their information about linear market demand with their rivals.

Each firm has to determine an output strategy σ^i by maximizing its expected profit with respect to it, given the signal received and the optimal strategy of its competitor. This expected profit $E(\Pi_i \mid s^i, \sigma^1, \sigma^2)$ is defined on a distribution which is supposed to be known, so as to transform the problem into one that can be solved. Here the trick is to suppose that each player knows the joint distribution of his or her signal s^i and the residual intercept $\alpha - \sigma^j$. The Cournot–Nash equilibrium is then such that, for each firm i and for each signal s^i, outputs σ^i maximize the expected individual profits.

Notice that the assumption about the players knowing a joint distribution does not imply that the signals about the true value of α turn out to be correct. (The assumption that bidders know the joint distribution of their private reservation values, made in Chapter 4, did not imply that they make correct guesses about the true values.) The assumption made here implies, however that, given the equilibrium, the expected joint evolution (the joint distribution) of a signal and the intercept on which it provides information is correct. (Similarly, Vickrey's analysis of a Dutch auction supposes that the postulated rectangular distribution is correct.) In this sense, expectations are said to be "fulfilled."

What is the equilibrium? If intercept α were perfectly known, the equilibrium strategies would be $q_1 = q_2 = \alpha/3$. Indeed, the profit functions would be $\Pi_1 = [\alpha - (q_1 + q_2)]q_1$ and $\Pi_2 = [\alpha - (q_1 + q_2)]q_2$, respectively, and the system of first-order conditions to be solved would be

$$\frac{\partial \Pi_1}{\partial q_1} = \alpha - 2q_1 - q_2 = 0,$$

$$\frac{\partial \Pi_2}{\partial q_2} = \alpha - 2q_2 - q_1 = 0.$$

From the second equation $q_2 = \alpha/2 - q_1/2$ so that $q_1 = \alpha/3$ (from the first equation) and $q_2 = \alpha/3$. In the Novshek–Sonnenschein model, the equilibrium pair is simply $\sigma^1 = s^1/3$ and $\sigma^2 = s^2/3$. The true value of α is replaced by the signal perceived by each duopolist.

To prove this, Novshek and Sonnenschein suppose that the conditional expectation of α, for firm 1, is

$$E(\alpha \mid s^1) = s^1 = E(s^2 \mid s^1)$$

for all values of signal s^1, and similarly

$$E(\alpha \mid s^2) = s^2 = E(s^1 \mid s^2)$$

for firm 2, for all values of signal s^2. This amounts to assuming that the signals are unbiased. This is not too unrealistic, if one admits that small errors can be neglected.

Suppose firm 1 chooses strategy $\sigma^1 = s^1/3$. Then, for all values of s^2, the expected profit of firm 2 is

$$q_2 E[(\alpha - \sigma^1 - q_2) \mid s^2] = q_2 E[(\alpha - \sigma^1) \mid s^2] - q_2^2.$$

The maximization of this expected profit with respect to q_2 gives

$$E[(\alpha - \sigma^1) \mid s^2] - 2q_2 = 0$$

or

$$
\begin{aligned}
q_2^* &= \frac{1}{2} E[(\alpha - \sigma^1) \mid s^2] \\
&= \frac{1}{2} E\left[\left(\alpha - \frac{s^1}{3} \right) \Big| s^2 \right] \\
&= \frac{1}{2} \left(s^2 - \frac{s^2}{3} \right) = \frac{s^2}{3}
\end{aligned}
$$

because $E(\alpha \mid s^2) = s^2$ and $E(s^1 \mid s^2) = s^2$ by assumption.[11]

6.2.3.   Acquisition and transmission of information

Given this result, a natural question is to ask whether noncolluding duopolists would wish to acquire more information and would be interested in pooling the available information. The answer is, if they know the joint distribution of their signals and the residual intercepts, they will want more information but will be indifferent with respect to the pooling.

To show this, Novshek and Sonnenschein specify their model a bit further. Each signal is defined as the simple average of a number of observations, drawn from a sample $t_1, t_2, \ldots, t_n$, on the intercept α. The total sample is generated and owned by an independent information agency. Each observation is defined as

$$t_k = \alpha + \epsilon_k \tag{6.12}$$

with $E(\epsilon_k) = 0$, $E(\alpha \epsilon_k) = 0$, $E(\epsilon_k, \epsilon_{k'}) = 0$, and $E(\epsilon_k^2) = v$. This amounts to supposing that t_k is unbiased, because $E(t_k) = \alpha$ if $E(\epsilon_k) = 0$, that α is uncorrelated with the error and that the errors are uncorrelated. Each error also has the same variance v.

---

[11] See Novshek and Sonnenschein (1982) for the proof that the equilibrium pair $\sigma^i = s^i/3$ is unique.

Suppose each duopolist signs a contract with the information agency. Firm 1 agrees to buy n_1 observations, of which it transmits m_1 to a common pool that is available to both. It thus keeps $n_1 - m_1$ observations as private information. Firm 2 makes a similar arrangement.

Suppose also that the agency labels these observations in the following order: First come the $m_1 + m_2$ pooled observations; then come the $n_1 - m_1$ private observations of firm 1; finally, there are the $n_2 - m_2$ private observations of firm 2.

Under these arrangements, signal s^1 is the simple average of the observations bought by firm 1, plus those transmitted to the pool by firm 2, and vice versa. Since the optimal strategies are functions of these signals, and the latter are functions of the error terms ϵ_k, the expected equilibrium profits can be expressed in terms of the ϵ_k's and their variances and covariances. The properties of these variances and covariances can thus be used to simplify the results and to crank out precise results. Formally,

$$s^1 = \frac{\displaystyle\sum_{k=1}^{n_1+m_2} t_k}{n_1 + m_2} = \alpha + \frac{\displaystyle\sum_{k=1}^{n_1+m_2} \epsilon_k}{n_1 + m_2} \tag{6.13}$$

and

$$s^2 = \frac{\displaystyle\sum_{k=1}^{m_1+m_2} t_k + \sum_{k=n_1+m_2+1}^{n_1+n_2} t_k}{n_2 + m_1}$$

$$= \alpha + \frac{\displaystyle\sum_{k=1}^{m_1+m_2} \epsilon_k + \sum_{k=n_1+m_2+1}^{n_1+n_2} \epsilon_k}{n_2 + m_1} \tag{6.14}$$

because firm 2 has access, in addition to the $m_1 + m_2$ pooled observations, to the observations that are not available to its competitor, that is, the observations from $n_1 + m_2 + 1$ to the last one, which is $n_1 + n_2$ because this is the grand total available. At the Cournot–Nash equilibrium computed earlier, the expected profit for firm 1 is

$$E(\Pi_1) = E\frac{s^1}{3}\left[\alpha - \left(\frac{s^1}{3} + \frac{s^2}{3}\right)\right]. \tag{6.15}$$

Insert results (6.13) and (6.14) into (6.15) and use the assumptions made about the error terms ϵ_k. You end up with

$$E(\Pi_1) = \frac{1}{9}\left[E(\alpha^2) - \frac{v}{n_1 + m_2} - \frac{(m_1 + m_2)v}{(n_1 + m_2)(n_2 + m_1)}\right] \tag{6.16}$$

for firm 1. By a similar procedure firm 2 is seen to have an expected profit that is structured in the same way. These profits can be differentiated with respect to n_1 or n_2 (a positive direct derivative indicates that the firm wishes to acquire information; a zero cross derivative indicates that the firm is indifferent to its competitor acquiring information) or with respect to m_1 or m_2 (to see whether it is profitable to transfer information to a pool).

It is clear that the expected profit of firm i increases in n_i, so that firms find information acquisition profitable. This doesn't imply, of course, that they wish to share this information totally or partially. Looking at the signs of the derivatives, one finds inter alia that the expected profit of firm i also increases in n_j, if part of it is pooled (i.e., if $m_j \neq 0$) but decreases in m_i when the other firm retains some private information.

As for contractual arrangements between the firms jointly to transfer information to the common pool, one finds that the duopolists are indifferent between pooling all information ($m_1 = n_1$ and $m_2 = n_2$) and no pooling at all ($m_1 = m_2 = 0$), because in both cases expected profits are the same when $n_1 = n_2$.

With a linear market demand curve such as (6.11), expected consumer's surplus is easy to compute. It is the triangle under the demand curve above p; that is,

$$\frac{1}{2} E(\alpha - p)q = \frac{1}{2} E(\alpha - \alpha + q)q = \frac{1}{2} E \left(\frac{s^1 + s^2}{3} \right)^2 .$$

Insertion of (6.13) and (6.14) shows that expected consumer's surplus

is lower the higher the value of n_1 and n_2. This is consistent with a familiar theme in the economics of uncertainty: in markets with uncertain demand, decreases in variance reduce expected consumer's surplus. Also, expected consumer's surplus is lower the higher the value of m_i when $m_j > (2n_j - n_i)/3$ (Novshek and Sonnenschein 1982, p. 218).

However, the total expected surplus in equilibrium (the sum of the expected profits and the expected consumer's surplus) turns out to be equal to $\frac{2}{3}E(\alpha^2)$ − {expected consumer's surplus} so that the effects of information acquisition and pooling on total surplus are exactly the opposite (of their effects on consumer's surplus).

The results are strengthened by Clarke (1983a,b), who replaces the fulfilled expectations assumption by a "Bayes–Cournot" assumption, implying that firms must make their quantity decisions based on their best Bayes estimates of their opponents' information. Using results obtained by Basar and Ho (1974), Clarke finds that in all cases where expectations are not actually fulfilled, firms would prefer not to share information,[12] even if they have less accurate information than their rivals, unless they may cooperate once information has been shared.[13]

We can summarize by quoting Clarke (1983b, p. 383): "This situation is unfortunate as society's welfare is maximized only when firms share information, but act competitively. Thus society faces a dilemma. Information pooling is good if firms behave competitively, but shared information makes anticompetitive agreements easier to construct."

6.3.   Tacit collusion

Explicit collusion aims at putting the members of an agreement at the point on the profit frontier at which joint profit is maximized. Tacit collusion aims at increasing the profits of the colluders above the level implied in the noncooperative Cournot–Nash equilibrium until hopefully the same joint profit maximizing point is reached. The objectives are thus basically the same. But with tacit collusion the task is complicated by the fact that no explicit agreement in the form of a legally enforceable contract is possible, typically because such contracts are illegal. This section will show that, from an economic point of view, explicit collusion and tacit collusion are not fundamentally different. Section 6.1 made it clear that contracts, however enforceable legally, will not be carried out if there is no mechanism that deters cheating and that it is this mechanism that makes the agreement binding. If the mechanism is a set of strategies (such as Osborne's rule) which together constitute a noncooperative Nash equilibrium, then the results of Section 6.1 implicitly suggest that the outcome associated with collusion can be obtained in a noncollusive way. That is exactly the message of the present section, with the important proviso that the dynamics of the problem should be carefully spelled out. In particular, oligopolists should be seen as meeting over and over again in the marketplace, so that the time sequence of the deterring mechanism can be made clear to all.

Perfect and complete information will again and not surprisingly appear as a necessary condition for the emergence of a collusive outcome. The more information is incomplete and imperfect, the more difficult it will be to get away from the Cournot–Nash equilibrium in the direction of the profit frontier.

---

[12] See also Crawford and Sobel (1982) and Palfrey (1982). Empirical evidence on the exchange of information and collusion can be found in Eisenberg (1980).

[13] Gal-Or (1985) and Vives (1983) find this result to hold only if the goods produced are substitutes, and to be reversed for the case of Bertrand price competition (with substitutes).

6.3.1. *A noncooperative collusive equilibrium*

Having discussed the respective informational requirements of a joint
profit maximizing equilibrium and of a noncooperative Cournot–Nash
equilibrium, it seems natural to try to bring the two equilibria together
and to ask whether they could not, possibly in a temporal sequence,
constitute the components of a dynamic game. J. Friedman was the
first[14] to work out such a solution. Time now explicitly enters the picture. Players are supposed to play the same game repeatedly (they are
said to play a stationary repeated game, also called a "supergame")
and to have an infinite horizon (to simplify the mathematics involved).
The strategic variables are either quantities (when the products are
homogeneous) or prices (when the products are differentiated). This
presentation concentrates on quantity (or "Cournot") strategies.

Instead of using an instantaneous deterring mechanism such as Osborne's rule (6.8), Friedman postulates the following intertemporal
strategy. In the first period of the game, all players choose the collusive
Pareto-optimal quantities q_i^0. In any subsequent period, they continue
to do so if, in all past periods, all players were loyal. If, however, this
is not the case, then all players shift to the Cournot–Nash quantities
q_i^c. The profit possibilities for a single period are represented in Figure
6.5, reprinted by permission from Friedman (1983, Figure 5.3).

Let $\Pi^0 = (\Pi_1^0, \Pi_2^0)$ be the profits realized in each period with the
quantities (q_1^0, q_2^0) so that $\Pi_i^0 = F_i(q_1^0, q_2^0)$. These profits are somewhere on the profit frontier, possibly on the point that maximizes joint
profits. The stationary assumption implies that the elements of the
game are the same in each period, so that the profit frontier remains
unchanged through time, and that each period is treated as completely
independent of every other one. In a similar way, let $\Pi^c = (\Pi_1^c, \Pi_2^c)$
be the profits realized in each period with the equilibrium Cournot–
Nash quantities (q_1^c, q_2^c) so that $\Pi_i^c = F_i(q_1^c, q_2^c)$.

Next define Π_1' as the maximum immediate profit firm 1 can make
by cheating (producing $q_1' > q_1^0$) when the other firm sticks to q_2^0, or
$\Pi_1' = \max F_1(q_1', q_2^0)$. We know from our discussion of the prisoner's
dilemma that $\Pi_1' > \Pi_1^0$ and that the other firm will make a smaller profit.
In Figure 6.5, Π_1' corresponds to point A on the profit frontier. Define
Π_2' similarly as $\max F_2(q_1^0, q_2')$.

---

[14] It was first presented by Friedman (1971) following an idea by Aumann (1960) and
then included in Friedman's 1977 textbook (chap. 8). A short summary is given in
Friedman and Hoggatt (1980, chap. 1). A very readable and reasonably complete
version can be found in Friedman (1972), and some further discussion is contained in
Rees (1985). See Friedman (1983, pp. 123–35) for a numerical illustration with price
strategies.

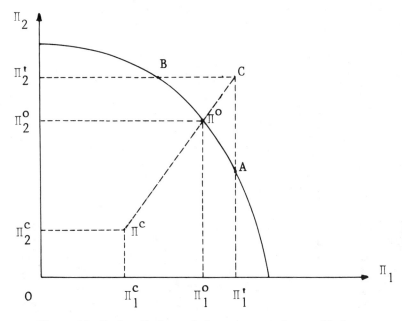

Figure 6.5. Tacit collusion: a balanced temptation equilibrium.

Each player's strategy σ^i is defined as

$$\sigma^i = \begin{cases} q_{i1} = q_i^0, & \\ q_{it} = q_i^0 & \text{if } q_{j\tau} = q_j^0 \ (j \neq i) \\ & \text{for } \tau = 1, \ldots, t-1, \\ q_{it} = q_i^c & \text{otherwise.} \end{cases} \qquad (6.17)$$

To decide whether cheating is worthwhile, each player compares the discounted value of his profits when these are equal to Π_i^0 in each period, or $\Pi_i^0/(1 - \alpha_i)$ where α_i is the discount factor used, with the discounted profits he would get if he were to choose q_i^0 for the first t periods and q_i^t in period $t + 1$. Because this deviation would be followed by a move to q_j^c by his competitor in period $t + 2$ and all subsequent periods, he would himself end up in q_i^c as of period $t + 2$ because that is his best reply, so his discounted profits would be

$$\Pi_i^0 + \alpha_i \Pi_i^0 + \cdots + \alpha_i^{t-1} \Pi_i^0 + \alpha_i^t \Pi_i^t + \alpha_i^{t+1} \Pi_i^c + \alpha_i^{t+2} \Pi_i^c + \cdots$$

or

$$\frac{1 - \alpha_i^t}{1 - \alpha_i} \Pi_i^0 + \alpha_i^t \Pi_i^t + \alpha_i^{t+1} \frac{1}{1 - \alpha_i} \Pi_i^c \,.$$

Nobody will want to cheat – there is tacit collusion, that is, a non-cooperative collusive equilibrium – if, for all players,

$$\frac{\Pi_i^0}{1 - \alpha_i} > \frac{1 - \alpha_i^t}{1 - \alpha_i} \Pi_i^0 + \alpha_i^t \Pi_i' + \alpha_i^{t+1} \frac{1}{1 - \alpha_i} \Pi_i^c$$

or

$$\Pi_i^0 > (1 - \alpha_i)\Pi_i' + \alpha_i \Pi_i^c,$$

$$\alpha_i(\Pi_i' - \Pi_i^c) > \Pi_i' - \Pi_i^0,$$

$$\alpha_i > \frac{\Pi_i' - \Pi_i^0}{\Pi_i' - \Pi_i^c}. \tag{6.18}$$

This is a particularly interesting result. The numerator $\Pi_i' - \Pi_i^0$ is the immediate extra gain from cheating. The denominator $\Pi_i' - \Pi_i^c$ is the per period decrease in profit in each succeeding period. Their ratio is compared with the discount factor. If the latter is sufficiently high, which means that a big enough weight is placed on the future, then cheating is not worthwhile. Firms that are not shortsighted but look far enough into the future will prefer tacit collusion to reaping immediate profits Π_i', and the vector[15] q^0 repeated in each time period is a noncooperative Nash equilibrium. Because $\alpha_i = 1/(1 + r)$, where r is the rate of interest chosen by the firm, it is clear that condition (6.18) is more likely to be satisfied in periods where the rate of interest is low. If the rate of interest is too high, it is optimal to set $t = 1$ and to cheat (choose q_i') in the first period, with the result that the industry is in a Cournot–Nash equilibrium as of period $t + 1$ and remains there.

When, in addition to (6.18),

$$\frac{\Pi_i' - \Pi_i^0}{\Pi_i' - \Pi_i^c} = \frac{\Pi_j' - \Pi_j^0}{\Pi_j' - \Pi_j^c} \qquad (i \neq j; \, i, j = 1, \ldots, n) \tag{6.19}$$

there is what may be called a "balanced temptation equilibrium": Each player has the same temptation to behave in a myopic way. Such an equilibrium is depicted in Figure 7.5. [In that figure, point C does *not* represented the profits when both are cheating; there can be no profits outside the profit frontier! Point C is useful only to show that condition (6.19) is satisfied.]

---

[15] Or any initial vector of quantities that gives higher profits than the vector q^c. In this sense, this is an early version of the "Folk Theorem" (Fudenberg and Maskin 1986).

6.3.2. Complete information

We can now further elaborate Osborne's remark that collusion is difficult when the oligopolists have different time horizons. If, in the present context, some firms use a smaller discount factor than their competitors, so that their time horizon is in fact shorter, condition (6.18) may be satisfied for some and not for others. Tacit collusion is then not workable: Before you conclude that cheating is not profitable in the long run, you better check that all your competitors come to the same conclusion.

In fact, tacit collusion requires complete information exactly like in the case of explicit collusion. The equilibria described "depend on each firm knowing the cost functions, demand functions, and discount parameters of all other firms for the present and all future periods. They depend also on the time lag during which a firm gains from deviation being of a known and fixed duration . . ." (Friedman 1983, p. 133). It is a difficult empirical question to ascertain under which conditions real-life firms have information that is sufficiently complete for this model to have descriptive value. Tacit collusion is likely to occur only in certain types of markets such as geographically segmented markets or markets with no rapid growth or slow technical progress, in which Friedman's inequality (6.18) is easy to compute in practice.

Because of its reliance on complete information, Friedman's super-game approach makes price wars appear as disequilibria. Although his approach has the advantage of giving a precise meaning to the concept of tacit collusion, it has the drawback that his noncooperative equilibrium solves the prisoner's dilemma too well: No firm ever has an incentive to cheat in this equilibrium! One might want to treat price wars as part of an intertemporal equilibrium.

This is what Porter (1983a,b) and Green and Porter (1984) do, by introducing an extra incentive to cheat, based on incomplete information, into the supergame. They allow for random shocks in demand so that firms have incomplete information about their rivals' output. An observed price decrease may then be blamed on the demand shock rather than on cheating, so the intertemporal strategy (go to q_i^c if somebody cheats) is redefined in terms of a trigger price: Switch to the Cournot–Nash equilibrium as soon the observed price is less than this trigger price. The equilibrium quantities are found to be above their joint profit-maximizing level and to tend toward this level as the variance of the unobserved disturbance term (of demand) goes to zero. Interestingly, price wars now occur with positive probability as the result of unusual demand shocks. But individual deviations due to the availability of new information and the corresponding revision of beliefs about rivals' behavior are not handled explicitly. Further work in this area will probably be devoted to the dynamic effects on cheating of the occurrence of new private information.[16]

This is not to suggest that price wars, treated as part of the intertemporal equilibrium, necessarily imply incomplete information. They can occur as well under complete (and perfect) information as part of noncooperative intertemporal equilibrium price strategies. Selten (1965) showed this to be the case in a dynamic oligopoly game in which demand inertia dynamizes consumer behavior.[17] When oligopolists know that market demand will jump upward in the near future, they will conclude that time has come to try to improve their market shares *now* by engaging in active competition, because the foreseen improvement in market demand will allow all of them to recoup today's reduced profits (or losses). Launching a price war now can be in everybody's individual interest!

6.3.3.   Tacit coordination and imperfect information

Reverting to tacit collusion, it is clear that it also requires perfect information about the actual outputs. How could the threat to retaliate to anybody's cheating be credible otherwise? All the comments made above about the informational requirements for cartel members remain valid. Without perfect information, profits must be off the profit frontier.

An interesting question is then to ask whether one could not define tacit collusion in a weaker sense. Rather than keeping oligopolists on the profit frontier (and thus solving the prisoner's dilemma), its more modest aim would be to get them somewhat away from the Cournot–Nash equilibrium in the direction of the frontier, without binding agreements. This type of tacit collusion doesn't seem to depend on precise intertemporal strategies. And it may not require complete or perfect information. Let us call it "tacit coordination," following Spence (1978).

Spence allows for incomplete information, by introducing event uncertainty into the profit functions. He simultaneously allows for im-

---

[16] As suggested by Fudenberg and Tirole (1986a). Slade (1987) analyzes price wars as information-seeking devices used after shifts in demand occurred.

[17] The same result obtains when, in addition, the supply side of the market is dynamized by allowing producers to carry inventories, as in the generalized Selten model setup by Phlips and Richard (1986).

perfect information, because firms do not observe rival behavior directly but receive market signals instead (such as those discussed by Stigler 1964).

The event uncertainty is represented by the random factor α [leading to unforeseen shifts in market demand, for example, such as changes in the intercept in equation (6.11)], so firm i's profit function is $\Pi_i = F_i(q_1, q_2, \alpha)$.

Imperfect information comes in because observed behavior is replaced by market signals $s_i = M_i(q_1, q_2, \alpha)$, which depend both on actual outputs and on the random factor. The reaction function[18] $R_i(q_j)$ of firm i becomes $R_i(s_i)$, in which the argument is the signal firm i receives about the behavior of its competitor. When the random factor α does not modify the signals, a status quo situation arises in which the signal provides information about the competitor's behavior and is not affected by the random shocks.

A tacit coordination equilibrium exists when, for all signals that can be observed when the status quo action pair is (q_1^*, q_2^*),

$$R_1(s_1) = q_1^*, \qquad R_2(s_2) = q_2^* \tag{6.20}$$

and

$$EF_i(q_i', R_j(q_i', q_j^*, \alpha), \alpha) \leq EF_i(q_1^*, q_2^*, \alpha),$$

or, in a simple notation,

$$D_i(q_i', q_j^*) \leq \overline{F}_i(q_1^*, q_2^*) \qquad (i \neq j; i, j = 1, 2). \tag{6.21}$$

Output q_i' represents a deviation from the equilibrium. Condition (6.21) says that tacit coordination requires a deviation to be less profitable than no deviation in terms of expected profits for both firms. Condition (6.20) requires the status quo quantities to be sustained over time by the reaction functions, given the information structure.

Conditions (6.20) and (6.21) are a generalization of the conditions defining a Nash equilibrium, much in the spirit of the analysis by Novshek and Sonnenschein (discussed in Section 6.2) of a Cournot–Nash equilibrium with incomplete information. Here signals about rival behavior are added to the randomness of α. (In Section 6.2, the focus was on signals about α.) Novshek and Sonnenschein's fulfilled expectations assumption made sure that players act according to the signals received. A similar condition is needed here, to guarantee that players act according to their reaction functions (defined in terms of signals, not actual behavior).

---

[18] The reaction function of firm i represents its output as a function of its competitor's output. It is obtained by rewriting the first-order condition for firm i, solving for q_i.

Notice, indeed, that even when randomness (α) does not modify the signals so that q_i^* is defined, these signals may give wrong information and, for example, suggest that (q_1^*, q_2^*) is being played when in fact (q_1', q_2^*) or (q_1^*, q_2') are occurring. Detection of cheating must therefore be considered again, and a condition must be found that makes undetected cheating unprofitable, so that signals become credible and players act according to the reaction functions as required.

Redefine therefore D_i as the expected profit when a deviation q_i' goes *undetected,* and suppose that it is larger than $\overline{F}_i$. Then cheating will depend on the probability of being detected (by a signal, again, but a signal that is not compatible with (q_1^*, q_2^*) being the actual outputs) and the penalty suffered when detected. Let λ be the probability[19] that a deviation is *not* detected, and let m_i be the minimum profit made by firm i if its gets caught and punished by its competitor. Then no deviation from the equilibrium will occur if, at the equilibrium, each firm is in a situation such that

$$\lambda D_i(q_i', q_j^*) + (1 - \lambda)m_i \leq \overline{F}_i(q_1^*, q_2^*),$$

or

$$\lambda[D_i(q_i', q_j^*) - m_i] \leq \overline{F}_i(q_1^*, q_2^*) - m_i,$$

or

$$\lambda \leq \frac{\overline{F}_i(q_1^*, q_2^*) - m_i}{D_i(q_i', q_j^*) - m_i}. \tag{6.22}$$

The probability of not being detected, λ, appears as a measure of the noise in the system. When $\lambda = 0$, condition (6.22) is always satisfied: Nobody ever cheats, because cheating is immediately detected and punished. When $\lambda = 1$, there is no way cheating could be detected and tacit coordination is impossible. The larger is D_i, the smaller λ has to be, that is, the larger the probability of getting caught should be. The larger is m_i, the smaller is the loss incurred when punished, and the smaller λ has to be for tacit collaboration to be workable.

When information is perfect ($\lambda = 0$) but incomplete (α random), tacit coordination simply requires $\overline{F}_i \geq m_i$. It suffices that the expected profit if one does not deviate be larger than the profit after punishment. Under perfect information there is much scope for tacit coordination! This result reinforces the negative conclusion reached above that duopolists do not wish to share information or are at least indifferent about information pooling in a noncooperative Cournot–Nash equilibrium.

---

[19] This probability depends on the extent to which α blurs the message received through signals about rival behavior.

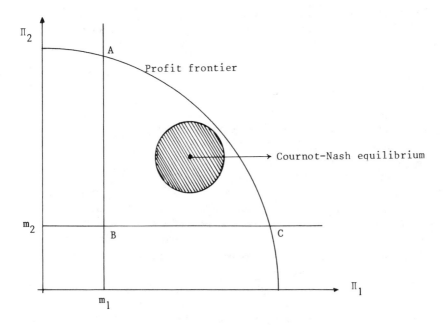

Figure 6.6. Tacit coordination under imperfect information.

Notice that the Cournot–Nash equilibrium with imperfect information is such that condition (6.22) is automatically satisfied. By definition, $\overline{F}_i(q_1^c, q_2^c) \geq \overline{F}_i(q_1', q_2^c)$, that is, the unconditional profit expectation when one deviates, whether detected or not. If the latter is no smaller than $D_i(q_i', q_j^c)$, the profit conditional on the deviation being undetected (which should normally be the case because detection does not matter here), then

$$\frac{\overline{F}_i(q_1^c, q_2^c)}{D_i(q_i', q_j^c)} \geq 1$$

while $0 \leq \lambda \leq 1$. Tacit coordination is automatic because there is no need to detect or punish.

Spence's general conclusion is that perfect information eliminates all the profit combinations where the temptation to cheat is too large in comparison with the probability of not being caught. Under imperfect information, tacit coordination is possible only in a restricted area around the noncooperative Cournot–Nash equilibrium profits (such as the shaded area in Figure 6.6) inside the profit frontier. With full information, all the payoffs in the region ABC can be equilibrium outcomes. With incomplete and imperfect information, this equilibrium set shrinks to the shaded area. The extent of the shrinkage is determined primarily by the extent to which randomness detroys the informational content of the signals.

6.4.   Antitrust implications

The antitrust implications of information sharing were discussed at length in the 1950s and 1960s. Precise policy implications were derived and implemented. In Europe the discussion was coached in terms of "market transparency" and the impact of improved transparency on the competitive behavior of oligopolists. In the United States the discussion centered on "open price systems." The embarrassing conclusion was that market transparency among competitors does not promote competition but, instead, makes tacit collusion among oligopolists easier. This was embarrassing because the Arrow–Debreu approach was riding high, so theoreticians were sticking to the belief that better information is welfare-improving per se and were superbly ignoring the conclusions of the debate among antitrust specialists. The latter, on the other hand, superbly ignored welfare economics and did not hesitate to make information-sharing agreements or devices among oligopolists illegal.

Today, we are confronted with what looks like an invasion of the field by game theorists, who, after playing for some time with the concepts of incomplete information and imperfect information, have come to sharpen their tools to the extent that they now seem capable of deriving policy conclusions that shed new light on the old topic and may even lead to a revision of antitrust policy. Since these conclusions have a strong theoretical foundation, there is some hope that antitrust policy might get linked, at last, with sound economic theory.

The purpose of this section is to make a heroic attempt at comparing the two approaches, to see to what extent some of the old wood has to be pruned and some of the new should be given a chance to grow. I shall first try to present the old intuitions in some detail, as they transpire in recent EEC antitrust decisions, and then compare these with possibly conflicting game-theoretic findings.

6.4.1.   Old intuitions

Current EEC antitrust policy is directly inspired by a voluminous literature, mostly of German origin, which is itself influenced by American writings. A typical and influential representative is Mestmäcker (1952), who carries the reasoning to the extreme conclusion that all forms of information transmission among oligopolists are to be made illegal. The opposite view, reflecting ideas that are widespread in industrial circles, is exposed by Behrens (1963). To be honest, I myself defended a viewpoint (in 1963) that is close to Mestmäcker's. If, in what follows, I were to criticize some of the antitrust actions currently taken, that would admittedly imply a change in beliefs.

6.4.2. The wood pulp decision

The position of the EEC Commission with respect to information transmission among oligopolists can be reconstructed by analyzing a number of decisions[20] taken since 1974. In each case, the basic criterion used is a situation of "normal competition," more or less synonymous (I guess) with the concept of "active competition." Before trying to determine what the Commission considers "normal," it may be of some help to take a closer look at the December 1984 wood pulp decision, in which the Commission's views are expressed in great detail.

In 1981, six Canadian wood pulp producers, ten American, eleven Finnish, ten Swedish, one Norwegian, one Portuguese, and one Spanish producer, plus the U.S. Pulp, Paper and Paperboard Association, the Finnish common sales agency and the Swedish association of wood pulp producers were informed that the Commission had found evidence of collusive behavior with regard to the prices of their exports to the EEC.

The main evidence given is the fact that, from 1975 to 1981, these prices moved in a parallel way. Indeed, these firms were observed to match competitors' price changes within hours or days. In fact, individual prices were announced to clients, agencies, or the press (verbally, by telephone, in writing, or by telex) a few weeks in advance for the next quarter. All competitors were thus immediately informed of a future price change and were given the opportunity to match it by announcing an identical change. As a result, the announced prices were identical in northwestern Europe and almost identical in southern Europe. Transaction prices were most often identical with the announced prices, because very few customers received "genuine" rebates (not just the usual payment facilities). All price announcements were in U.S. dollars rather than in the local European currencies.

---

[20] See the IFTRA decision of 15 May 1974 (*Official Journal* No L 160), the Cobelpa decision (*O.J.* No L 242 of 21.3.1977), the vegetal parchment decision (*O.J.* No L 70 of 13.3.1978), the Céruse decision of 12 December 1978 (*O.J.* no L 21), the zinc decision of 14 December 1982 (*O.J.* No L 362), and most recently the wood pulp decision of 19 December 1984 (*O.J.* No L 85/1).

All addressees, except one American, the Norwegian, the Portuguese, and the Spanish producers, had to pay (within three months) fines ranging between 50,000 and 500,000 ECU (European Currency Unit). The fines imposed on the Finnish and Swedish producers were reduced to take account of the fact that they agreed to reduce the "artificial transparency" of the market by quoting prices in local currencies and to refrain from making announcements on a quarterly basis, from exchanging information about prices or other confidential data and from colluding.

6.4.3. Normal competition

A careful reading of the decision suggests that in the Commission's view, normal competition is characterized by the following ingredients.

Proposition 1. Normal competition implies the freedom, for each individual firm, to change its prices independently.

Anything that affects this freedom is an illegal restriction of competition. This includes price agreements, needless to say, but also any discussion, between competitors, of their current or future prices *and* of the market conditions that make it possible for a firm to change or not to change its prices.

Proposition 2. Price competition between oligopolists typically takes the form of secret rebates, given for particular transactions, on list prices.

Secrecy of the rebate is the feature that prevents oligopolistic competitors from reacting immediately to a price reduction by one of them and thus makes price competition effective. Without secrecy, the reaction would be immediate and therefore the price reduction would not be granted. In addition, these rebates should be "real" rebates, not just payment facilities granted to a select group of large customers. (The fact that such rebates imply price discrimination, which is illegal, is not stressed.)

Proposition 3. Normal competition is not compatible with simultaneous moves of transaction prices (and thus of secret rebates) or list prices.

Indeed, if each firm is free to change its prices, simultaneous moves are not to be expected. Each firm will act according to its own individual interest, changing its list price or its transaction price at the optimal point in time. As a result, if oligopolistic prices display parallel moves, this very fact proves that there is collusion.

Proposition 4. Imperfect information among sellers strengthens the bargaining position of their customers and thus leads to lower transaction prices.

Indeed, it is costly for a firm to check whether a competitor is quoting a low price, as claimed by its customers, so that it will more readily concede a price reduction. When customers are able to play this game simultaneously, average price will go down.

Proposition 5. Perfect information among competitors is not only a necessary condition for collusion but also a sufficient condition, because oligopolists want to collude.

Without market transparency about prices or quantities, colluders cannot enforce a price agreement, that is, punish the cheater. With market transparency, they will maximize joint profits overtly or tacitly or follow the price leader's moves without delay.

Proposition 6. Multilateral information transmission among oligopolists is therefore per se evidence of collusion.

The transmission of information about *current* prices or quantities is a substitute for a formal price agreement because this information is all that is needed for collusion to work.

Proposition 7. Multilateral information transmission about *future* prices is, a fortiori, per se evidence of collusion.

To discuss or communicate current prices or production rates is bad. To discuss or communicate future prices or production rates is even worse, since the freedom to change in the future is thus also restricted. More or less simultaneous announcements are substitutes for dinner meetings of colluding oligopolists.

Proposition 8. Unilateral information transmission about future prices is also per se evidence of collusion, because it could have no other purpose.

Why, indeed, would an individual firm bother to announce a price change publicly (by issuing a press release, circulating a new price list, sending telexes to customers or agents) if not to make sure that competitors be informed in time to be able to make similar moves?

6.4.4. The possibility of noncooperative equilibria

This enumeration of the informational requirements of active competition is not meant to be exhaustive. It is sufficient, though, to leave one with uneasy feelings.

First, there obviously is no reference to a possible noncooperative equilibrium. Normal competition is seen as active competition, as implying independent moves by individual firms resulting from bargaining between a particular seller and a particular buyer and leading to price undercutting.

Second, no mention is made of a lower limit at which there would be no possibility of further price decreases. Theoreticians will no doubt emphasize that the lower limit is price equal marginal cost. But marginal cost is not generally taken as a legal criterion in court discussions or in official decisions by the Commission of the EEC. Admittedly, the idea that a price is above marginal cost and therefore too high may pop up occasionally, but it seems fair to say that Pareto optimality is not the stated objective of current antitrust policy.

Third, the implicit assumption seems to be that the only conceivable oligopolistic equilibrium is the collusive one. If prices do not move, there must be a collusive equilibrium. If prices move simultaneously, or almost simultaneously, this must be a move from one collusive equilibrium to another collusive equilibrium. If one firm changes its price, and the others follow immediately or almost immediately, this must be interpreted as a defensive reaction to maintain the agreed market shares. Consequently, competition among oligopolists is possible only through (what game theorists call) cheating. Therefore cheating has to be encouraged by all means. And the best encouragement is to create or maintain imperfect information among competitors.

The time has come to turn toward game theory and to throw in the now trivial idea that an oligopolistic industry can be in equilibrium, so no firm has any incentive to change its price or production rate, without there being any collusion. There is no cooperation whatsoever neither tacit nor explicit and yet no firm actively tries to increase its market share! There is competition, and yet no firm actively fights its competitors, because it is in no firm's individual interest to engage in active competition! Needless to say, I am referring to the *noncooperative Nash equilibrium* introduced in Section 1.3 and discussed in Section 6.2 with respect to its informational requirements.

The least I hope for is that it should be clear that antitrust authorities, lawyers, judges, and experts cannot continue to ignore the concept of a Nash equilibrium, which is at least as much a theoretical possibility as the equality of price and marginal cost. But I am ready to go many steps further, even though I know that much work remains to be done on practical questions, such as how a given industry can be identified as being in a Nash equilibrium, how it gets into such an equilibrium, how it gets out of it, and how it moves from one such equilibrium to another one. Progress in this direction will be made only to the extent that the people involved in antitrust cases begin to take the concept seriously.

Even if many of these questions cannot yet be answered in practice, I am arguing that the present state of the art allows us to go a few steps further. The first thing we can do – and I shall make an effort in that direction in a moment – is to study the properties of a Nash equilibrium and compare these with those of a collusive equilibrium, to see for example which types of behavior or which informational requirements, if any, are typical for the latter and can thus be identified clearly as implying collusion. If both equilibria turn out to have the same informational requirements or to imply the same behavior, it should be doubtful that parallel behavior and information transmission are per se evidence of collusion.

The next step is a more difficult one to agree on. I consider active competition as one way to get an industry out of a collusive equilibrium and move it into a Nash equilibrium. I therefore am ready to argue that the Nash equilibrium provides the equilibrium concept that is missing in the propositions listed above and defines the lower limit to which active competition should reduce industry prices or the upper limit to which active competition should push industry production. Once this limit is reached, no oligopolist has an incentive to break through it. To break through it would be against everybody's interest. Perhaps this is what industry circles call "ruinous competition" (although the same word could designate the collapse of a collusive equilibrium). At any rate, nothing allows us to interpret such terminology as obviously referring to the breakdown of collusion. The words could have their true meaning. Now that the concept of a Nash equilibrium exists, and that the possibility of its occurring in the real world must be granted, it seems unfair not to allow for this possibility.

My last step is likely to meet strong opposition. To state it bluntly: To reach a noncooperative Nash equilibrium is the best antitrust policy can hope for in oligopolistic markets (which is a far-reaching statement, given that most real life markets are oligopolistic). Therefore, if normal competition is the objective of antitrust policy, it should be defined as and have the properties of a noncooperative Nash equilibrium.

Let me make this statement a bit more precise and insist that, given the multiplicity of possible Nash equilibria, I mean a "perfect" non-cooperative Nash equilibrium (in quantities or prices, according to the strategies chosen by the industry). Such a perfect Nash equilibrium is part of a two-stage equilibrium,[21] in which the other stage implies a market structure that is endogenously determined by the given technology and given tastes. If, at a point in time, demand is such and technology is such that, with free entry, there is room for say only two firms with a given number of products each, and if prices and quantities are at the noncooperative Nash equilibrium levels, what more can antitrust authorities ask for? Should it call for active competition that would bring prices down to even lower levels? Should it object to the absence of price changes if market conditions are such that no price changes are called for?

Pervasive to the entire argument is the idea that antitrust authorities are *not* social planners. A social planner wants price equal to marginal cost, plus optimal taxes or subsidies. Antitrust authorities want the best possible market structure given technology and tastes, and, given this market structure, as much competition as is compatible with it and with entrepreneurial freedom. But that is precisely, it seems to me, what is described by a perfect noncooperative Nash equilibrium.

A final warning is in order. In the preceding discussion, "the" non-cooperative Nash equilibrium has been contrasted with collusion. The time has come to recall that, alas, collusive outcomes may be sustained at a noncooperative Nash equilibrium, when a game is played repeatedly, so that none of the colluders has an incentive to cheat, as explained in some detail in Section 6.3. In particular, one possible collusive outcome that is directly relevant here and is known as "conscious parallelism" – the matching of price changes announced in advance by competitors – can be modeled as a (perfect) noncooperative dynamic Nash equilibrium (MacLeod 1985). It is this type of combination of a collusive outcome with noncooperative behavior that gives a precise meaning to the otherwise vague concept of "tacit collusion."

---

[21] See Shaked and Sutton (1987).

It should be clear, therefore, that the Nash equilibrium referred to is a particular one: It is a perfect noncooperative *and* noncollusive Nash equilibrium (whether static or dynamic). To avoid tedious repetition, this particular equilibrium will be designated in what follows as an NE.

Again, such an NE may be a set of quantity strategies or a set of price strategies. (In this sense, it is not unique either.) This should not trouble us, contrary to a still widespread opinion, because the nature of the product (the extent of product differentiation and storability) determines which of these strategies (quantity or price) is relevant.

6.4.5. New insights

To check whether all this is more than loose speculation, I suggest the following exercise. Let us consider such an NE and write down a set of propositions that correspond, one by one, to the Propositions 1–8 and describe its relevant properties. I will have reached my objective if the simple juxtaposition of these makes you doubt the truth of at least one proposition stated above. I must confess I have doubts about several.

Proposition 1a. In an NE, each individual firm is free to change its prices (or quantities), but it is in the interest of none to do so independently.

Agreements to set or maintain prices are of course by definition incompatible with an NE. To raise or lower one's price makes sense only if all other competitors do the same, because one firm is in NE only on the condition that all others are. To act independently is foolish because no firm is independent of the others.

Proposition 2a. In an NE, there is no room for secret rebates.

Cheating makes sense only if there is collusion. Since there is no collusion here, there is no need either to prevent cheating or to make secret moves to prevent competitors from reacting immediately. On the contrary, if one firm moves it expects its competitors to move in the same direction. If they don't, it must conclude that it misinterpreted the market situation. Yet, nothing prevents the firms involved from giving "genuine" rebates in the open; that is, price discrimination is compatible with an NE.

Proposition 3a. Successive Nash equilibria are compatible with simultaneous moves of list prices and transaction prices.

Although there are no secret rebates, transaction prices can differ from list prices, for example if a rebate is required in a particular transaction (for a particular location, say, or for a particular delivery date). At any rate, if market conditions change in the same direction for all (aggregate demand increases or falls, or wage rates move up in the same way for all), simultaneous moves are to be expected. If the first to move makes the correct decision, one should expect all competitors to follow within days or hours. If the same firm is repeatedly the first to move, what looks like price leadership develops. Simultaneous moves are not per se evidence of collusion.[22]

Proposition 4a. An NE requires neither perfect nor complete information.

Analytically, the NE of a game can be found (by game theorists) even if the players do not know each other's profit functions or strategies with certainty (this is a game with "incomplete" information). The same is true for games in which the history of the game, including today's moves, is not perfectly observable (these are games with "imperfect" information). Hopefully, real-life oligopolists are able to find their NE in the same circumstances using some rule of thumb such as cost-plus or normal costing. It is doubtful, therefore, that the strengthening of the buyers' bargaining position (emphasized in Proposition 4) must lead to a price war.

Proposition 5a. The implementation of tacit or explicit collusion requires perfect information, because colluders have an incentive to cheat. In addition, however, the difficulties due to incomplete information have to be solved.

Proposition 5 ignored the fact that potential colluders may not be able to observe each other's preferences (profit functions), and reduced the problem of implementing collusion to the detection and punishment of cheating. Proposition 5a recognizes the importance of perfect in-

---

[22] MacLeod (1985, p. 41) arrives at the same conclusion: "Given that an industry faces a common shock, such as a change in demand or an increase in factor costs, can one distinguish between the static Nash equilibrium . . . and the collusive equilibrium based only on observed price responses? We would say no . . . in terms of *timing* one would expect all firms to respond at the same time to exogenous shocks, regardless whether collusion is occurring or not. In terms of the size of price changes, again little can be said . . . without specific knowledge of the profit functions there would be no systematic differences between the size of price responses at the non-cooperative and collusive equilibria."

formation, but insists that, even if information is perfect, collusion does not automatically result. If potential colluders are not able to observe each other's profit functions, they each have private information and must be given an incentive to reveal it correctly (on this, see Roberts 1985). While Proposition 5 gives the impression that collusion is easy and therefore ubiquitous, Proposition 5a reminds us that collusion is not only difficult to implement, once reached, because of the prisoner's dilemma,[23] but is also difficult to achieve because there are two types of information involved. To be well informed about how competitors are currently behaving is not the same thing as being well informed about the competitors' decision parameters. Market transparency therefore does not guarantee that there is collusion. The presumption that market transparency (among oligopolists) is evidence of collusion should rather be based on the following proposition.

Proposition 6a. In an NE, it is not in the oligopolists' interest to share information, but it is in their individual interest to acquire more information.

This proposition was discussed at length in Section 6.2. If information sharing leads to perfect information, if perfect information is a necessary ingredient of collusion, *and* if a noncooperative equilibrium provides no incentive for such information sharing (or even an incentive not to share information, as argued by Clarke), then the current distrust of information sharing agreements can be given a sound theoretical foundation.[24] However, this conclusion is valid for schemes that systematically pool all current information available to all colluders, so information *is* perfect. A case in point, which almost literally illustrates the model set up by Novshek, Sonnenschein, and Clarke, is the agreement between OPEC and an independent agency that will collect complete daily information on oil extraction and shipments by OPEC members.

I wonder whether Proposition 6a applies to the transmission of price or quantity data, by individual firms, via press releases, telexes, or

---

[23] See Section 6.1.

[24] Clarke (1983b, p. 392) concludes: "If all industry firms are observed to pool information without paying each other compensation, they must be setting quantities cooperatively on the basis of the homogenized information. Hence information-pooling mechanisms like trade associations can be considered *prima facie* evidence that firms are illegally cooperating to restrict output. This result strengthens Posner's (1976) informal analysis of the desirability of information-sharing agreements. On the other hand, lack of information-pooling mechanisms can be taken as fairly good evidence that cooperative behavior is impeded."

letters or even to meetings where competitors discuss their price or production policies. When a pooling scheme is in operation, such messages or meetings are superfluous. Couldn't these messages or meetings simply reflect everybody's interest in getting more information – the more so as one cannot presume that more information is all that is needed for collusion to work?

Proposition 7a. Communication about future prices may be a way of getting better information about a new NE.

Suppose industry demand displays seasonal fluctuations, as in the wood pulp industry. Under explicit collusion, the cartel would collectively announce in advance a price schedule covering the entire year. (The announced price changes would be smaller or larger, depending on the possibility of building up inventories and depending on whether inventories are built up at the producer or at the customer level.[25]) Perfect intertemporal information (complete certainty) about prices is thus obtained, in the same way as a pooling scheme provides perfect information about current prices, and the freedom to change prices in the future is collectively restricted.

If, now, firms individually announce prices valid for the next quarter only, not the next year, and do this in rapid succession within hours or days, this is a substitute for a discussion at a meeting. (In an explicit collusive arrangement, such signaling would be superfluous.) A price announcement may be a way of implementing "conscious parallelism," that is, tacit collusion. But the message may as well be that a firm thinks the old NE needs to be changed and wishes the others to confirm or contradict. If firms go through the trouble of announcing future quarterly prices in advance, so that competitors have time to confirm or not, this is therefore not evidence of collusion. And if the same first is always first, there is market dominance, but even that is not collusion.

Proposition 8a. Advance notice of price changes may serve all sorts of purposes.

Advance notice of a price increase is a classic device to encourage customers to buy now rather than later: The flow of orders is smoothed over time so that the cost of carrying inventories is shifted from the seller to the buyer. Advance notice of a price decrease provides an

---

[25] See Phlips and Thisse (1981).

incentive to buy later and smooths the rate of production over time. A better understanding of intertemporal profit maximization and of the economics of inventory building may take away some of the current distrust.

To sum up, we cannot avoid the conclusion that the current antitrust attitude with respect to information acquisition and pooling rests on shaky grounds, to the extent that it considers any communication between oligopolists as evidence of collusion. Careful distinctions have to be drawn. The quest for perfect information on current behavior has to be distinguished from transmission of information about "preferences" (i.e., the quest for "complete" information about profit functions and strategies). Pooling schemes are not synonymous with discussions about current or future prices or quantities: The former are proof of collusion; the latter may occur between noncooperating competitors. Advance notification cannot be said to be bad as such. And information about prices should not, in principle, be considered more "dangerous" than information about quantities, because quantity can be a strategic variable as well as price, especially for homogeneous goods.

Are we to conclude that per se rules are to be avoided and that we should more carefully weigh the pros and cons in each case? I would hate such a conclusion, not only because it is no conclusion at all, but especially because it leaves business with no indication about what is legal and what is not. We must, somehow, sharpen our economics to the extent that per se illegal behavior can be defined.

6.4.6. Collusive information transmission

It is easy to establish a list of explicitly collusive types of behavior that are illegal. Nobody disputes the fact that signing a cartel agreement is illegal. The question really is which types of behavior are *tacitly* collusive and therefore also illegal. In our discussion one such type was identified – a scheme for the systematic pooling of current information with the purpose of creating perfect information – by comparing the incentives for information transmission in an NE with the incentive properties of a collusive outcome. Can we identify other such practices by the same method?

6.4.7. Tying clauses

Nonsystematic transmission of current information (i.e., sporadic transmission by a particular firm to another) by direct or indirect ways has been seen to be compatible with the search for a noncooperative equilibrium in the discussion of Proposition 6a. The same must be true for nonsystematic acquisition of current information.

An example that comes to mind is a provision that requires buyers of Northern Pacific's land to ship timber produced on this land via the Northern Pacific Railway *unless lower rates or better services were available from competing railway lines.* As argued by Cummings and Ruther (1979), the main purpose of such clauses is not to tie the shipping with the purchase of land, but to compel buyers to disclose the lower rate or better service offered by competing carriers. (The tying arrangement simply provided protection against nonreporting). Such contracts imply no obligation for the seller to meet lower prices, so there is no automatic deterrence of cheating (in contrast with "meet competition" clauses). As such, they are competitive rather than collusive.

Another classic example is the *International Salt* case. Following Peterman (1979), the tying clause used by the International Salt Company can be interpreted as a device to ensure good reporting by the lessees (of a machine that dissolves rock salt) of the competitor's prices of salt, because lessees were free to buy on the open market whenever International Salt failed to meet these prices.

6.4.8.   "Meet competition" clauses

A "meet competition" clause entitles a buyer who finds another seller offering a lower price to this same lower price. If the clause also contains a "release" option, so that the buyer can choose to be released from his contractual obligation, I am ready to argue that this is again an innocent information acquisition device: It is only by informing the original supplier that the buyer can escape from an obligation to purchase. But the buyer can escape from this obligation, and this freedom gives the buyer an incentive to enter long-term arrangements that it might otherwise be hesitant to sign.

Deletion of the release option, however, transforms the clause into a powerful deterrent to cheating. Now the competitors know that this firm will retaliate to any detected price reduction and that customers will report any price reduction immediately to it. The deterrence effect is maximized. And because deterrence is a problem only in a collusive arrangement, the clause (without release) must be collusive.

Salop (1985) has illustrated the deterrence effect with respect to the prisoner's dilemma in a game with two players (Ethyl and DuPont, say). First, the achievement of a collusive equilibrium is facilitated, because one firm can raise its price to the collusive level without losing any sales to a lower-priced rival in the transition period during which the rival sticks to the lower price. In addition, the rival is encouraged not to delay a matching price increase, because the transitional gains that could result from his lower price are eliminated by the clause. Second, once the collusive outcome is reached, it is stabilized. Indeed, with no-release meeting competition clauses on both sides, it becomes impossible for one player to undercut the other. The only possibilities are to stick to the collusive equilibrium or to shift to an NE. The threat of such a shift is very credible and therefore effective. It can be reinforced by a "most favored nation" (MFN) clause.

6.4.9. "Most favored nation" clauses

An MFN clause guarantees the buyer any discount offered to another buyer by the (same) seller under the terms of the contract. The clause can be retroactive or contemporaneous.

Consider *retroactive* MFN clauses first. These prevent price reductions in case the market deteriorates, because later price reductions must be applied to some past sales. Their objective is thus to make prices stickier over time and to keep them at the collusive level. Salop (1985, table 3) again illustrates the mechanism with respect to the prisoner's dilemma by showing that, with a retroactive MFN clause, gains from retaliating are relatively smaller than in the absence of such clauses. Adjustments to changing market conditions (typical for non-collusive Nash equilibria) are prevented. In particular, a shift to the noncollusive NE is made relatively more unprofitable. The effect of a meeting competition clause is thus reinforced.

A *contemporaneous* MFN clause penalizes and deters only price cuts that are restricted to a limited number of customers. Retaliation with a general price reduction is not penalized.

If nobody offers an MFN, selective discounts may develop and imperfect information may destabilize a collusive equilibrium. If one firm unilaterally institutes a contemporaneous MFN, it commits itself to retaliating only with a general price cut to all its customers (a price war, in fact). Its rivals will conclude that, because a general price cut is costly and easily detected, there will be no retaliation if they approach only a limited number of customers of the firm that instituted the MFN. Collusion is thus reinforced. If all competitors institute an MFN, selective discounts will not be matched (because this would imply a general price cut) if they are restricted to a limited number of the rivals' customers. On the one hand, price undercutting is restricted in scope. On the other hand, the threat of a shift to a noncooperative NE is made more credible. Finally, if an MFN clause is combined with a meeting competition clause, the threat is reinforced and the need to actually carry it out may be reduced (Salop 1985).

CHAPTER 7

Predatory pricing

7.1. Theory

The theory of economic predation has a special and rather uncommon feature: Great sophistication is needed to show that predation can occur at all, and perhaps even greater sophistication is needed to show what distinguishes predatory prices from other types of prices. One reason is that predation appears, on simple intuitive grounds, as irrational or at least as impossible to reconcile with profit maximization. Another reason is that one well-known line of reasoning in game theory leads to the conclusion that predation cannot be an equilibrium strategy.

To show that predation can be a profit-maximizing equilibrium strategy, a number of particular circumstances have to be modeled.

To begin with, for predation to make sense it has to be defined as an attack (in the form of a low price) by a monopolist against an entrant, *after* the latter has actually entered one of the monopolist's markets. Otherwise predation would be synonymous with entry-preventing limit pricing.

Second, this aggressor is typically a *multimarket* monopolist. If the aggressor operates in one market only, it can always protect it profitably by absorbing the entrant. Predatory pricing without merger has a chance to be the best strategy only if a low profit (or a loss) in one market can be compensated by larger profits in other markets. Predation thus appears in one market in order to protect the aggressor's other markets.

A further feature is that entrants must have *incomplete information*. If they know that predation is profitable, they will not enter and predatory prices will never be observed. If they know that predation is not profitable, they will enter without hesitation and, again, predation will not be observed. It is essential, therefore, that entrants have some doubts about the monopolist's response and are not sure that predation will occur. The standard way to model this is to assume that the monopolist they are facing may belong to different more or less aggressive "types" and that they cannot distinguish these types. A probability is therefore attached to each type. At most, the entrants know the probability distribution of these types. An additional sophistication is to model the fact that the entrant may find it difficult to identify low prices set by the monopolist as being predatory rather than the result of normal competition, that is, prices corresponding to a noncooperative Nash equilibrium in their local market.

Entry implies not only a fixed cost but also an adjustment cost: It is not instantaneous – hence the assumption that a particular entrant can *enter at most one market in any period.* (The question then arises whether each entrant should be allowed to enter several markets or just one market.)

What about the predator? Should one try to allow for (and to rationalize) the possibility that, after one or several attacks, the predator *stops* preying? This seems more realistic than a solution in which the predator continues to prey once preying has begun. Similarly, it seems more realistic to look for a model in which the predator's aim is to *slow down* entry (in other markets) rather than to stop entry entirely.

Finally, the predator's markets can be supposed to be *identical,* in order to emphasize the purely intertemporal aspect of the problem, according to which a low profit today (in any market) is more than compensated by a flow of higher profits later (in the other markets). However, part of this compensation may not be due to predation as such but to (nonpredatory) geographical price discrimination based on differences in demand elasticities. The question then arises how predatory and nonpredatory price discrimination can be distinguished.

7.1.1. Why predatory pricing is rare and unimportant

The *Standard Oil* case[1] of 1911 is probably the best known and most widely discussed case of predatory pricing. Allegedly, Standard established a monopoly in oil refining and maintained it mainly through the systematic use of a particular type of geographical price discrimination, namely local price cutting. It thus eliminated its competitors in one local market at a time and preserved its monopoly by selective price cuts wherever entry occurred.

McGee (1958) made himself a reputation by challenging this commonly held view. He not only showed that the available evidence brought before the court was not convincing, but also accumulated sound economic reasons why predatory pricing is, in general, rare and not an important problem for competition.

Evidently, he says, because the predator is supposed to have im-

---

[1] *Standard Oil Co. of New Jersey v. United States,* 221 U.S.1 (1911).

portant monopoly power (the "war chest" for supporting the unprofitable raids and forays), local price cutting cannot explain the monopolization of a market. But suppose sufficient monopoly power is achieved through some other means. How would this monopolist go about using predatory techniques? McGee (1958, pp. 139–140) writes

Assume that Standard has an absolute monopoly in some important markets, and was earning substantial profits there. Assume that in another market there are several competitors, all of whom Standard wants to get out of the way. Standard cuts the price below cost. Everyone suffers losses. Standard would, of course, suffer losses even though it has other profitable markets: it could have been earning at least competitive returns and is not. The war could go until average variable costs are not covered and are not expected to be covered; and the competitors drop out. In the meanwhile, the predator would have been pouring money in to crush them. If, instead of fighting, the would-be monopolist bought out his competitors directly, he could afford to pay them up to the discounted value of the expected monopoly profits to be gotten as a result of their extinction. Anything above the competitive value of their firms should be enough to buy them. In the purchase case, monopoly profits could begin at once; in the predatory case, large losses would first have to be incurred. Losses would have to be set off against the prospective monopoly profits, discounted appropriately. Even supposing that the competitors would not sell for competitive value, it is difficult to see why the predator would be unwilling to take the amount that he would otherwise spend in price wars and pay it as a bonus.

Acquisition or merger is thus a feasible alternative to local price cutting. It always gives a higher present value, because revenues during the price war are always less than revenues gotten immediately through purchase and are not higher after the war is concluded. Predation can therefore make sense only if the direct costs of a price war were small compared to the difference between the takeover price to be paid to a competing firm and its competitive value. However, this can never happen, because the costs of the price war must be higher for the predator than for the individual competitors. As McGee (1958, p. 140) puts it:

To lure customers away from somebody, he must be prepared to serve them himself. The monopolist thus finds himself in the position of selling more – and therefore losing more – than his competitors. Standard's market share was often 75 per cent or more. In the 75 per cent case the monopolizer would sell three times as much as all competitors taken together, and, on the assumption of equal unit costs, would lose roughly three times as much as all of them taken together.

Purchase must be cheaper than price cutting. Since competitors know this, they will simply stick it out. Or they will shut down operations temporarily, letting the predator take all the business and all the losses, and resume operations when he raises prices again. Indeed, plants do not necessarily wear down and may be reopened at low cost, by the same owner or by some opportunist who knows that the predator will have, sooner or later, to buy these up. And it is not likely that a price war would sufficiently depress the purchase price of these properties, because everybody knows that the artificially low price cannot be permanent.

It remains true that Standard did, in fact, discriminate geographically by local price cutting, as in the case in some form or another in most historical examples of alleged predatory pricing. To rationalize this discriminatory behavior, McGee notices that these discriminatory prices simply reflect changes in local demand elasticities, but do not imply or establish that anybody is preying on anybody else. In today's terminology, the argument would be reformulated by saying that geographical price discrimination is a property of a noncooperative Nash equilibrium when oligopolists are serving submarkets in which demand elasticities differ.[2]

Twenty years after his initial article, McGee (1980) still maintains his position against an impressive flood of articles in which predation is taken seriously and numerous (competing) rules for establishing whether predation has occurred are proposed. He also offers a string of arguments, some old and some new, among which I pinpoint the following.

The predator may, because of its size and activities in other markets, have larger financial reserves – a "longer purse" – and thus be able to sustain larger losses and sustain them longer. McGee (1980, p. 297) answers:

> Military analogies are not apt. Among other differences, business lacks pipes, drums, and flags, and it does not have conscription. A firm plotting a predatory campaign would *require* disproportionately greater liquid reserves, and, in one way or another, it will have to pay for them. Liquid reserves are costly, and disproportionately large reserves are disproportionately costly. Reserves are a cost, not an inherent advantage. No one has yet demonstrated why predators could acquire the reserves they will need, while victims cannot. In any case, if this is predation, the present value of assets in this trade is positive. Why not stick it out, since the long-run returns are there?

McGee (1980, p. 300) also notes that the very presence of an antitrust rule against predation creates an incentive for a small firm to make a complaint to the antitrust authority in order to prevent a big competitor from undercutting it:

[2] Neven and Phlips (1985) have worked out an example.

. . . so long as people in authority can be made to listen and perhaps persuaded to do something, it may pay competitors to complain that someone is preying on them. They have a natural interest in tying the hands of those who compete for consumers' favors. If law permits, they also have an interest in collecting damages from those who compete with them. These are good reasons for doubting that predation claimed is predation proved. These are also good reasons to be cautious in developing rules against "predatory" conduct.

Finally, let me quote a passage (McGee 1980, p. 296) in which McGee hints at the role of incomplete information and suggests that if the game is played under complete and perfect information, then predation is impossible for the simple reason that the victim will not give up, so there is no point in even trying to kill it:

> [The predator] will be disappointed, if for no other reason than that it will pay the victim to stick it out. If things go back to where they were before the predatory price cut, it would pay both the predator and victim to replace their plants. And, of course, if prices were somehow raised even more. It only *seems* paradoxical, therefore, that if a victim were sure this is a predatory campaign, rather than normal competition or a response to a collapsing market, he would *surely* want to stick it out.

If, under complete information, predation is impossible – an intuition that will be shown to be correct for game-theoretic reasons in what follows – then predation can occur only to the extent that the potential victim has doubts about the predatory nature of a price cut and that the predator manages to manipulate these doubts to its own advantage – another intuition that is at the core of the discussion that follows.

7.1.2. *The chain store paradox or the impossibility of predation*

To show that predation is logically impossible from a game-theoretic point of view, Selten (1978) imagines the following game, in which a firm operates in a number of identical markets. For concreteness, he supposes it is a chain store, also called player A, which has branches in twenty towns, numbered from 1 to 20. The game is played over a sequence of twenty consecutive periods 1, . . . , 20. In each of the towns there is a small businessman, called player k, who might raise money to establish a shop of the same kind.

As time goes on, each of these businessmen will, in turn, have accumulated enough capital to start a new business so that they must in turn – first player 1, in town 1, then player 2, in town 2, and so on – decide whether they want to enter the local market or use their capital in some other business. In other words, at the beginning of period k, player k must decide between IN or OUT. Player k's decision is immediately known to all players. Incumbent A enjoys its monopoly position without further threat if player k, at time k, decides not to enter.

Incumbent A can react in two ways in each market. It either decides to "cooperate," that is, to share the market, or to be "aggressive," that is, to prey on the entrant. Again, this decision is immediately common knowledge so that information is perfect. The incumbent gets the highest immediate profit, in period k, if player k stays out. If he enters, and if A's reaction is cooperative, then A's immediate profit is lower. But it is even lower if A's reaction is aggressive, because predation is costly (McGee's argument!). As for player k, his profit is the highest if his entry is met by a cooperative response. When it is met by predation, his interest is to stay out and invest his capital elsewhere.

The problem for the incumbent is to maximize the sum of the immediate payoffs over the periods 1 to 20. It would be the highest if all twenty potential entrants decided to stay out. If all decided to enter, then this sum is the highest if player A cooperates with all of them. If some decided to enter, it might be worthwhile to prey on them, although that gives A the lowest immediate profit, if that could convince the others to stay out. The trouble is that each one-period game has to be played after the other in a sequence, and that in each of these the then potential entrant has an interest to come in *if* the incumbent cooperates.

Notice that the game is to be played in a noncooperative way, that the players cannot commit themselves to threats and promises, and, in particular, that the chain store cannot purchase the shops possibly opened by the entrants (to ignore the McGee argument that acquisition is cheaper than predation and thus to be able to analyze the profitability of predation as such in the long run). More generally, binding contracts and side payments are not permitted. Selten also emphasizes that the players are not allowed to talk during the game.

The numbers in the payoff matrix in Figure 7.1 represent the potential predator's immediate payoffs (in the upper left corner) and the payoffs of player k (in the lower right corner). These numbers are known to all players, so that information is complete. In this example, the prey loses as much (-2) as the predator.

If all potential entrants decide to stay out, player A's intertemporal profit is $20 \times 5 = 100$. If all decide to enter and A shares a local market with each of them, then A gets $20 \times 2 = 40$. If all enter and A preys on each of them, A's total profit is $20 \times 0 = 0$. (There is no discounting to simplify the argument.)

What is A's best policy? Notice that A cannot hope to make a total profit of 20×5, because to keep potential entrants out, at least one

	IN	OUT
COOPERATIVE	2 2	5 1
AGGRESSIVE	0 0	5 1

Figure 7.1. Player A's immediate payoffs and player k's payoffs.

aggression is necessary. And this implies that at least one entry has occurred, leaving a profit of at most $0 + (19 \times 5) = 95$. At best, this one predation in period 1 might create such a reputation of aggressiveness that players 2 to 20 prefer to stay out. Perhaps a sequence of 2 or more predatory acts (each giving zero profit) might be necessary to build up such a reputation. But even then, why should the remaining players be afraid? They know the rules of the game as well as player A. In particular, they know the numbers in Figure 7.1 as well as the incumbent. They therefore realize that the best policy for A is never to prey at all and to share all markets with the local entrant, because it is profit maximizing for each potential entrant to actually enter.

To see this, consider what must happen in market 20 in the last period. Selten (1978, p. 131) writes the following:

If in period 20 player 20 selects IN, then the best choice for player A is the COOPERATIVE response. The COOPERATIVE response yields a higher payoff. Long run considerations do not come in, since after period 20 the game is over. This shows that it is best for player 20 to choose IN. Obviously the strategic situation of period 20 does not depend on the players' decisions in periods 1, . . . , 19.

Now consider period 19. The decisions in period 19 have no influence on the strategic situation in period 20. If player 19 selects IN, then the CO-OPERATIVE response is best for player A. The AGGRESSIVE response would not deter player 20.

It is clear that in this way we can go on to conclude by induction that each player k should choose IN and each time player A should use the COOPER-ATIVE response. The strategic situation in the remainder of the game does not depend on the decisions up to period k. If it is already known that in periods $k + 1, . . . , 20$ players $k + 1, . . . , 20$ will choose IN and player A will always select the COOPERATIVE choice, then it follows that also in period k a choice of IN should lead to a COOPERATIVE response.

The induction theory comes to the conclusion that each of the players 1, . . . , 20 should choose IN and player A should always react with his CO-

OPERATIVE response to the choice of IN. If the game is played in this way, then each of the players 1, . . . , 20 receives a payoff of 2 and player A receives a total payoff of 40.

The logic of this reasoning is implacable: In equilibrium, predation cannot occur, because the equilibrium strategies of the game (over twenty periods) must also be equilibrium strategies for every subgame (a game starting at any period k and ending at period 20). This is the "perfect equilibrium" concept for noncooperative games introduced by Selten (1965). Even if the players were to observe A to behave differently, for example, to prey systematically during the initial periods, they would not be impressed and the next potential entrant would expect its entry not to meet an aggressive response.

The entire reasoning clearly hinges on the assumption that all players know everything: They know all possible strategies and all possible outcomes (such as in Figure 7.1), so that their information is "complete"; they also are immediately informed about all decisions, so the history of the game as it is being played is perfectly known and information is "perfect." When this assumption is relaxed, the logic of backwards induction (starting with period 20 and then going backwards to period 19, 18, etc.) breaks down, because actions taken in the past may become a useful guide to future behavior. If one wants past predation to impress potential entrants, it is necessary therefore to admit some incompleteness or imperfectness of the available information. Only then could something like a reputation of aggressiveness effectively deter entry.

7.1.3. The lack of common knowledge can generate predation

It is easy to imagine a game in which a slight imperfection of the information can lead to predation in equilibrium. Consider the following example, based on Milgrom and Roberts (1982a, Appendix B). For simplicity, the chain store (player A) faces only two possible entrants, player 1 and player 2, in that order. However, the situation is complicated by the fact that there are three possible states of the world, a, b, and c, all equally likely, and by the fact that the three players differ in their information. Although firm 1 has perfect information and is thus able to distinguish a, b, and c, firm 2 cannot distinguish between states a and b. The chain store, on the contrary, cannot distinguish between b and c. The information structure is thus

> player A: [{a}, {b, c}],
>
> player 1:   [{a}, {b}, {c}],
>
> player 2:   [{a, b}, {c}].

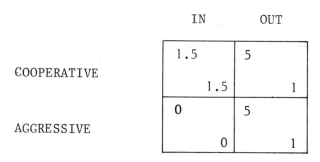

Figure 7.2. Player A's immediate payoffs and the payoffs for players 1 and 2.

The three states could be three events leading to price cutting. State b could be a cost decrease and state c could be a demand decrease, but any other interpretation could do. At any rate, state a is such that entry results automatically in predation. The chain store is a fanatic predator. In the other states, predation (AGGRESSIVE) is one of two possible strategies (COOPERATIVE is the other one) according to the payoff matrix in Figure 7.2, which applies to players 1 and 2.

The only difference with Figure 7.1 is that the market-sharing payoffs are slightly reduced, for a reason that will become clear in the discussion.

What is the chain store's best long-run policy? It is to prey if firm 1 enters,[3] whatever the state! And since firm 1 knows this, it is deterred from entering! As for firm 2, it will enter only in state c.

To see this, note first that A cannot distinguish states b and c and must therefore take the same act in both states. It can prey against firm 1 in both states or in neither. If it does not prey against firm 1, its expected return is 3. Indeed, if c is the actual state, firm 2 recognizes it and also enters so that A's return is $1.5 + 1.5 = 3$. If the state is b, failure to prey against 1 allows 2 to infer that the state is b, that it will therefore not meet predation and that it should enter. Again, A's return is $1.5 + 1.5 = 3$.

However, if A does prey against firm 1, then A's expected return is 3.25. Indeed, if the state is b, firm 2 cannot distinguish a and b and must allow for the possibility that it might meet predation (case a), in which case its return is zero. If A is not a fanatic predator (state b), then entry would give firm 2 a return of 1.5. Its expected return is thus, because a and b are equally likely $\frac{1}{2}(0 + 1.5) = 0.75$. This is less than

---

[3] If firm 2 enters, A preys automatically in state a. If the state is b or c, it should not prey, because this is the last period of the game.

the return (1) if it stays out. So firm 2 prefers to stay out. On the contrary, if the state is c, which firm 2 recognizes, it enters without fear. So, from A's point of view, predation yields equal chances of firm 2 staying out or not, so that A's expected return is $\frac{1}{2}(0 + 5) + \frac{1}{2}(0 + 1.5) = 3.25$. Because this exceeds the return of 3 resulting from failure to prey, A preys no matter what the state. Therefore firm 1 does not enter.[4]

Note that firm 1 is deterred from entering although there still is a lot of common knowledge in this game. It is common knowledge between firm 1, firm 2, and the chain store that the latter is not a fanatic predator, when state c occurs. In period 1, both firm 1 and the chain store know that to share the market is directly more profitable for the latter. Yet, the confusion of the chain store about b and c and the confusion of entrant 2 about a and b, which require both to reason in terms of expected returns, suffices to turn predation into an equilibrium strategy.

7.1.4. Reputation and predation

In a sense, the example just given worked too well. Predation had a deterrent effect without even having to actually occur! It was the common understanding that predation is A's equilibrium policy that prevented entry. One might wish to construct a game whose equilibrium implies that predation has to occur at least once in order to have a deterrent effect. Intuition suggests that the real-life solution to the chain store's problem is to be aggressive in the early stages of the game and to share the market (be "cooperative") when the game comes close to its end. And intuition is, for once, more convincing than correct game-theoretic reasoning. This is, by the way, the opinion of Selten himself and the reason why he called his game the chain store "paradox."

It thus remains to show how the lack of complete information can imply an equilibrium in which entry is not only deterred by predation but predation has to actually be practiced. Kreps and Wilson (1982a) and Milgrom and Roberts (1982a) construct models that have these properties. What drives them is the idea that to establish a reputation (that will make further punishments unnecessary) it is necessary to first

---

[4] If I were to keep the market sharing payoffs at 2, failure to prey would give A the largest return. A would not prey, firm 2 would be indifferent between IN and OUT, and firm 1 would enter in equilibrium. So the equilibrium is sensitive to the numbers chosen.

carry out a few punishments,[5] because any other attitude would be misinterpreted as weakness and encourage further disobedience (entry). This in turn implies that some potential entrants did prefer to enter in the early stages of the game although they could expect to be attacked. Such entry seems to make sense only in a very lucrative market.

One possible approach, followed by Kreps and Wilson, is to allow for some positive probability that predation is immediately more profitable, in any given period, than peaceful market sharing. This assumption looks rather unrealistic and, furthermore, leads to complicated arguments. I shall therefore follow the Milgrom–Roberts approach, which sticks to the idea that predation is always costly in the short run but allows that the entrants entertain some possibility that the chain store may follow some simple behavioral rule, such as being a fanatic predator or a fanatic pacifist.

Take Selten's chain store model but modify it in the following two ways. First, introduce the possibility that past behavior is relevant in forecasting future behavior, to destroy the induction argument. For this purpose, allow the entrants to think that a predatory response, if they meet one, might be part of a general aggressive pattern (the chain store is a fanatic predator) and a cooperative response might be part of a general cooperative pattern (the chain store is a fanatic pacifist). This amounts to admitting that one of three possible games (with twenty periods each) are played and that only the chain store knows which of the three actually obtains. The first game has a one-period payoff matrix structured as in Figure 7.1 or 7.2; the second game only admits the aggressive response (and the corresponding payoffs); the third game only admits the cooperative response (and the corresponding payoffs). The entrants attach a probability to each of these three possibilities, say of ·

$1/(1 + \epsilon + \delta)$ to the first game
$\epsilon/(1 + \epsilon + \delta)$ to the second game (automatic predation)
$\delta/(1 + \epsilon + \delta)$ to the third game (automatic sharing)

so that the three values add up to 1. Think of ϵ and δ as being small. In Selten's model $\epsilon = \delta = 0$, so there is no reason for an entrant to suspect that any observed behavioral pattern might continue.

To this uncertainty on the entrant side, a second modification of the chain store model adds a lack of information that affects all players

[5] See also Scharfstein (1984), Roberts (1986), Fudenberg and Tirole (1986b), and Milgrom and Roberts (1987).

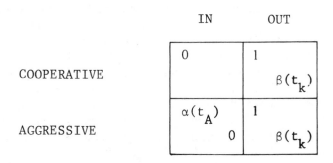

Figure 7.3. Player A's immediate payoffs and player k's payoffs.

and relates to the other players. Suppose the entrants are not sure about the costs of predation for the chain store, and the chain store is not sure about the payoffs of the potential entrants if they stay out. To model this, suppose that to each player is associated a random variable τ_i which is uniformly distributed on [0, 1] and independent of the τ_j associated with the other players. Refer to a realization t_i of τ_i as the "type" of player i ($i = A, 1, \ldots, 20$). The cost of predation $\alpha(t_A)$ is then a function of the type of chain store, increasing with t_A between $-\infty$ and 0 (0 not included, i.e., always negative; see McGee!). The payoff of staying out is then $\beta(t_k)$, where $k = 1, \ldots, 20$, and is normalized between $-\infty$ and 1 (not included). This payoff also increases with the type of entrant. The entrant of type $t_k = 1$ has the highest opportunity cost of entry. The assumption that β may be negative allows for the possibility that a particular entrant might prefer to enter even if preyed upon, so predation may fail against a particular entrant.

If the first game is played, player A's immediate payoffs and player k's payoffs are given in Figure 7.3, in period k. If the second game is played, only the "aggressive" payoffs indicated are possible. If the third game is played, only the "cooperative" payoffs are possible. Player A's intertemporal profit is the discounted value of its profits over the twenty periods calculated with the discount factor ρ.

The numbers in Figure 7.3 have been normalized (compare with the previous tables) so that the chain store gets 1 in any period in which it does not experience entry and 0 in case of peaceful market sharing. Similarly, player k gets 0 if it meets predation and 1 if its entry elicits a nonaggressive response. These numbers are chosen solely to ease computations. I could have retained the corresponding numbers of the previous payoff matrices.

It is worth emphasizing that all players know the values of δ and ϵ, the α and β functions, the distributions of the τ_i, and Figure 7.3. The rules of the game are thus known by all players, so a situation with incomplete information is modeled as a game with complete information as far as these rules are concerned. However, the model is simultaneously a game with imperfect information, because the historical realizations are not known to all players. Only the chain store knows which of the three games is being played (was selected by Nature, which could be treated as an additional player). Only player k knows his type (realization t_k, drawn by Nature from the distribution of τ_k) and the corresponding payoff $\beta(t_k)$. Only player A knows his type and the corresponding payoff $\alpha(t_A)$. Although each player is immediately informed about the moves of all other players, and thus knows the history of the moves taken to each point in the game by it and the other players, the history of player A's payoffs is not known to the others.

In this game, predation *must* occur! The basic intuition is that if, during the game, the chain store ever failed to prey all other players immediately know with certainty that it is not a fanatic predator. And then the chain store paradox is valid again!

Let us therefore begin by examining the equilibrium of the game if A ever fails to prey. Knowing that it is not a fanatic predator, player 20 enters because everybody knows that A will not prey in period 20 (Selten's argument applies). But then, A cannot gain by preying in period 19, nor in period 18, nor in any other period. Thus if A ever fails to prey, it will never prey again in equilibrium. And entry will occur in every period, because $\beta(t_k)$ is always less than 1 (the payoff for unopposed entry). Then the present value of A's intertemporal profit is zero (a sum of 0's).

On the contrary, if entry just occurred in period k *and firm A has never failed to prey*, then one or more successive predatory aggressions gives an intertemporal profit to firm A of $P\alpha(t_A) + M$, where P is the number of future predatory acts and M is the number of future periods with unshared markets (in which A's payoff is 1 each time).

Since P is a number equal or larger than 1, and $\alpha(t_A)$ is increasing in t_A, the whole payoff is increasing in t_A. If this payoff is positive for a value $\tau_A = t$ at period k, it is therefore also positive (it pays to prey) if $\tau_A = t' > t$. On the other hand, if future payoffs increase with t_A, their maximized value also increases with t_A. The strategy to follow (to prey or not) can thus be determined without ambiguity for each type of chain store: It is a "pure" strategy (as opposed to a "mixed" strategy which would involve choosing different strategies with a probability attached to each).

If we then consider the history of play up to period k and the collection of critical values that triggered off predation, it makes sense to call the highest of these values firm A's current "reputation" x.

Call the maximized value of the expected future payoffs $V(t, x)$, noting that it depends only on the value (t) taken by τ_A and firm A's current reputation x [because entrants only look at the chain store's reputation, whereas the revision of the latter's reputation depends only on its current actions (prey or share)]. Firm A will prey at period k if and only if its current return plus the maximum present value of future payoffs, that is $\alpha(t) + \rho V_{k+1}(t, x_{k+1})$, is larger than the value of the payoffs resulting from failure to prey (which are zero), or

$$\alpha(t) + \rho V_{k+1}(t, x_{k+1}) > 0. \tag{7.1}$$

What is firm A's reputation when period $k + 1$ starts, x_{k+1}? If no entry occurred in period k, its reputation is still x (we assume throughout that it has never failed to prey in the past). If entry did occur in period k and firm A did not fight, everybody knows it will never fight in the future and it has lost its reputation. If entry occurred and firm A did fight, then x_{k+1} is at least as high as a value of t just large enough to make predation worthwhile, that is, to satisfy the profitability condition given earlier. If its reputation x was in fact larger than this minimum, it remains intact at the beginning of period $k + 1$.

Therefore, predation necessarily occurs in period k if firm A is at least of type $t = x_{k+1}$. A fortiori, there is predation if its current reputation x is larger, because $V_{k+1}(t, x_{k+1})$ is increasing in t. And this aggressive strategy in period k implies that firm A at least keeps its reputation of aggressiveness during the next period, so its reputation is either constant or growing over time by repeated predation. Whenever future entrants observe a predator, they can correctly forecast that he will continue to predate. [Whether they enter or not depends on whether their expected payoff in case of entry exceeds their $\beta(t_k)$.]

The entire reasoning was based on a given discount factor ρ. When this factor increases, because the interest rate decreases, then the future reward to preying increases in present value terms and the chain store is willing to incur larger immediate losses. A reduction in interest rates thus allows the predator to use the reputation effect with less delay between uses, because an increase in ρ in period k makes predation more attractive in period $k + 1$. The incentive for building and maintaining a reputation increases.

We thus get an effect that goes in the opposite direction of the effect established by Friedman (1972) with relation to the incentive for colluders to deviate from a collusive price. A reduction of the interest rate increases the present value of a deviator's future losses due to retaliation by loyal colluders (who push the price down to its Nash equilibrium level). Low interest rates thus make immediate gains due to cheating less worthwhile, so cartels are more stable and price wars (leading to Nash equilibria) less likely. We just saw that low interest rates simultaneously make predatory price cutting more likely, because future gains get a higher weight compared to immediate losses for the predator. The argument is entirely symmetric.

7.1.5. Nash equilibria and predation

The Milgrom–Roberts model has the merit of showing that predation in one market to protect another market is theoretically possible. However, it does this at the cost of a number of restrictive assumptions, which it shares in part with the Selten model. First, there is the assumption that entry occurs sequentially, in one market at a time by a different entrant. (In each period a new entrant appears.) Consequently, if predation occurs today, its aim is to prevent entry in a later period, not to prevent simultaneous entry in other markets. In addition, if predation has begun in any market there is no reason why it should stop. Finally, though it seems inevitable to assume that there are different types of monopolists between which entrants cannot distinguish before they have revealed themselves, it is unfortunate and unsatisfactory that these types correspond to pathological cases (a fanatic predator or a fanatic pacifist).

Easley, Masson, and Reynolds (1985) have managed to relax these assumptions. They allow for the possibility that entry may occur simultaneously[6] in several of the monopolist's markets, possibly to stop or prevent predation. They allow for a monopolist to prey only to gain extra time, that is, to slow down entry in other markets, with full knowledge that eventually entry will occur. They also are able to explain why a monopolist may decide to stop preying after preying once or twice, and so on. Above all, Easley et al. define different types of monopolists (which the entrant cannot distinguish) according to the nature of the postentry nonpredatory Nash equilibrium that would occur in the entrant's local market if a particular type of monopolist were active in it. This definition of types has the advantage of incorporating (admittedly in a complicated way) the often observed simple fact that, in practice, predatory prices are difficult to distinguish from

---

[6] Each entrant can enter at most one market in any period, though, to take adjustment costs into account.

prices corresponding to a local noncooperative Nash equilibrium (or "normal" competition).

Indeed, suppose the monopolist is drawn from a sample composed of "type 1" and "type 2" monopolists. If he is a type 1, then the local market considered in isolation has a postentry Nash equilibrium that yields a negative entry value to any of the potential entrants. Entry is nonremunerative in the present value sense. Profits are competitive, and the present value of their future flow is smaller than the fixed sunk entry costs of any potential entrant. If he is a type 2, then the local Nash equilibrium considered in isolation yields a positive entry value (defined in the same present value sense).

Predation occurs when the monopolist is a type 2, which means that entry is remunerative in the local market considered in isolation, but acts as a type 1 in that market to make entry nonremunerative. (For that purpose, the monopolist must sacrifice immediate local profits.) When the entrant observes a positive entry value, it can conclude without error that the monopolist is not a predator (that he is a type 2 monopolist and acts as such). But when the entrant observes a negative entry value, it has no way of figuring out whether this is the result of predation (a type 2 monopolist feigning the reaction of a type 1) or whether the market it entered in is inherently competitive (the monopolist *is* a type 1).

At this point, the reader will have realized that the reasoning in terms of different types of monopolists is a technical necessity, in order to be able to model the incompleteness of the entrants' information in terms of a known probability distribution over types (from which probabilities can be taken to compute expected values and so on). In simple words, the preceding paragraph says that entry into a local market would be profitable in the long run without predation (and without collusion), but predation makes it unprofitable in a way that cannot be distinguished from normal competition by the entrant, because the latter does not know whether the monopolist acts to prevent (or slow down) entry in its other markets or not.

Can such predatory pricing be an equilibrium of a game? Yes.[7] Given a particular distribution of types and a behavior rule for each monopolist type, Easley et al. (1985, p. 451) are able to show,[8] in a first step of the proof, that the best replies for the entrants can lead to the following entry sequence, on the assumption that the monopolist has three markets:

---

[7] It can be a "sequential equilibrium" in the sense of Kreps and Wilson (1982b).
[8] By computing entrants' expected entry values.

Time 1: entrant 1 enters market 1.

Time 2: entrant 1 enters market 2.

Time 3: if the entry value is positive in markets 1 and 2, then entrant 2 enters market 3. If the entry value is negative in markets 1 and 2, there is no further entry.

Time 4 (anon): No entry. The profit steady state is that of time 3.

Given this entry sequence, the best reply for a type 2 monopolist could be to prey in response to a period 1 entry and to not prey in response to the second entry.

To prey in period 1 is profitable if the period 1 profits foregone are smaller than the gains made by retarding entry into market 3 by one period. These gains and foregone profits can be computed by comparing the flow of profits in the three markets with and without period 1 predation.

If this type 2 monopolist *does not* prey in period 1, entry has a positive present value, and this fact reveals that the monopolist is not of type 1. As a result, all other markets will be entered in period 2, and the situation is represented by the matrix in Figure 7.4. $\Pi 2$ is the monopolist's postentry profit (when he does not prey), and ΠM is his profit in the absence of entry. If this monopolist *does* prey in period 1, however, his profits in his different markets evolve over time as depicted in Figure 7.5. Predation in period 1 is profitable if

$$\Pi 2 - \Pi P < \frac{\Pi M - \Pi 2}{1 + r}, \tag{7.2}$$

where ΠP designates the profits made in market 1 with predation (possibly their absolute value if they are negative), ΠM is the additional period 2 monopoly profit made in market 3 because entry into that market is retarded by one period, and r is the real rate of interest.

Not to prey in period 2 is certainly profitable if preying also in the second market leads to foregone profits that are higher than the gains made if this were to stop all future entry in market 3. Figure 7.6 represents the flow of profits resulting from two successive predations, continued over time to make sure that no entry occurs in market 3. (The additional infinite sequence of columns which replicate the time 3 profits is not represented, because the profit steady state is reached after time 3.)

The foregone profits by preying twice are found by comparing Figures 7.5 and 7.6. They are equal to the difference between $\Pi 2$ and ΠP in markets 1 and 2 in perpetuity as of time 2 and thus have a present

Market \ Time	1	2	3
1	Π2	Π2	Π2
2	ΠM	Π2	Π2
3	ΠM	Π2	Π2

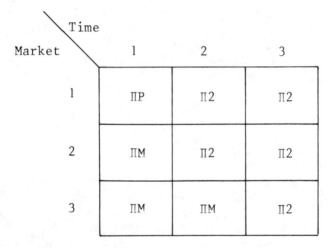

Figure 7.4. No predation in period 1.

Market \ Time	1	2	3
1	ΠP	Π2	Π2
2	ΠM	Π2	Π2
3	ΠM	ΠM	Π2

Figure 7.5. Predation in period 1.

value of $2(\Pi 2 - \Pi P)/r$. The gains are equal to $\Pi M - \Pi 2$ in the third market in perpetuity (starting at time 3) and have a present value of $(\Pi M - \Pi 2)/r(1 + r)$. Not to prey twice is therefore profitable if

$$\frac{2(\Pi 2 - \Pi P)}{r} > \frac{\Pi M - \Pi 2}{r(1 + r)} . \tag{7.3}$$

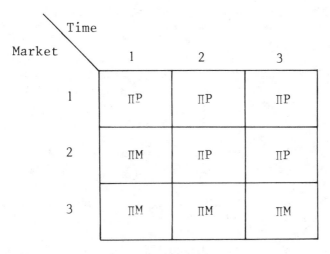

Figure 7.6. Preying twice to stop all entry.

Putting conditions (7.2) and (7.3) together and multiplying by r, we see that a type 2 monopolist preys once in a way that mimics a type 1 Nash equilibrium (negative entry value) and then stops preying if

$$2(\Pi 2 - \Pi P) > \frac{\Pi M - \Pi 2}{1 + r} > \Pi 2 - \Pi P, \qquad (7.4)$$

because conditions (7.2) and (7.3) are thus seen to be consistent. The foregone profits by preying twice must be larger than the gains from retarding entry, which must be larger than profit foregone by preying only once.

Of course, this is not the only possible predatory strategy. Easley et al. also show that an equilibrium strategy may be to prey in some markets (two in the example given) in perpetuity to protect others (the third market in the example) in perpetuity. To that effect, they introduce a "type 3" in the sample from which the monopolist is supposed to be drawn.

7.1.6. Geographical price discrimination and predation

The reader who takes McGee's arguments against the possibility of collusion seriously, as we do, may wonder how, at the end of this lengthy discussion we can nevertheless conclude that both transitory and permanent predation is a real possibility. There is no contradiction, because McGee reasons under two restrictive assumptions which were relaxed during the discussion.

The first assumption is that of complete information on the entrant side. McGee himself made the qualification that his impossibility arguments are based on the condition that his businessman (the entrant) is ". . . sure this is a predatory campaign, rather than normal competition. . . ." He thus pointed the way to the discovery of the chain store paradox and to the subsequent game-theoretic treatment under incomplete information.

The second assumption has become clear in the presentation of the model by Easley et al. Although McGee talks about a multimarket monopolist, especially when he mentions the possibility of geographical price discrimination, he ignores the fact that the control of several markets provides the possibility of compensating immediate foregone profits (or losses) in one market by future gains in other markets. This possibility is at the core of the model by Easley et al.

Notice that it is different from the "long purse" argument, which says that the predator must have larger financial reserves because of its activities in other markets. McGee correctly rejects this argument, and so do Easley et al. (1985, p. 453):

> In "deep-pockets" predation firms are alleged to use earnings from profitable markets to finance predation in others. That is certainly not the causality underlying this example. In fact the predatory markets may yield non-negative cash flows ($\Pi P \geq 0$). Thus, a "long purse" (see [Telser 1966]) is not required for predation to have anticompetitive effects in some markets in perpetuity.

However, to demonstrate this feature of multimarket control, Easley et al. make another simplification, which should be emphasized now. They suppose that all the markets controlled by the monopolist are identical. This makes it possible to consider the entrant's market in isolation and to define a Nash equilibrium for it as if the monopolist was active in this market only. (Each monopolist type is defined that way.) Indeed, when all markets are identical, then the Nash equilibrium in one market is not affected by the fact that the monopolist also operates in other markets.

This amounts to excluding the possibility that the local Nash equilibrium may imply a price that is discriminatory when compared with the equilibrium prices in the other markets. Indeed, when markets are different (display different demand elasticities) for the same commodity and the marginal cost of production is not constant, then the monopolist will find it profitable to price discriminate by equating marginal revenues across markets.[9] Then the price in one market is linked to the

[9] See Neven and Phlips (1985).

prices in the other markets, the maximization of profits over all markets is not synonymous with profit maximization in each market separately, and its implications are to be added to those, emphasized by Easley et al., of intertemporal profit maximization over all periods in a number of identical markets.

As a consequence, part (or all) of what may appear as foregone immediate profits, as a result of a low price in the entrant's market, may in fact reflect the low ex post profit made in that market that is necessary (to maximize profits over all geographical markets) because demand is more elastic in that local market. Indeed, entry in a market should make the demand for the monopolist's product more elastic in that market, so price discrimination is to be expected.

When the Nash equilibrium implies discriminatory prices, predation must be redefined as implying a price cut below the (already low local) discriminatory price to make the entry value negative in present value terms. In the terminology of Easley et al., a discriminatory type 2 monopolist (positive entry value at the local discriminatory Nash equilibrium) behaves like a discriminatory type 1 monopolist. To distinguish this behavior from normal discriminatory competition must be difficult for the entrant; hence, incomplete information is likely and the possibility of predation is greater than in a world of identical markets. The actual occurrence of predation presupposes that the discriminatory Nash equilibrium in the entrant's market implies a positive entry value. Predation then appears as a particular case of geographical price discrimination, made possible by the possibility to compensate immediate foregone profits by later gains in other markets.

Along the same lines, one might consider a monopolist that sells different commodities in different markets. Such a multimarket monopolist is also a multiproduct monopolist. All that has been said about a price-discriminating monopolist carries over to this case, because the prices of a multimarket monopolist deviate from marginal cost in the same way as discriminatory prices – they have the common property that their percentage deviation from marginal cost is inversely proportional to the absolute value of the price elasticity.[10]

7.1.7. Necessary conditions for predatory pricing

To sum up, economic theory suggests that predatory pricing is a real possibility only when the following five conditions are simultaneously met:

[10] See Phlips (1986, sec. 3.3).

1. The aggressor is a multimarket firm (possibly a multiproduct firm).
2. The predator attacks after entry has occurred in one of its markets.
3. The attack takes the form of a price cut in one of the predator's markets, which brings this price below a current noncooperative Nash equilibrium price at which the entry value is positive for the entrant (possibly below a discriminatory current Nash equilibrium price with the same property).
4. The price cut makes the entry value negative (in present value terms) in the market in which predation occurs.
5. Yet the victim is not sure that the price cut is predatory. The price cut could be interpreted by the entrant as implying that its entry value is negative under normal competition. In other words, the victim entertains the possibility that there is no room for it in the market under competitive conditions.

Notice that immediate exit of the entrant from the market it entered into, as a result of predation, is not essential because predation, as defined, does not necessarily make the postentry cash flow negative for the entrant. Similarly, the price cut does not have to take the price below the predator's marginal cost. Notice also that the market in which the attack takes place is not necessarily the one in which entry occurred. It may be another market in which the entrant was already established (for example, entry in market 2 leads to predation in market 1 in which the entrant entered earlier). On the other hand, although the theory is cast in terms of an incumbent who has the monopoly of the submarket in which entry occurs, this does not exclude the possibility that "the monopolist" (or "the chain store") is in fact an oligopolist. The presumption is then that it has a dominant position. Finally, predation is more likely in periods when the real rate of interest is low.

7.2.   Evidence

In the previous section, I asked whether predation is a theoretical possibility. In this section, I search for empirical evidence on predatory pricing, using the conclusion of the theory (in particular the five necessary conditions for predatory pricing) as a guideline.

Three sources of evidence will be discussed. The potentially most interesting source is of an experimental nature. It asks whether predatory pricing is an observable phenomenon that can be induced in a laboratory environment. Its interest stems from the fact that a direct link with economic theory can be established by imposing a set of structural features that are favorable to the emergence of predatory pricing on theoretical grounds.

I then move to an overview of American antitrust litigation, to get an idea of the relative importance of the number of cases of alleged predation brought before court, knowing that predation claimed is not predation proved.

Finally, direct evidence is gathered by analyzing some of the famous historical cases that are referred to in the literature.

7.2.1. Experimental evidence

Experimental games[11] have provided new insights in the working of industrial markets. Instead of collecting statistical industry data and computing econometric estimates or running numerical simulations, the idea is to let people play games under conditions which the experimenter has under control. The experimenter can thus reproduce the assumptions made by the theory that is to be verified and come close to the laboratory environment set up by experimenters in the so-called exact sciences.

The results of one such experiment on the possibility of predatory pricing, conducted by Isaac and Smith (1985), are available. Isaac and Smith organize a series of market games lasting at most twenty-five periods each. The sellers are two graduate students. They receive information about their own costs of production (and possibly about the costs of production of their competitor), are given initial endowments (and possibly cash bonuses), and are required in some games to pay entry permits. In each period, they must post a price, which constitutes an irrevocable offer, after a computer has given them the corresponding quantity sold and the corresponding immediate profit.

Since they are in search of predatory pricing, as the title of the paper indicates, Isaac and Smith introduce a number of features that they think are favorable to predation. In all games played, there is one large firm (firm A) and one small firm (firm B). The larger firm is given a cost advantage, in the sense that its marginal cost and its average cost of production are always below those of the smaller firm. (At a competitive equilibrium there is room for a profitable firm B.) If predation

---

[11] An overview and general discussion of experiments in the field of industrial organization can be found in Plott (1982). Section 4.1 above reports experimental results on auctions with private values. Section 6.2 refers to a number of experiments on Nash equilibria under imperfect information.

occurs, A is the predator. In addition, A is given a "deep pocket," that is, the initial endowment to A is double the endowment to firm B.

In some games, additional features are added to make predation more likely to occur. One feature is the introduction of sunk entry costs. It is achieved by requiring the two firms to buy an "entry permit" before they are allowed to participate in the market. Each permit is good for only five consecutive periods. The incumbency advantage is created by requiring A to purchase two permits (good for periods 1 to 10) and not allowing B the option of entering until period 6.

In the games just described, the firms did not know one another's cost structure and neither knew demand. Three further games were played with complete cost information, the assumption being that predation is more likely if the potential aggressor (firm A) knows that the prey (firm B) has a cost disadvantage. (In all games, the demand curve remains unknown. All a firm knows is what quantity will be sold at a particular posted price.)

In further games, a motivation other than profit maximization is introduced, to allow for the possibility that fanaticism or any abnormal intent may cause predation. For this purpose, player A is told privately that he or she will receive a cash bonus for each period in which B chooses not to enter the market.

To make sure that nothing artifactual about the experimental design inhibits B's being driven out of the market, secret instructions were given to A, in further games, to post predatory prices (and quantities sold) in periods 1 to 11. (As a result, B refused to renew his entry permit in period 11, which shows that the experimental design did not prevent B from exiting).

Finally, an antitrust program was incorporated in the game with sunk entry costs and uncertainty about the cost structure, to see how the firms would spontaneously react to antitrust rules. According to the rules imposed, A faces (a) an output expansion limitation for two periods whenever B enters, and (b) a price reduction regulation. If A reduces its price during periods in which B could be in the market, A is required by this regulation to maintain the low price for at least five consecutive periods. The authors' conjecture (p. 333) is that tacit collusion would be more likely under these rules:

> At a collusive high price this constraint makes it more costly for A to punish B for defection. Firm B, knowing that any cut in price by A cannot be reversed for 5 periods, may be hesitant to defect and risk being locked into a lower price pattern. Similarly, at low prices if A signals with a price increase, this action may have greater credibility under the PPAP [Predatory pricing antitrust program] for firm B and may increase the probability that B will follow.

Unfortunately, after creating these conditions favorable to predatory pricing, Isaac and Smith define it in a very restrictive way. For them there is predation if two conditions are satisfied. First, the predator's price p_A must be below the predator's marginal cost of production (measured at the announced quantity sold q_A). The assumption is one of short-run (myopic) profit maximizing by a firm that cannot produce for inventory (the quantity sold is equal to the quantity produced). The authors therefore ignore the possibility of intertemporal profit maximization, which was found to be essential in the theoretical analysis above, and the resulting possibility of foregone immediate profits being compensated by later gains. The second condition for a price to be predatory is that it should be lower than B's average cost (AC_B), so that either B's entry is prevented, or B is driven out or its reentry is prevented. Again, this condition ignores the possibility that (a) B may also maximize intertemporal profits and may rather be concerned about the sign of its entry value (in present value terms), (b) predation may be compatible with a positive cash flow ($p_A > AC_B$), and (c) predation may aim at delaying rather than preventing entry.

Isaac and Smith acknowledge the fact that they ignore reputation effects. What they do not seem to realize, however, is that the *multimarket* aspect of the problem is essential. Each of their firms has only one market! It is not too surprising, then, that *predatory behavior did not show up in any of their experimental games*. (In fact, the predominant outcome is that of a dominant firm equilibrium, in which the leader A moves first and B moves last, responding with the quantity that maximizes instantaneous profit given the price quoted by A.) This result does not imply that predatory pricing is impossible, but rather suggests that a narrow concept of predation based on a single-market monopolist that maximizes instantaneous profits is not likely to have descriptive value.

Since the antitrust rules introduced *in fine* are valid for several periods, so that players may be supposed to consider long-run effects, as hinted at in the given quotation, the outcome of the games played under these rules may be of greater practical relevance. Figure 7.7 reproduces the evolution of a typical game played under cost uncertainty with sunk entry costs, and Figure 7.8 displays the evolution of the same game under the two antitrust rules described. The upper horizontal line represents the monopoly price p_M that firm A would charge if all production were allocated to it given the supposed cost and demand parameters. The dominant firm equilibrium price is then p_{df}. The competitive equilibrium price must lie in the interval 2.66 to 2.76, and the potential predatory price range is 2.60–2.66. (Prices in that range

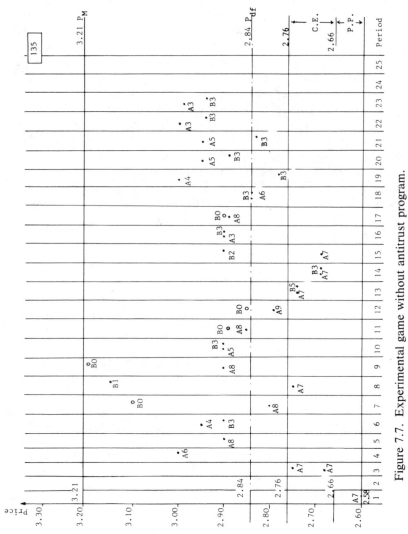

Figure 7.7. Experimental game without antitrust program.

153

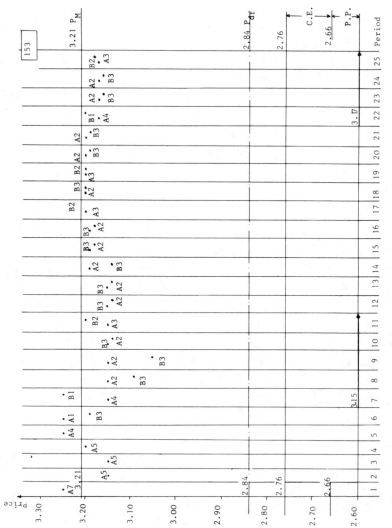

Figure 7.8. Experimental game with antitrust program.

are below marginal cost if the quantity sold is at least equal to 8 units.) The prices posted by A and B are indicated by the solid and open circles. The circle is open when the quantity sold is zero. (Remember that B enters in period 6 in these games.) The letters A and B are followed by a number that indicates the number of units sold by each firm.[12] Isaac and Smith's conjecture that tacit collusion is facilitated by the antitrust program is confirmed. In Figure 7.7, the prices fluctuate mostly around p_{df}; in Figure 7.8 they cluster around the monopoly price!

7.2.2. Antitrust litigation

Although predation has not yet shown up in a laboratory environment, it must have made an appearance in courtrooms, or at least in the mind of plaintiffs and the opinion of judges. Are complaints based on predatory pricing relatively important? Are there more and more complaints of that nature? Are judgments generally favorable to plaintiffs? No systematic evidence on these questions seems to be available for Europe. For the United States, the answers are no.

The Georgetown Project on Private Antitrust Litigation collected suitable data on all private antitrust cases filed in the years 1973–83 in five district courts chosen to provide breadth and depth to the sample. The following tables are taken from an introductory presentation of this material by Salop and White (1988).

Table 7.1 shows that horizontal price fixing was the most frequent primary allegation (18%), with predatory pricing representing only 3%, and Table 7.2 confirms the intuition that competitors are the main parties who allege predatory pricing.

Table 7.3 shows that the share of (primary and secondary) allegations of predatory pricing has fallen sharply in the 1980s. Salop and White suggest that this may be due to the spread of the Areeda–Turner predatory pricing rule (according to which there is a presumption of predation when a large firm prices below its marginal cost, as in the Isaac–Smith definition). To the extent that this rule was accepted by an increasing number of courts, the burden of proof on plaintiffs was increased.

Finally, Table 7.4 indicates that settlement rates in cases of predatory pricing were above average, with plaintiff win rates deviating in the opposite direction. We know, from theory, that such pricing can arise only in situations where the victim is not sure about its predatory na-

---

[12] The heavy black arrows near the bottom of Figure 7.8 denote periods in which A has triggered a price ceiling on himself (of 3.15 and 3.17, respectively).

Table 7.1. *Illegal practices alleged in complaints*

	Primary allegations	Combined primary and secondary allegations
Horizontal price fixing	15.7%	21.3%
Vertical price fixing	3.5	10.3
Dealer termination	4.4	8.9
Refusal to deal	12.0	25.4
Predatory pricing	3.1	10.4
Asset or patent accumulation	2.5	5.6
Price discrimination	5.0	16.4
Vertical price discrimination	1.7	5.8
Tying or exclusive dealing	9.6	21.1
Merger or joint venture	2.6	5.8
Inducing government action	0.5	0.8
"Conspiracy"	3.0	5.9
"Restraint of trade"	4.3	10.0
"Monopoly" or "monopolization"	3.7	8.8
Other	8.6	8.9
No information	25.2	13.4

Note: Percentages sum to more than 100% because a complaint may have more than one allegation.
Source: Salop and White (1988).

ture. One may suspect, therefore, that some litigations are initiated with the sole purpose of obtaining a settlement favorable to the plaintiff.

On the other hand, when there is a conviction, this is not proof that the plaintiff was aggressed in a predatory way. Koller (1971) studied twenty-three cases of convictions in detail and found that, indeed, only dubious cases come before the courts. According to Bork (1978, p. 155), Koller concluded that "predatory price cutting was attempted in only seven cases, succeeded to some extent in four, and had harmful effects upon resource allocation in only three (and these three involved predation not to eliminate a rival but to precipitate merger or collusion)." However, it should also be said that Koller's criteria were too severe, because he recognized predation only when a competitor was eliminated or merged or when "improved market discipline" resulted.

7.2.3. The historical record

After all these negative considerations, one wonders whether the historical record does not contain well-documented cases in which all the

Table 7.2. *Cross-tabulation of business relationships and alleged illegal practices*

	Horiz. price fix	Vert. price fix	Dealer term	Refusal to deal	Pred. price	Asset accum.	Price discrim.	Vert. price discrim.	Tie; excl. dealing	Merger; joint vent.	Induce govt. action	Consp., restr., monop.	Other	No info.	Total
Competitor	141	68	36	214	138	77	141	53	161	82	10	240	83	18	1462
Dealer	105	112	159	211	56	19	138	68	165	19	2	125	30	5	1214
Customer comp.	85	39	8	102	23	13	63	17	55	11	0	44	10	3	473
Franchisee	3	3	6	9	6	1	12	3	23	1	0	5	3	0	75
Licensee	2	1	1	3	1	2	0	0	12	0	0	25	2	0	49
Final cust.	97	4	0	25	7	6	29	4	35	6	0	39	13	3	268
Supplier	23	8	3	35	10	3	23	4	0	4	1	25	15	2	176
Employee	10	3	4	18	8	8	6	3	11	6	1	15	15	1	109
State/local govt.	13	0	0	1	0	3	0	0	0	2	2	9	3	1	34
Other	48	14	6	59	4	11	15	14	39	10	3	86	55	7	371
No information	13	2	2	2	4	3	6	2	10	1	0	20	3	228	296
Total	540	254	225	679	257	146	433	168	531	142	19	633	232	268	4527

Note: The totals of the cross-tabulations sum to more than 1959 because individual cases can have more than one type of business relationship and/or more than one alleged business practice.

Source: Salop and White (1988).

Table 7.3. *Frequency of alleged illegal practices,[a] by year of filing*

	Horizontal price fixing (%)	Vertical price fixing (%)	Dealer termination (%)	Refusal to deal (%)	Predatory pricing (%)	Price discrimination (%)	Tying or exclusive dealing (%)
1973 and before	24.4	16.3	9.1	26.3	12.4	23.4	29.2
1974	25.7	13.6	12.1	28.0	9.8	18.7	26.6
1975	20.5	7.3	11.7	25.4	10.2	20.0	29.8
1976	28.6	8.5	7.7	21.4	10.7	14.1	19.2
1977	17.3	7.3	6.4	21.8	11.4	17.7	18.2
1978	18.9	15.8	10.0	34.7	11.6	14.7	18.9
1979	18.2	13.3	11.5	33.9	13.3	21.8	19.4
1980	17.2	4.5	8.2	26.1	9.7	13.4	15.7
1981	19.6	7.1	10.1	24.4	8.3	10.1	16.7
1982	23.1	8.3	4.6	15.7	7.4	9.2	12.0
1983	32.1	8.0	2.7	15.2	5.4	9.8	17.9
All cases	21.3	10.3	8.9	25.4	10.4	16.4	21.1

[a] Combined primary and secondary allegations.
Source: Salop and White (1988).

Table 7.4. *Settlements and judgments, by alleged statute violation, alleged illegal practice, and business relationships*

	Broad definition of settlement[a]		Narrow definition of settlement[b]	
	Settlement as a % of terminated cases	% of judgments favorable to plaintiffs	Settlement as a % of terminated cases	% of judgments favorable to plaintiffs
Alleged statute violation				
Sherman, Sec. 1	87.7	27.9	70.7	11.8
Sherman, Sec. 2	88.6	27.4	71.7	11.0
Clayton, Sec. 2	91.0	34.5	73.4	11.4
Clayton, Sec. 3	84.9	26.7	71.4	14.0
Clayton, Sec. 7	92.5	37.5	74.8	11.2
Alleged illegal practice[c]				
Horizontal price fixing	84.2	24.6	68.3	12.3
Vertical price fixing	88.5	19.0	72.5	8.0
Dealer termination	86.2	43.5	74.5	23.8
Refusal to deal	85.6	25.4	68.6	11.6
Predatory pricing	92.9	23.1	77.6	7.3
Price discrimination	88.9	34.4	73.0	14.1
Tying or exclusive dealing	87.7	28.9	72.2	12.7
All horizontal	88.5	23.8	72.2	9.8
All vertical	86.9	27.9	72.3	12.7
Plaintiff's business relationship to defendant				
Competitor	91.1	20.8	73.4	7.4
Dealer	86.2	23.9	69.8	11.1
Customer company	92.0	5.9	77.9	2.1
Final customer	86.6	26.3	74.9	10.9
Supplier	96.9	25.0	74.4	4.5
All cases	88.2	28.1	70.8	11.3

[a] Includes dismissals in settlements.
[b] Includes dismissals in judgments for defendants.
[c] Combined primary and secondary allegations.
Source: Salop and White (1988).

ingredients of predatory pricing are clearly present. One thus looks for cases where a multimarket firm attacks an entrant by cutting the price in the latter's local market (possibly for a particular product or brand) to make his entry value negative in a way that could be interpreted as normal competition, without necessarily forcing the entrant to exit. A few such cases were put forward by Yamey (1972).

One convincing example is provided by the use of "fighting brands" by a monopolist to meet the competition of an entrant in those parts of the market where it is trying to become established or to extend its operations. In Yamey's words (1972, p. 136),

A special brand is introduced for the purpose. Its sale is confined to the affected areas; the quantities offered are controlled so as not to make unnecessary sacrifices of profit; and it is withdrawn as soon as the objective has been attained, namely the acquisition of the independent by the monopolist, or the withdrawal of the independent, or its abandonment of plans of enlarging its share of the market. Good examples of the use of fighting brands are provided by the activities of the match monopoly in Canada from its creation, by merger, in 1927 to the outbreak of the Second World War. The dominant firm used the device at various times, and this suggests that the firm was convinced of its efficacy.

Another well documented example is the use of "fighting ships" by shipping cartels (conferences) as in the Mogul case, which Yamey (1972, pp. 138–42) describes as follows.

In December 1891 the law lords in the House of Lords pronounced upon the activities of a conference of shipowners in the China-England trade designed to exclude competitors so as to maintain a monopoly. This important decision, *Mogul Steamship Co. v. McGregore, Gow and Co. et al.*, terminated litigation which had been started in 1885 and concerned events of that year.

Shipowners regularly engaged in the China trade had formed a conference in 1879 to regulate freight rate and the sailings of the ships of each member. The object was to improve the profitability of the trade by removing competition among members, especially at the height of the tea harvest (May and June) when large quantities of tea were shipped from Hankow and elsewhere down the Yang-tse-Kiang river to Shangai, and thence to London. At some time before 1884 the conference introduced a 5 per cent rebate payable to such shippers as gave all their business to conference companies during the particular year. This was designed to discourage shippers from giving business to interlopers who might be attracted into the trade, particularly at the height of the tea season when demand for shipping space was high and, presumably, also relatively inelastic.

The plaintiff company, Mogul, was formed in 1883, with ships engaged primarily in the Australia trade. It had an interest in picking up freights in China at the time of the year when homeward freight was plentiful in China but hard to come by in Australia. In the 1884 season the conference allowed two sailings to Mogul ships, although the company was not admitted as a full member. In the next year Mogul asked to be admitted as a full member of the conference, and threatened to cut rates if its request was not granted. The conference refused the request, and decided to treat Mogul as an outsider which had to be excluded from the trade. . . .

In 1885 the conference decided "that if any non-Conference steamer should proceed to Hankow to load independently the necessary number of Conference steamers should be sent at the same time to Hankow, in order to underbid the freight which the independent shipowners might offer, without any regard to whether the freight they should bid would be remunerative or not." Three independent ships were sent to Hankow, two of them being Mogul ships; and the agents for the conference lines responded by sending such ships as they thought necessary. Freight rates fell dramatically. . . . Apparently in the event the losses of the conference were larger than those of the outsiders, since some conference ships sailed empty from Hankow, while all the outsiders' vessels were able to load up with some cargo and did not have to sail in ballast. . . .

The fact that shipping companies continued to use fighting ships after the Mogul affair suggests that predatory pricing and the standing threat of such action were considered efficacious. . . .

The point is frequently made in the literature on predatory pricing that the practice makes little sense where entry into the industry or trade in question is easy. However, the Mogul story serves to illustrate a general point, namely, that predatory pricing, or the threat of its use, *may* itself operate as an effective hindrance to new entry even in situations where the conventional barriers to entry are weak or absent. In this request predatory pricing, like certain other pricing practices, should be given a place in the analysis of barriers to entry.

This lively story was worth telling, because it brings together all basic ingredients. The aggressor is a multimarket cartel. The victim is also a multimarket firm. The direct aim of the price cut is to slow down entry by the latter into a submarket and to deter further entry into that submarket. The fight could be interpreted as normal competition. Only the shipping conference knew whether the immediate foregone profits are compensated by later gains in the China trade. That it did consider such intertemporal compensation to be possible is indicated (though not proved, of course) by the fact that it continued to send fighting ships.

McGee might object that this alleged predation was a failure, because the losses for the shipping conference were eventually larger, while the outsiders might have made some small immediate profit. That is, at any rate, one of the conclusions of his 1960 study of the ocean freight rate conferences and of his 1964 study of the history of the Spanish sugar industry. My answer is that it is immaterial whether the immediate cash flow is negative for the victim or the predator. The key features are the possibility, for the predator, to compensate immediate losses or foregone profits by other gains in the long run, and the deterrence of further entry.

7.3.   Antitrust implications

As shown in Section 7.1, recent game theory is able to demonstrate that predatory pricing can be rationalized in an intertemporal profit maximization approach, when a number of conditions are met. The essential conditions are that the predator be a multimarket firm, otherwise McGee's objections apply, and that his pricing behavior can be misinterpreted by an entrant as normal competition. Although the first is easy to recognize in practice, the second implies that identification of predatory behavior is a fortiori inherently difficult for both the economist and the antitrust authority. Yet, difficult to identify or not, predatory pricing is a real possibility.

Section 7.2 suggests that clearly identified cases of predatory pricing are very hard to find. In the vast majority of cases, alleged predation is doubtful predation, which should not come as a surprise given that true predation requires the presence of such doubts. For the very same reason, predatory pricing may be more frequent, in the real world, than is generally thought.

Even if it were in fact rare, antitrust authorities could not simply disregard it. Indeed, to preserve free entry is one of the main objectives of any antitrust policy. When there is room in a market for new entrants (their entry value is positive under normal competition), predation should not be allowed to make this entry value negative and thus to discourage or delay further entry (or, in the limit, force exit). The issue is an essential one. One should at least try to see what policy implications can be derived from the recent theoretical advances. Hopefully, they should indicate what can be done in an operational way, which policy actions could deter predation, and what side effects these actions could have. At any rate, they should indicate what antitrust authorities should not do.

At least three policy attitudes are possible. The simplest is to do nothing and hope that "market forces" will do the job in the long run. A second attitude is to devise a per se rule, according to which a dividing line between legitimately competitive prices and prices that are properly regarded as predatory is drawn and/or well-defined obligations are imposed on potential predators. The third attitude is to use a *rule of reason,* implying that each case is judged on its own merits, using all the available evidence.

7.3.1. *No standard*

According to McGee (1980, p. 317), the best thing to do is to do nothing – the best standard against predation is no standard at all. The
argument is that predatory pricing *is* rare, while the danger of con-
demning what is in fact active competition by the more efficient firm
is great, so more harm than good is likely to be done. I cannot follow
this argument in view of the unduly restrictive assumptions of McGee's
analysis *and* in view of the fact we do not and cannot know how rare
predation actually is. Not detecting the guilty is as probable as pun-
ishing the innocent.

Another argument also leads to the conclusion that no standard
should be used. It says that a prohibition, even if it is effective, does
not necessarily lead to more entry, because predatory pricing is but
one of a series of means to deter entry. A prohibition of predatory
pricing may increase the incentive for a dominant firm to make investments prior to entry (e.g., investments in productive capacity, in
advertising, in retail capacity, in R & D) to reduce the need for predatory pricing after entry has occurred. And it may be impossible to
provide policy rules about such preentry investments. As argued by
Spence (1981) an attack on predation may therefore not be the most
important weapon in dealing with abuses of market dominance. Again,
this argument is not convincing. It is of the same nature as the one that
says that price agreements should not be made illegal because such a
prohibition will promote mergers. With this type of argument, the
whole of antitrust policy is under attack.

7.3.2. *Price below marginal cost*

It would be nice if a neat dividing line could be drawn between a price
resulting from normal competition and a predatory price. Areeda and
Turner (1975) have proposed what they call a meaningful and workable
test[13] for making such a distinction, to replace such empty formule as
"below cost" pricing, ruinous competition, or predatory intent. The
simplicity of their test may explain why it was adopted with remarkable
speed by American judicial circles. (It has become *the* standard in a
number of cases.) The test provides a floor below which a price is
presumed predatory: "Unless at or above average cost, a price below
reasonably anticipated (1) shortrun marginal costs or (2) average variable costs should be deemed predatory, and the monopolist may not

---

[13] Alterations and refinements by Posner (1976) and Greer (1979) will not be discussed
here.

defend on the grounds that his price was "promotional" or merely met an equally low price of a competitor" (Areeda and Turner, 1975, p. 733). To establish predation, the antitrust authority "simply" has to show that a price is below (reasonably anticipated) average variable cost, treated as a proxy for marginal cost. To escape indictment, the alleged predator "simply" has to show that his price is not below (reasonably anticipated) average variable cost. Consideration of threats is disallowed.

After recalling the standard textbook definitions of fixed and variable costs, Areeda and Turner first discuss a general price reduction by a single-product single-market monopolist. (We know that predatory pricing cannot be rationalized under these circumstances.) Predatory pricing is defined (p. 698) as

a temporary sacrifice of net revenues in the expectation of greater future gains. Indeed, the classically-feared case of predation has been the deliberate sacrifice of present revenues for the purpose of driving rivals out of the market and then regrouping the losses through higher profits earned in the absence of competition.

Although the elimination of the victim is an unduly severe criterion, this definition has at least the merit of being cast in terms of intertemporal profit maximization (future profits compensate immediate losses). Quite surprisingly, however, Areeda and Turner then proceed to analyze predation in terms of myopic instantaneous profit maximization and concentrate entirely on the sacrifice of short-run profits (p. 703):

We would normally expect a profit-maximizing firm, within the limits of data and convenience, to attempt to maximize profits or minimize losses in the short run – the competitive firm by producing where marginal cost equals price, and the monopolist by producing where marginal cost equals marginal revenue.

Two exceptions to short-run profit maximization are deemed nonpredatory. One is "limit pricing," that is, a price permanently set above average cost but below the profit-maximizing price to prevent entry (that has not yet occurred) by newcomers with a higher average cost. The other one is a temporary price reduction to average cost when entry is relatively costly. These two pricing policies are deemed analytically indistinguishable and are not presumed illegal because they exclude only less efficient rivals and would require continuous supervision by the antitrust authority. (One might as well argue that they are also indistinguishable from predatory pricing.)

What is presumed illegal is pricing below marginal cost, *when marginal cost is below average cost* – pricing at marginal cost being tolerated (p. 712):

We have concluded above that marginal-cost pricing by a monopolist should be tolerated even though losses could be minimized or profits increased at a lower output and higher price, for the reasons, among others, that marginal-cost pricing leads to a proper resource allocation and is consistent with competition on the merits. Neither reason obtains when the monopolist prices below marginal cost. The monopolist is not only incurring private losses but wasting social resources when marginal cost exceeds the value of what is produced. And pricing below marginal cost greatly increases the possibility that rivalry will be extinguished or prevented for reasons unrelated to the efficiency of the monopolist. Accordingly, a monopolist pricing below marginal cost should be presumed to have engaged in a predatory or exclusionary practice.

Subsequently, Areeda and Turner consider devices other than a "general" price cut, namely, selective price cuts on particular products or particular geographical markets. In both cases, it is claimed that the same conclusions apply (except that a monopolist should have the benefit of any defenses, such as "promotional" pricing or "meeting competition," available to other sellers in any market in which he lacks monopoly power).

In view of our theoretical analysis, the Areeda–Turner approach obviously lacks serious analytical underpinning, even if a "general" price cut by a single-product single-market monopolist is left out of the analysis. To begin with, I can hardly think of an economist who would be willing, today, to interpret the marginal-revenue–equal-marginal-cost rule as more than a mathematical tautology without descriptive value.[14] But above all, Areeda and Turner totally ignore the behavior of firms as sophisticated players in an intertemporal game and the requirements of a noncooperative Nash equilibrium between such players. From a game-theoretic point of view, the distinction made between the elimination of newcomers with higher average costs than the incumbents (called "competition on the merits," apparently) and the elimination of at least equally efficient newcomers seems pointless. What matters is whether there is room for the newcomer in a competitive Nash equilibrium, that is, whether its entry value is positive, and whether the incumbent's pricing policy makes this entry value negative, that is, whether the entrant's fixed sunk entry costs are no longer compensated by the present value of future profits. The precise relationship between price and marginal cost plays no essential role at such a competitive equilibrium as far as predatory pricing is concerned.

From a policy point of view, the line drawn by Areeda and Turner

---

[14] On this, see Chapter 6 of my 1983 book on price discrimination.

is underinclusive. As noted by Easley et al. (1985, p. 457), none of the predators described in their model could be held in violation of the Areeda–Turner standard or similar standards defined in terms of price–cost relationships. Prices are not below average variable cost or marginal cost in their model, and exit is not induced. Ironically, standards such as Areeda and Turner's "may constitute the instruction manual on how to prey with impunity."

On a pragmatic "administrative" level (Areeda and Turner put heavy weight on the costs of administrative supervision and litigation), it may be added that average variable costs are not as easily defined in practice as they are in elementary textbooks. In addition, no judge, or academic or antitrust authority has adequate means of checking the correctness of a defendant's evaluation of average variable costs (whether "reasonably anticipated" or not). For all practical purposes, the Areeda–Turner price–cost relationship is impossible to measure and makes the proof of predation too difficult.

7.3.3. Limit pricing and output restrictions

Instead of a dividing line between a price that is predatory and a price that is not, as in the Areeda–Turner rule, Williamson (1977) proposes an "output restriction rule" which stipulates that a dominant firm cannot, in the period after entry occurs, increase output above the preentry level even if the resulting market price exceeds the dominant firm's average variable cost. This rule results from a reasoning in terms of limit pricing, which is apparently considered by Williamson as the type of pricing that correctly describes the behavior of dominant firms (or collusive oligopolists). It is necessary, therefore, to briefly discuss limit pricing.

Limit pricing has been a major topic in industrial economics. It goes back at least to Modigliani's classic 1958 paper "New Developments on the Oligopoly Front." The basic idea is that "potential entrants behave as though they expected existing firms to adopt the policy most unfavorable to them, namely, the policy of maintaining output while reducing the price (or accepting reductions) to the extent required to enforce such an output policy" (Modigliani, 1958, p. 217, note 26).

Figure 7.9 makes this statement more precise. The incumbent is supposed to maintain output (sales) at the level Q_L to which corresponds the limit price p_L. This price is below the monopoly price p_M, which the incumbent would fix if there is no prospective entry and no fear of it. The limit price (and the corresponding output Q_L) is found by drawing a line that is parallel to the industry demand curve AB and

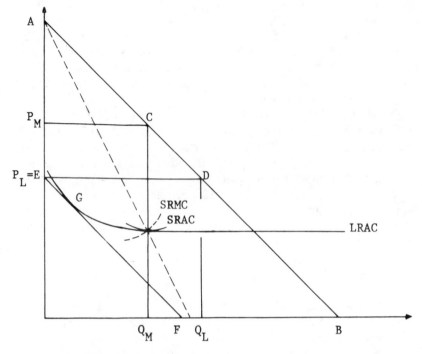

Figure 7.9. Limit pricing.

simultaneously tangent to the given long-run average cost curve (*LRAC*). The parallelism results from the assumption that the incumbent maintains sales at Q_L, so that *DB* is the residual demand curve on which the entrant can operate. This segment *DB* is shifted to the left. The tangency with the *LRAC* curve (which is the same for the potential entrant and for the existing firm) represents the policy most unfavorable to the potential entrant. Indeed, any quantity of the (homogeneous) commodity put on the market by an entrant leads to losses or at most to the break-even point *G*. Entry is thus deterred. The incumbent prefers the immediate reduction in profit (due to the fact that $p_L < p_M$) to the larger reduction in profit that would result if entry occurred.

Suppose entry somehow occurs. Then the dominant firm will allegedly flood the market to reduce the price below the entrant's *LRAC* curve and force it to exit. An output expansion is necessary, because lowering the price without increasing sales would create excess demand and make it easier for the entrant to establish itself. Hence the rule that a postentry output expansion above the preentry level Q_L should be presumed predatory, even if the resulting price were still above the dominant firm's average variable cost.

Needless to say, this is an oversimplified presentation of limit pricing[15] and of the output restriction rule.[16] It will do for my present purpose, because I do not believe limit pricing to be a valid rationalization of the pricing policy of dominant firms, nor an output restriction rule to be a valid standard against predatory pricing.

First of all, limit-pricing theories are hard to reconcile with empirical evidence. In McGee's strong words (1980, pp. 312–3)

> . . . if – as the theory asserts – long-run average costs are flat beyond the minimum efficient size, taken as it stands the theory cannot explain why there is anything but single-firm monopoly everywhere. If limit pricing works, why did not the first member of each industry practice it from the beginning and keep everyone else out forever? This is a serious question because, among other things, the limit price is determined by the *slope* of industry demand, no matter how big the market is. It would be difficult to explain the evolution, prosperity, and present structure of the U.S. economy if limit-pricing theories were right.

In particular, one wonders how entry and hence predation could ever occur.

On a more analytical level, McGee (1980, p. 311) notes that limit pricing rests upon an implicit threat which is not credible:

> The monopoly threatens that it will not reduce output if entry should occur. Under the circumstances posited, the threat is not credible because it would not pay to carry it out. Suppose an entrant decides that it will come in at the smallest scale at which it can achieve minimum average cost. As Figure III [see my Figure 7.9] shows, it is true that if the monopolist holds output constant in the face of entry, the entrant would lose money. But so would the monopoly. Indeed, the monopoly would lose much more than the entrant. Holding its output constant at that scale would hurt the monopoly more than it hurts the entrant, and the ex-monopoly has more attractive alternatives if entry actually does occur. As a result, the entrant should assume that the monopoly will not act like that. More attractive alternatives may include so-called dominant-firm pricing, Cournot-style duopoly pricing, a cartel, or other attempts to divide the market peacefully, and so on.

At this point, it should be clear that a game-theoretic treatment of limit pricing is the only way to disentangle the rights and the wrongs.

---

[15] For important refinements see Gaskins (1971), Kamien and Schwartz (1971), Pyatt (1971), and Salop (1979).
[16] Williamson (1977) also discusses rules which allow postentry output expansion on the condition that price does not fall below short-run marginal cost or below short-run average cost.

Both the existing firm and the potential entrant should be treated as rational players in a well-defined game, and one should study the properties of the resulting equilibrium, to clarify the "strategic" possibilities alluded to by both McGee and Williamson.

This is exactly what Friedman (1979) has done. His conclusion is that *if the incumbent and the entrant are completely informed* about demand and about each other's costs, as is implicitly assumed in the foregoing discussion and in the construction of Figure 7.9, *no limit pricing can emerge in equilibrium.*

The argument is essentially the same as the argument leading to the chain store paradox. Postentry profits are completely independent of the preentry price, under the usual assumption that preentry price does not affect postentry demand. Under complete information, the postentry profits are also fully known when the entry decision is made. Hence the entry decision is independent of the preentry price. Reducing this price to the limit price p_L amounts to throwing preentry profits away. As long as preentry actions do not influence postentry costs and demand, this argument is valid and the traditional theory of limit pricing has no game-theoretic foundation.

The implication is that limit pricing can be rationalized only if information is incomplete, exactly as is the case with predatory pricing. It then remains to see how limit pricing could arise in equilibrium under incomplete information and especially whether such deviation from myopic profit maximization would effectively deter entry in equilibrium. Milgrom and Roberts (1982b) have tackled these questions and shown that, while traditional limit pricing can arise under incomplete information, it does *not* bias the entrant's expectations of the profitability of entry. The only consequence of limit pricing, when it occurs, is therefore to reduce the price without limiting entry. Antitrust authorities should thus not worry about it. A reduction in price with no effects on entry cannot be objectionable from their point of view.

In the games analyzed by Milgrom and Roberts (1982b), neither the incumbent nor the potential entrant is perfectly informed about the other firm's unit costs. Therefore, no player is able to compute the postentry profits with certainty. However, the preentry price becomes a *signal* concerning the incumbent's costs and thus concerning the price and market share to be expected after entry. By signaling lower costs, a lower preentry price is an attempt to influence the entry decision.

The modeling is done, as in the analysis of predatory pricing, with the help of a probability distribution, which is here defined over the possible values of the unit costs of the players. A third player, "Nature," moves first and draws a particular value of the unit costs out of the given probability distribution. The incumbent is informed about its own unit cost, but not about the unit cost of the potential entrant, and vice versa. In addition to its own unit cost, the potential entrant can observe the preentry output chosen by the incumbent. The game is thus transformed into a game with "complete" information (the probability distribution is known to all, so all possible outcomes are known). But the information is "imperfect" in the sense that the players must make a move at some point without having been fully informed about all the previous moves by the other players (including Nature). The equilibria can then be computed as pairs of strategies (based on what each player knows) such that each player maximizes his expected payoff, given that the other is using a particular strategy.[17]

As for Williamson's output restriction rule, note that it is as underinclusive as the Areeda–Turner rule. There is no reason why a predator, as defined here, should necessarily violate it, that is, should necessarily expand output above its preentry level. It is also worth recalling that such a rule is likely to facilitate tacit collusion, as shown in the Isaac–Smith experiment. Conversely, as noted by Baumol (1979, p. 3, note 8), the rule prevents entry from serving its purpose of forcing price reductions upon the incumbent and "inhibits price wars among large incumbent firms, who are constrained, in effect, to retain their initial market shares, at least for the immediate post-entry period."

7.3.4. Limit pricing and quasi-permanent price reductions

Baumol (1979) therefore proposes a rule that, instead of preventing output increases, forbids price increases after the entrant has been forced to cease operations. In this way, price reductions are made "quasi-permanent." Though left free to respond to entry by a price cut, in contrast to Williamson's output restriction rule, the established firm can no longer do so without fear of long-term repercussions, because it must take the long-run cost of a permanent reduction in price into account. This quasi-permanence rule could be supplemented, according to Baumol, with a test like the Areeda–Turner test to determine whether profits on other outputs or markets are used to subsidize predatory prices. Of course, the defendant should be allowed to provide evidence that a postentry increase is justified by cost increases or by other autonomous developments. The burden of proof should thus be on the defendant.

Baumol's quasi-permanency rule is deemed consistent with the re-

---

[17] The interested reader is referred to Milgrom and Roberts (1982b) for further details.

quirements of allocative efficiency because it closely approximates the optimality properties of stationary limit pricing. This type of limit pricing, in turn, is possible only if the incumbent is a natural monopoly, that is, if several firms cannot produce the industry's output at least as cheaply. Indeed, in that situation, stationary limit prices are such that entry can be prevented without changing them in response to an attempted entrant's moves. The incumbent "can sit back and await the entrant's financial failure" (Baumol, 1979, p. 18). When a prospective predator, who, by definition, is not a natural monopoly, knows that it cannot raise its price after a predatory campaign, it will automatically abandon the idea of preying upon an entrant!

Baumol's rule is thus embedded in a particular form of limit pricing. No game-theoretic explanation on how such pricing could occur in equilibrium is given. Awaiting such explanation, the critiques formulated above against traditional limit pricing apply. In addition, this rule is as underinclusive as Williamson's (predation does not necessarily induce exit and a subsequent rise in prices) and is equally likely to facilitate collusion.

7.3.5. *Abuse of a dominant position*

I must conclude that none of the per se rules under discussion can be adopted as a useful weapon against predatory pricing. The only available alternative seems to be to use a rule of reason, that is, to establish predation with all available evidence at hand. In the case of the Treaty of Rome, this amounts to treating predatory pricing as a case of "abuse of a dominant position" in application of article 86 of the EEC treaty.

From our discussion it should be clear that proof, by the defendant, that the allegedly predatory price is above marginal cost or average variable cost should be treated as inconclusive and discarded. Argumentation about relevant costs and their measurements can and should be avoided. In a similar vein, discussions about whether a postentry price increase (or sales expansion) by the predator was justified by cost increases (or decreases) can and should be avoided. The same is true, more generally, for arguments cast in terms of limit pricing. The only way out is to collect evidence that is related to the game-theoretic arguments presented.

Game theory admittedly requires a great deal of sophistication. Its implications, however, are clear and simple, at least in principle. The negative implications are that it is immaterial whether the alleged victim was forced out of the market it entered in and whether its cash flow (current profits) remained positive. As for the alleged predator, when this turns out to be a single-market firm, the presumption should be that predation is irrational.

The positive implication is that the plaintiff (or the antitrust authority) should provide evidence to the effect that an alleged predatory price cut turned a positive entry value into a negative one for the alleged victim. It should be shown that the present value of future profits is larger than the fixed sunk entry costs of the victim under normal competition and that the price cut made this value smaller than the fixed sunk entry cost. In simple words, this amounts to showing that, without the price cut, there was room in the market for an additional firm under normal competition, that is, in a noncooperative Nash equilibrium. And that, as a result of the price cutting, the price went below the noncooperative Nash equilibrium price.

The difficulty is that such proof is hard to provide in practice, because predation can occur only when there is uncertainty about whether the price cutting is the result of normal competition, that is, whether the postentry noncooperative Nash equilibrium implies a negative entry value, or not. The alleged predator will inevitably argue that its price *is* the noncooperative Nash equilibrium price (so that it is normal competition that made the entrant's entry value negative) while the alleged victim will pretend it is not. Nevertheless, I wish to emphasize that the postentry noncooperative Nash equilibrium, with the implied price (or prices, if the commodity is nonhomogeneous) and market shares (for the incumbent and the entrant), should be the theoretical yardstick. The discussion should be on the issue whether this equilibrium leaves room for the entrant, in the sense that entry is profitable in the long run under normal competition.

One might object that, in addition to the inherent uncertainty about the predatory nature of a price cut, information about the competitors' cost and demand is generally incomplete (how could the victim know the predator's profits in its different markets?), so the relevant Nash equilibrium cannot be computed. This objection will not do. It is well established and well known[18] that oligopolists can find it in practice, even if they are not perfectly informed about each others' profits, costs and/or demands. In fact, the noncooperative equilibrium is the natural outcome of oligopolistic competition under *incomplete* information! The entrant and the alleged predator *are* therefore able to say what the postentry competitive price is, in the market in which entry occurred, in the absence of predation, and what the corresponding market shares are. The least the Commission should do is to ask that these numbers be revealed.

[18] See Section 6.2.

In particular, the victim should be asked to show (a) that its postentry equilibrium market share and the equilibrium price(s) are, in this market, such that its entry value was positive and (b) that, at the predator's price, this value became negative. The alleged predator's defense would be to show that its postentry price, in the local market in which entry occurred, *is* the noncooperative equilibrium price in this market, in the absence of compensations in its other markets. Its best defense would be to show that its postentry price in the entrant's market does *not* imply immediate foregone profits that are compensated by larger profits in its other markets, now or in the future. (The defendant could show, for example, that the alleged victim or other producers of the same commodity entered successfully, simultaneously or subsequently, in its other markets and reduced its profits there.)

Although this requires putting figures about future total revenues and total production costs on the table, and discounting these in an appropriate way, irrelevant discussions about what is a variable cost are avoided. The discussion should center on discounted profits at alternative prices and on the relevant discount factor to use. The emphasis should thus be very different from what it currently is in cases of alleged predation.

CHAPTER 8

Efficient double auctions

8.1. Efficient capital markets

The auctions discussed in Chapter 4 were "simple" in the sense that there was one seller and several buyers or one purchaser and several suppliers. Let there be several market participants on both sides of the market who publicly announce their demand and supply prices so that the market price (also publicly announced) is the one that equates supply and demand. We then have an open "double" auction. This type of institutional setup characterizes capital markets (stock exchanges) and markets for basic commodities (such as the London Metal Exchange).

At least three questions arise. First, could one argue that these markets are "efficient" in the sense that their prices reflect all available information? Second, do their current prices transmit the private information of the better-informed dealers to the less-informed? Third, can these prices be said to correctly aggregate the possibly conflicting information available to the individual participants?

We begin with the efficiency question and center the discussion on the capital market, because that is the institutional setup for which the concept was first defined.

Fama (1970, p. 383) defines an efficient capital market as follows:

> The primary role of the capital market is allocation of ownership of the economy's capital stock. In general, the ideal is a market in which prices provide accurate signals for resource allocation: that is, a market in which firms can make production-investment decisions, and investors can choose among the securities that represent ownership of firms' activities under the assumption that security prices at any time "fully reflect" all available information. A market in which prices always "fully reflect" available information is called "efficient."

This definition is rather vague. One wonders what the meaning is of "to fully reflect." One also wonders what exactly is the "available information." Interesting conclusions can be derived only when the information structure of a problem is described with sufficient precision.

It is only after a long and often confused debate, summarized in Fama (1970), that some progress to a better understanding of the problem was made. In fact, three types of efficiency emerge: (1) a *weak* form, which considers only information gathered from *historical* price movements; (2) a semistrong form, in which prices reflect all information that is *public*; (3) a *strong* form, in which both *private* and public information is supposed to be reflected in the market price. To understand this trichotomization, we must look closer at the implications of each type of efficiency.

8.1.1.   Weak efficiency: the random walk hypothesis

Historically, the first (and most numerous) studies of the capital market's efficiency were concerned with the question whether information obtained from the study of historical security price movements can enable investors to realize above normal returns. The basic intuition is that, if market prices do *not* fully reflect all available information, a clever investor could make profits by running a model that would forecast future prices using historic price series. He or she would thus outperform the less-well-informed investors and "beat the market." If, however, the market is efficient, then such models should not yield information that could be used to improve investment decisions. Speculation should be a "fair game": The expected profits to a speculator should be zero.

This intuition leads to an empirical test that is rather indirect, in that it aims at verifying an informational efficiency rather than the information transmission itself. The hypothesis to be tested is specified as a "random walk." Formally, the (random) return r_{jt} of a security j at time t is generated by a random walk process if

$$f(r_{jt+1} \mid \Phi_t) = f(r_{jt+1}); \tag{8.1}$$

that is, if its probability distribution conditional on the set of available information Φ_t is equal to its marginal probability distribution, and if the density function f is the same for all t. The information set is assumed to include only the past history $r_{jt}, r_{jt-1}, r_{jt-2}, \ldots$ The conditional distribution $f(r_{jt+1} \mid \Phi_t)$ implies that this historical information is "fully reflected" in the market returns.

Empirically, the implication is that in the regression model

$$E(r_{jt} \mid r_{jt-\tau}) = \alpha_\tau + \beta_\tau r_{jt-\tau} \tag{8.2}$$

the autocorrelation coefficient β_τ should be zero for any τ. All autocorrelations of any order should be zero. Accordingly, percentage

changes in share prices of commodity prices should look like independent random numbers drawn from a symmetric distribution with
constant variance, and their serial correlation coefficients should not
be statistically different from zero. (One looks at percentage changes
to eliminate trends which the random walk hypothesis ignores because
it assumes that the expected return is stationary through time: α_t is
supposed constant.) In his seminal 1965 paper, Fama found first-order
serial correlation coefficients for one-, four-, nine-, and sixteen-day
changes in the natural log of price (for each of the thirty stocks of the
Dow Jones Industrial Average) that were always close to zero. However, a number of correlations were statistically different from zero,
as was the case in similar studies listed in Fama's 1970 survey. The
empirical evidence is thus not entirely convincing.

8.1.2. Semistrong efficiency

Fortunately, it is possible to go one step further and test directly the
extent to which market prices reflect new information that is made
public through announcements in the press (such as new security issues, the publication of financial reports by firms, or stock splits). The
analysis of stock splits, initiated by Fama, Fisher, Jensen, and Roll
(FFJR) in 1969 is perhaps the most illustrative.

A stock split is an operation by which a company distributes new
shares to its shareholders without raising capital. These shares represent the incorporation of internal resources such as reserves. Technically, existing shares are fractioned (two for one, for example).

How does the stock market react to the announcement of such a
split, (which is generally made two to three months ahead)? If the
market is efficient, security prices will adjust fully to the split as soon
as it is announced, so no individual investor could make a profit by
buying the security after the announcement and selling it somewhat
later.

To test this idea empirically, FFJR examined the residuals of the
regression model

$$r_{jt} = \alpha_j + \beta_j r_{mt} + \epsilon_{jt} \tag{8.3}$$

where j is a company, and r_{mt} is the average return at period t in the
sample of company returns and measures the overall state of the market. Instead of looking at the residuals of individual companies, FFJR
take the average residual of the companies that announced a split. The
date (month) at which the split is carried out defines the origin of time
for each firm. (Thus $t = 0$ differs from company to company.) The

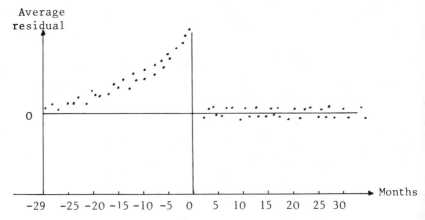

Figure 8.1. Average residual returns of companies announcing a split.

average residual of the companies that announced a split looks as in Figure 8.1 in the New York Stock Exchange.[1] Before the split is carried out, all average residual returns are positive. They are the highest in the months between the announcement $(-4, -3, -2, -1)$ and the actual split. After the split month the average return fluctuates randomly around zero. The market adjustment is thus completed before the occurrence of the event.

The difference between the "negative" and "positive" months is striking, but the length of the adjustment (twenty-nine months!) suggests that other forces are at work, and, in particular, that a split is announced during periods when the price of the share has increased more than the market average. In addition, there seems to be a gradual increase between the announcement and the split month. Couldn't a better-informed investor possibly make a profit during this period? Is the announcement "fully" reflected? Again, the empirical evidence could be interpreted for or against the efficiency assumption.

8.1.3. Strong efficiency

The more one thinks about this issue the more it becomes apparent that the interesting question is not so much the extent to which the market adjusts to public information but rather the extent to which private information can be acquired and kept private by insiders. In other words, to what extent is private information made public through

---

[1] Brehain (1980) found similar results for the Brussels stock exchange.

the price mechanism? To what extent should it be made public for a market to be efficient? A less than full adjustment may turn out to be necessary for a competitive market to work efficiently, just as less than full information transmission is necessary for an oligopolistic market to operate competitively.

On this point, the Fama survey simply notes that there is some evidence that specialists on the New York Stock Exchange can use inside information to make monopoly profits and that the same is true for officers of corporations. Whatever the empirical evidence, some additional theory would be welcome. The next section presents more recent efforts in that direction. Let me close the present section with a quotation from a letter (by a C. Warren Nooker) to the *International Herald Tribune*:

> The Efficient Market Theory states that stock or commodity market prices always reflect everything known about prospects of companies, commodities and the economy as a whole. Therefore, prices are not predictable, so it is impossible to beat the markets.
>
> This hypothesis is ridiculous. As a private investor, I have made an easy and riskless living for years because of the inefficiency of the market.
>
> The Efficient Market Theory assumes that all information (and misinformation) is dealt with in an intelligent manner. But most market participants are unable to successfully weigh market information against the basics of the situation, or else they completely misinterpret information – especially regarding the economy as a whole. As a result, stock or commodity prices often move initially in the wrong direction. Later, when time clarifies the situation, prices reverse direction – sometimes violently.
>
> How, in such an atmosphere, can efficiency exist?

8.1.4. *The impossibility of efficient capital markets*

In two important papers, Grossman and Stiglitz (1976, 1980) have addressed the "strong efficiency" question and convincingly developed two ideas. First, the current competitive price indeed makes *some* private information public and thus transmits *some* information from the better-informed to the less-informed market agents. But this does not lead to full public information. Second, only a fraction of those that were uninformed initially become informed at equilibrium. Indeed, equilibrium implies that a fraction of the market agents remain *uninformed*!

To understand the first point, suppose the return r of a security has an observable component η and an unobservable component ϵ, or

$$r = \eta + \epsilon, \tag{8.4}$$

where both η and ϵ are random independently and normally distributed variables. All investors that operate on this capital market are identical, except that some are informed and others are uninformed. The informed investors are those who observe η. For example, they acquire information about the profits, exports, production, and so on, of the company that issued the security. Their demand for the security is

$$X_I = X_I(p, \eta) \tag{8.5}$$

and thus depends on the component η and on the security's market price p. The uninformed agents observe only the price p so that their demand is $X_U = X_U(p)$. Suppose further that X_I increases with η and decreases when the price increases.[2]

In each period, market equilibrium implies that aggregate demand be equal to aggregate supply or

$$\lambda X_I(p, \eta) + (1 - \lambda)X_U(p) = X^s, \tag{8.6}$$

where λ is the fraction of informed investors, $1 - \lambda$ is the fraction of uninformed investors, and X^s is the aggregate supply.

If X^s were a fixed quantity, then one could argue that private information is fully made public by the price mechanism in the following sense. When the market price rises, the uninformed investors could deduce that η increased, because X_I increases with η and because a higher price implies a larger aggregate demand. All the information that the informed investors have would thus be transmitted. Indeed, to each value of the market price p would correspond only one value of η. In other words, the conditional distribution of r, for given η, would be identical to the conditional distribution of p, for given η.

However, X^s is not a fixed quantity; the supply also behaves randomly. As a consequence, the market price may be higher, either because η increased or because X^s decreased. (The link between p and η would similarly be blurred if an additional random component were introduced in X_I or X_U.) For each value of p, there is a distribution of possible values of η. A price increase remains a signal, but it is a noisy signal. All the information is not transmitted in the sense that, if the market price increases, η and r increase only on average. All one can say is that p and η are correlated.

Grossman and Stiglitz's second point rests on the fact that information is costly to gather. Given a positive cost of gathering information about η, and given that p is correlated with η when a fraction of investors pay this cost, it must be that at equilibrium, when equation

[2] See Grossman and Stiglitz (1980) for a discussion of this assumption.

(8.6) holds, some investors do not find it worthwhile to pay this cost and prefer to remain uninformed. The higher the cost, the smaller is the fraction λ that prefers to get informed.

The theory of market efficiency ignores this. That is why it runs into the famous paradox which says: "At equilibrium, the market is efficient, $\lambda = 1$, nobody has private information, and arbitrage is perfect. But if all information is public, arbitrage is unprofitable, and the market cannot operate." To explain why investors can, in fact, make a profit, the theory of efficient markets is obliged to say that (unexplained) "desequilibria" make this possible. It is much more satisfactory to recognize that market equilibrium does not imply full information transmission and that capital markets are efficient only to the extent that those who pay to become informed are rewarded for this. The simplest is to admit that capital markets are not and cannot be efficient.

Another interesting property of the Grossman–Stiglitz model should be noted. Supply and demand are no longer separated: One cannot draw independent supply and demand curves. Imagine a decrease in X^s raises the equilibrium price. This indicates that η has increased and that r is therefore higher *on average*. Since the uninformed evaluate r on the basis of p, their demand X_U increases. Demand thus depends on the probability distribution of supply and increases with the price, as is typical for speculators.

8.1.5. *Rational-expectations equilibria and experimental markets*

A further feature of the Grossman–Stiglitz model is that its equilibrium is a *rational-expectations* (RE) *equilibrium*. We noted that uninformed traders base their expectations about η (and therefore the return r) on the equilibrium price. In more general terms, this means that expectations about the state of nature (here the value of the random coefficient η) are conditional on the equilibrium value of the endogenous variables of the model (here the price p). On the other hand, the equilibrium price was seen to be consistent with the expectations based on it and to adjust to changing expectations. The combination of these two conditions (expectations conditional on equilibrium values and equilibrium values consistent with adjusting expectations) defines the RE equilibrium.

This adaptative behavior implies that prices *tend* to reveal the true state of nature (η) and that private information *tends* to be revealed through the price mechanism. Therefore, a market in RE equilibrium resembles a market that is "strongly efficient" in that there is a tendency for private information to be made public through the price evolution. The difference, however, is that private information is not made public immediately nor entirely in an RE equilibrium. To emphasize the resemblance and the difference, one could, as some authors actually do, define a strongly efficient market as a market in a "strong" RE equilibrium.

On the basis of what was said before, it seems clear that the RE equilibrium is more likely to characterize real-life double auction markets than strong efficiency. Yet, some readers may feel that the concept of RE equilibrium is still too demanding, because uninformed traders may in fact be unable to adjust their expectations (about the state of nature) to the equilibrium price, with the implication that the equilibrium price itself is not consistent with the expectations. It may be useful, therefore, to contrast the RE equilibrium with a "naive" equilibrium in which expectations do not depend on the prices (but on some given prior information), and prices are determined by independent demand and supply schedules in the traditional way, once the expectations are formed. Let us call this a "prior-information (PI) equilibrium."

Three characterizations of double auction markets are thus available: the strong efficiency (or strong RE) equilibrium, the RE equilibrium, and the PI equilibrium. It is of considerable interest to find out to what extent traders are in fact capable of adjusting their expectations and to what extent and how fast equilibrium prices adjust in turn. Since this is an empirical question, a natural way of answering it is to organize experimental markets in a laboratory environment and to see what happens. This is what Plott and Sunder (1982) have done. Their results indicate that the strong RE model and the PI model can be rejected in favor of the RE model. This is not to say that the RE model applies to existing capital markets or futures markets, because the experimental markets are very simple and stylized in comparison. But it is hoped that the understanding gained will be useful for the analysis of more complex markets.

Plott and Sunder designed their experiments as follows. Each experiment involved several periods. In each period securities which had one-period lives were traded (by students of the Graduate School of Business of the University of Chicago). Each security paid a dividend to its holder at the end of the period. The dividend from holding a security differed across individuals and depended upon the randomly drawn state of nature. To illustrate, I shall concentrate on the features and results of one of the experiments made (called "market 2"), in which two states of nature (X and Y) and three types of investors (I, II, and III) were defined. The actual numbers chosen appear in Table

Table 8.1. *Dividends in experimental double auction*

Investor type	Dividend		Prior probability		Expected dividend
	X	Y	X	Y	
I	100	350			100 ($\frac{1}{3}$) + 350 ($\frac{2}{3}$) = 266.7
II	200	300	$\frac{1}{3}$	$\frac{2}{3}$	200 ($\frac{1}{3}$) + 300 ($\frac{2}{3}$) = 266.7
III	240	175			240 ($\frac{1}{3}$) + 175 ($\frac{2}{3}$) = 196.6

8.1. Differences in dividends and possibly expectations lead to the existence of gains from exchange and market activity. The market is organized as an oral double auction.

At the beginning of each period, each player received two securities plus an initial endowment of working capital (Fr 10,000) which was sufficiently large never to serve as a binding constraint on purchases of securities.

The information structure was as follows. All players were aware of the mechanism used to determine the state of nature. During the first four periods, no player received information about the realized state of nature. In periods 4 and 5, all players were privately given information about the realized state. In periods 6 to 11, however, only six players (one half of the twelve players, two out of four of each type) were informed of the realized state of nature and thus became "insiders." In this way, information became "asymmetric." Every player knew (from the instructions given) that no one knew the number or identity of insiders. During periods 1 to 4, the fact that no one had any information was announced. From the nature of the instructions given, all could deduce that the dividend values for every player remained constant from period to period. But nobody knew the number of agent types nor the fact that the insiders were the same players throughout the relevant periods.

What outcomes are to be expected, that is, what is the equilibrium price and which type of players will end up holding certificates in equilibrium?

Consider the PI equilibrium first. Here (uninformed) players act according to their prior information and therefore according to their expected dividend (in the absence of risk aversion). At any price below the expected dividend value, they demand as many units as their working capital permits. At prices above their expected dividend values, they sell the two securities initially endowed. Prices are determined

Table 8.2. *Prices and allocations in the PI and RE models,*
depending upon the information of the insiders

Equilibrium	Price		Type of agent holding certificates	
	X	Y	X	Y
PI	266	350	I and II uninformed	I insiders
RE	240	350	III	I

by the equality of aggregate demand and supply. Equilibrium prices
are therefore equal to the expected dividend value of the agent type
with the *highest* expected dividend. When all players are uninformed,
the PI equilibrium implies a price of 266, with all type I and type II
players holding certificates. When some are informed, and the state of
nature is X, then 266 is still the equilibrium price, because the uninformed continue to demand at any price below 266. Now the uninformed of type I and type II end up holding certificates in equilibrium.
When some are uninformed, and the state of nature is Y, then 350 is
the equilibrium price and only the insiders of type I hold certificates
in equilibrium.

Next, consider the RE equilibrium in the case where there are insiders while the other players are uninformed. The latter are supposed
to be capable of inferring the state of nature from the observed transactions and to revise their expectations accordingly. When the state
of nature is X, the uninformed learn about this, revise their expected
dividend, and let the price fall from 266 to 240 (see Table 8.1). As a
consequence, only investors of type III (whether insiders or not) end
up holding securities. When the state of nature is Y, the uninformed
again learn and revise their expectations. The equilibrium price is 350
(the same as in the PI equilibrium), and all investors of type I (whether
insiders or not) end up holding securities in equilibrium.

These price and allocation predictions of the PI and the RE model
are reproduced in Table 8.2. Note that the equilibrium prices differ
only when the state of nature is X, whereas the pattern of holdings
predicted differs in each of the states. This difference in holdings results
from the fact that the uninformed end up behaving the same as the
insiders in the RE model.

Finally, the strong efficiency (or strong RE) equilibrium predicts that
prices adjust instantaneously to all available information and thus will
jump from 240 to 350 as soon insiders receive the information that the
state of nature changed from X to Y.

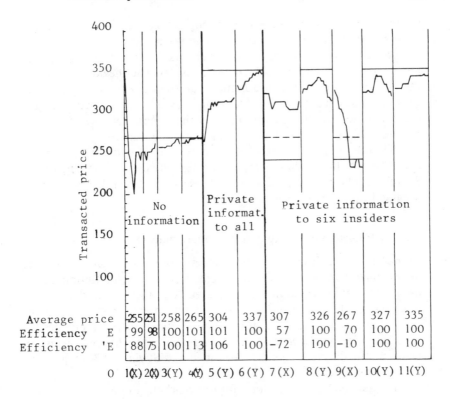

Figure 8.2. Results of the Plott–Sunder experiment.

The results of the Plott–Sunder experiment are reproduced in Figure 8.2. During the first four periods no information was given, so that the equilibrium price was 266. During periods 5 and 6, all players were told that Y was the state of nature, so 350 was the equilibrium. Periods 7 to 11 allow us to compare the predictions of the RE model and the PI model, because the insiders were informed about the state of nature, which was alternatively X or Y. The horizontal solid lines represent the predictions of the RE model (prices of 240 or 350) during periods 7 to 11. The horizontal dashed line gives the price predictions of the PI models (266) when different from those of the RE model.

Obviously, the strong RE model can be rejected: Prices did not adjust instantaneously. But they converged over time toward the RE predictions. (This tendency was confirmed by the other experiments conducted by Plott and Sunders.) The security holdings also converged to the RE values given in Table 8.2. In addition, profits of insiders and uninformed players converged to equality as the experience in the market accumulated. During initial periods insiders had the advantage. But the advantages of inside information vanished completely after replication. Finally, the values of two efficiency measures listed in Figure 8.2 converged to 100%, as implied by the RE model. (See Plott and Sunder 1982, p. 672 for details about these measures.)

The experiment discussed here was replicated with six students in economics at the Catholic University of Louvain by B. Noël. Figure 8.3 represents the contract prices. The results in general confirm those obtained by Plott and Sunders.

8.2.*   Information aggregation in futures markets

In the preceding discussion, some agents are informed and others are uninformed. Consider now another situation in which different agents have *different* information. Can one argue that the current equilibrium price aggregates these different bits of information correctly, in the sense that one can, from the current equilibrium price, correctly predict what the price will be in the future as a result of the different decisions made by the different agents? Grossman and Stiglitz (1976) argue that the answer is yes.

The question is relevant for a futures market.[3] Suppose there exists a futures market for an agricultural commodity grown by a large number (n) of isolated farmers. At the time of the harvest, there will be an equilibrium spot price p_s at which the total crop $Y = \sum_{i=1}^{n} y_i$ will be sold. Before harvest time, there is a current futures price p_f. Does this futures price p_f aggregate correctly the currently available bits of information on which the aggregate crop and therefore the spot price p_s will depend? Suppose that the demand for the aggregate crop is linear, or $Y = a - bp_s$, so that $p_s = (a - Y)/b$. In order to derive $E(p_s \mid y_i)$, the expected spot price for farmer i, given his crop y_i, Grossman and Stiglitz suppose that Y is normally distributed because each y_i can be described, at any date, by

$$y_i = \alpha + \epsilon_i. \tag{8.7}$$

Each crop is composed of a common component α and a specific error term ϵ. Both components are independent, normally distributed random variables with means $(\overline{\alpha}, 0)$ and constant variances. In addition,

---

[3] Further developments can be found in Danthine (1978) and Bray (1981).

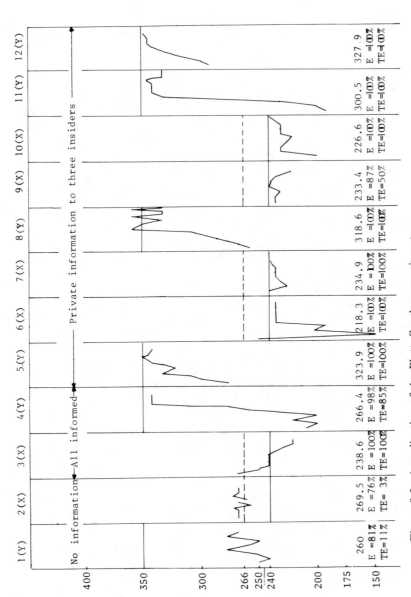

Figure 8.3. A replication of the Plott–Sunder experiment.

there is no correlation between ϵ_i and ϵ_j. Then the subjective distribution of p_s is also normal, with mean $(a - E[Y | y_i])/b$ and variance σ_p^2, which is independent of y_i.

To determine his demand for futures contracts f_i, each farmer must maximize his expected profit with respect to f_i. The individual profit function is the sum of profits (or losses) made on the futures market, $f_i(p_f - p_s)$, and on the goods market at harvest time, $p_s y_i$. Under normality of p_1 and constant absolute risk aversion k, the expected profit to be maximized is[4]

$$f_i[p_f - E(p_s | y_i)] + E(p_s | y_i)y_i - \frac{k}{2}(y_i - f_i)^2\sigma_p^2. \qquad (8.8)$$

On putting its first derivative with respect to f_i equal to zero, one finds

$$f_i = y_i - \frac{E(p_s | y_i) - p_f}{k\sigma_p^2}. \qquad (8.9)$$

If the current p_f is larger than the expected spot price, it is profitable to sell futures contracts (and buy them back at the delivery date at the price p_s, because at that date $p_f = p_s$). Because $[p_f - E(p_s | y_i)] > 0$, this implies $f_i > 0$ (for the expected profit to be positive). When the current p_f is smaller than $E(p_s | y_i)$, it is profitable to buy futures contracts and $f_i < 0$. (When one sells futures, one is said to go "short." When one buys futures, one is said to go "long.")

The futures market is in equilibrium when $\sum_{i=1}^{n} f_i = 0$ or, using equation (8.9), when

$$Y + \sum_{i=1}^{n} \left[\frac{E(p_s | y_i) - p_f}{k\sigma_p^2} \right] = 0, \qquad (8.10)$$

using the fact that farmers will normally go "short," that is, hedge against a low p_s. We know that $E(p_s | y_i) = (a - E[Y | y_i])/b$. On the other hand, it can be shown that $E[Y | y_i]$ is a linear function of the individual y_i, or $E[Y | y_i] = h_1 + h_2 y_i$. We also have $\sum_{i=1}^{n} y_i = a - bp_s$. Substitution of these expressions into (8.10) gives

$$Y + \frac{n}{k\sigma_p^2} \left[\frac{a - h_1 - h_2(a - bp_s)}{b} - p_f \right] = 0$$

(because each individual has the same k and σ_p^2) or

$$p_f = \left[\frac{k\sigma_p^2}{n} Y + \frac{a - h_1 - h_2 a}{b} \right] + h_2 p_s. \qquad (8.11)$$

[4] See Newbery and Stiglitz (1981, p. 85).

The futures price is a linear function of the spot price and the total crop. It is a perfect aggregator of the information collected by the different individuals. By observing p_f, one can predict the quantity that will be available in the spot market and what the spot price will be.

Notice, however, that the futures market works only to the extent that individual agents take positions based on their private information and not on the futures price. For a futures market to exist at all, some traders must be convinced that they can outperform the market, for example because they think they can predict the aggregate crop Y better than the market (and thus have a better prediction of p_1, given the current p_f). On both sides of the market, some traders must think that the futures price is a wrong forecast, to put it sharply.

Streit (1983, p. 8) develops the implications of this view as follows:

This view has interesting implications both for the interpretation of futures prices and also for the modelling of their formation. According to this view, prices at which transactions have taken place before the maturity of a contract represent wrong forecasts of future market conditions to traders who have made transactions at those prices. The implicit forecasts have been acceptable only to those who refrained from trading at those prices. As far as price changes indicate changes in information situations, those who trade tend to disagree that the observable price changes reflect accurately the changes in information. This has a further implication. Suppose it turns out, empirically, that the futures prices in a particular market over a particular period prove to have been good forecasts and that the market has to be judged efficient in the informational sense. This observed result would have been brought about by the actions of market participants who in fact disputed the forecasts implicit in the various futures prices. Thus the favourable "performance" of the market would be the unintended outcome of numerous decisions of the many participants who traded precisely because they considered various prices to be inappropriate and unjustified, not least in the light of information available to them, and who intended to profit from the mistakes. The rationale for active market participation differs completely from the observable market result.

The econometric results of Tomek and Gray (1970), Kofi (1973), and Giles and Goss (1980) show that futures prices at various dates before maturity are in fact accurate forecasts of the spot price at maturity for commodities such as wool and live beef. The null hypothesis that the regression coefficient of p_{st} on p_{ft-i} is equal to 1 (i designating particular months before maturity) cannot be rejected. The same is true for the null hypothesis that the regression intercept is 0. These observed results are brought about unintentionally by traders who thought their forecast is better than the one implied in the current futures price.

References

Aharon, R. and E. C. H. Veendorp. (1983). "Sequential search with a budget constraint." *Economics Letters, 11*, 81–85.

Akerlof, G. A. (1970). "The market for 'lemons': quality uncertainty and the market mechanism." *Quarterly Journal of Economics, 84*, 488–500. (Reprinted in Diamond and Rothschild 1978)

Akerlof, G. A. and W. T. Dickens. (1982). "The economic consequences of cognitive dissonance." *American Economic Review, 72*, 307–19.

Allen, F. (1984). "Reputation and product quality." *Rand Journal of Economics, 15*, 311–27.

Areeda, P. and D. F. Turner. (1975). "Predatory pricing and related practices under section 2 of the Sherman act." *Harvard Law Review, 88*, 697–733.

Arrow, K. J. (1959). "Toward a theory of price adjustment." *The Allocation of Economic Resources* (M. Abramovitz, ed.). Stanford: Stanford University Press.

Aumann, R. J. (1960). "Acceptable points in games of perfect information." *Pacific Journal of Mathematics, 10*, 381–417.

Baron, D. P. (1972). "Incentive contracts and competitive bidding." *American Economic Review, 62*, 384–94.

Barthélémy, P. (1981). "Une application du problème des deux bandits armés: un modèle simplifié de job search." *Analyse du Déséquilibre* (G. Bramoullé and J.-P. Giran, eds.), pp. 29–40. Paris: Economica.

Basar, T. and Y. C. Ho. (1974). "Informational properties of the Nash solutions of two nonzero-sum games." *Journal of Economic Theory, 7*, 370–387.

Baumol, W. J. (1979). "Quasi-permanence of price reductions: a policy for prevention of predatory pricing." *Yale Law Journal, 89*, 1–26.

Behrens, F. S. (1963). *Marktinformation und Wettbewerb*. Köln: Carl Heymans.

Bester, H. (1985). "Screening vs. rationing in credit markets with imperfect information." *American Economic Review, 75*, 850–5.

Bester, H. (1987). "The role of collateral in credit markets with imperfect information." *European Economic Review, 31*, 887–99.

Bond, E. W. (1982). "A direct test of the 'lemons' model: the market for used pickup trucks." *American Economic Review, 72*, 836–40.

Bond, E. W. (1984). "Test of the lemons model: reply." *American Economic Review, 74*, 801–4.

Bork, R. H. (1978). *The Antitrust Paradox*. New York: Basic Books.

Braverman, A., J. L. Guasch, and S. Salop. (1983). "Defects in Disneyland: quality control as a two-part tariff." *Review of Economic Studies, 50,* 121–31.

Bray, M. (1981). "Futures trading, rational expectations and the efficient market hypothesis." *Econometrica, 49,* 575–96.

Brehain, P. (1980). *Les modifications internes du capital et de sa représentation. l'efficience de la Bourse de Bruxelles.* Unpublished doctoral dissertation, Université Catholique de Louvain, Louvain-la-Neuve.

Bucovetsky, S. (1983). "Price dispersion and stockpiling by consumers." *Review of Economic Studies, 50,* 443–65.

Burdett, K. and D. A. Malueg. (1981). "The theory of search for several goods." *Journal of Economic Theory, 24,* 362–76.

Butters, G. R. (1977). "Equilibrium distributions of sales and advertising prices." *Review of Economic Studies, 44,* 465–91.

Cassady, R. (1967). *Auctions and Auctioneering.* Berkeley and Los Angeles: University of California.

Chalkley, M. (1984). "Adaptive job search and null offers: a model of quantity constrained search." *The Economic Journal, Conference Papers, 94* (Supplement), 148–57.

Cho, I.-K. and D. M. Kreps. (1987). "Signaling games and stable equilibria." *Quarterly Journal of Economics, 102,* 179–221.

Clarke, R. N. (1983a). "Collusion and the incentives for information sharing." *Bell Journal of Economics, 14,* 383–94.

Clarke, R. N. (1983b). "Duopolists don't wish to share information." *Economics Letters, 11,* 33–36.

Cooper, R. and T. W. Ross. (1984). "Prices, product qualities and asymmetric information: the competitive case." *Review of Economic Studies, 51,* 197–207.

Cooper, R. and T. W. Ross. (1985). "Product warranties and double moral hazard." *Rand Journal of Economics, 16,* 103–13.

Coppinger, V. M., V. L. Smith, and J. A. Titus. (1980). "Incentives and behavior in English, Dutch and sealed-bid auctions." *Economic Inquiry, 18,* 1–22.

Cox, J. C., B. Roberson, and V. L. Smith. (1982). "Theory and behavior of single object auctions." *Research in Experimental Economics, Vol. 2,* Greenwich, Conn.: JAI Press.

Cox, J. C., V. L. Smith, and J. M. Walker. (1982). "Auction market theory of heterogeneous bidders." *Economics Letters, 9,* 319–25.

Cox, J. C., V. L. Smith, and J. M. Walker. (1983). "Tests of a heterogeneous bidder's theory of first price auctions." *Economics Letters, 12* (Papers and Proceedings), 207–12.

Cox, J. C., V. L. Smith, and J. M. Walker. (1985). "Experimental development of sealed-bid auction theory: calibrating controls for risk aversion." *American Economic Review, 75* (Papers and Proceedings), 160–5.

Crawford, V. and J. Sobel. (1982). "Strategic information transmission." *Econometrica, 50,* 1431–51.

Cremer, J. (1984). "On the economics of repeat buying." *Rand Journal of Economics, 15,* 396–403.

Cremer, J. and R. P. McLean. (1985). "Optimal selling strategies under uncertainty for a discriminating monopolist when demands are interdependent." *Econometrica, 53,* 345–61.

Crocker, K. J. and A. Snow. (1986). "The efficiency effects of categorical discrimination in the insurance industry." *Journal of Political Economy, 94,* 321–44.

Cummins, J. M. (1977). "Incentive contracting for national defense: a problem of optimal risk sharing." *Bell Journal of Economics, 8,* 168–85.

Cummings, F. J. and W. E. Ruther. (1979). "The Northern Pacific case." *Journal of Law and Economics, 22,* 329–50.

d'Aspremont, C., J. J. Gabszewicz, and J. Thisse. (1979). "On Hotelling's stability in competition." *Econometrica, 47,* 1145–50.

d'Aspremont, C. and L. A. Gérard-Varet. (1979). "Incentives and incomplete information." *Journal of Public Economics, 11,* 25–45.

d'Aspremont, C., A. Jacquemin, J. J. Gabszewicz, and J. Weymark. (1983). "On the stability of collusive price leadership." *Canadian Journal of Economics, 14,* 17–25.

Dam, K. W. (1965). "Oil and gas licensing and the North Sea." *Journal of Law and Economics, 8,* 51–59.

Dam, K. W. (1974). "The evolution of North Sea licensing policy in Bratain and Norway." *Journal of Law and Economics, 17,* 213–63.

Danthine, J.-P. (1978). "Information, futures prices and stabilizing speculation." *Journal of Economic Theory, 17,* 79–98.

Deaton, A. and J. Muellbauer. (1980). *Economics and Consumer Behavior.* Cambridge: Cambridge University Press.

DeBrock, L. M. and J. L. Smith. (1983). "Joint bidding, information pooling, and the performance of petroleum lease auctions." *Bell Journal of Economics, 14,* 395–404.

de Palma, A., V. Ginsburgh, Y. Papageorgiou, and J.-F. Thisse. (1983). "The principle of minimum differentiation holds under sufficient heterogeneity." *CORE Discussion Paper 8339.* Louvain-la-Neuve: Université Catholique de Louvain.

Devine, D. G. and B. W. Marion. (1979). "The influence of consumer price information on retail and consumer behavior." *American Journal of Agricultural Economics, 61,* 228–37.

Diamond, P. (1971). "A model of price adjustment." *Journal of Economic Theory, 3,* 156–68.

Diamond, P. and M. Rothschild (1978). *Uncertainty in Economics.* New York: Academic Press.

Dionne, G. and P. Lasserre. (1987). "Adverse selection and finite-horizon insurance contracts." *European Economic Review, 31,* 843–61.

Dolbear, F., L. Lave, and G. Bowman. (1968). "Collusion in oligopoly: an experiment on the effect of numbers and information." *Quarterly Journal of Economics, 82,* 240–59.

Easley, D., R. T. Masson, and R. J. Reynolds. (1985). "Preying for time." *Journal of Industrial Economics, 33*, 445–60.

Eaton, C. B. and R. G. Lipsey. (1979). "Comparison shopping and the clustering of homogeneous firms." *Journal of Regional Science, 19*, 421–35.

Eisenberg, B. S. (1980). "Information exchange among competitors: the issue of relative value scales for physicians' services." *Journal of Law and Economics, 23*, 441–60.

Engelbrecht-Wiggans, R. (1980). "Auctions and bidding models: a survey." *Management Science, 26*, 119–42.

Epple, D. and A. Raviv. (1978). "Product safety: liability rules, market structure, and imperfect information." *American Economic Review, 68*, 80–95.

Fama, E. F. (1965). "The behavior of stock market prices." *Journal of Business, 38*, 34–105.

Fama, E. F. (1970). "Efficient capital markets: a review of theory and empirical work." *Journal of Finance, 25*, 383–417.

Fama, E. F. (1979). *Foundations of Finance.* Oxford: Blackwell.

Fama, E. F., and M. Blume. (1966). "Filter rules and stock market trading profits." *Journal of Business, 39*, 226–41. (Special Supplement, January)

Fama, E. F., L. Fisher, M. Jensen, and R. Roll. (1969). "The adjustment of stock prices to new information." *International Economic Review, 10*, 1–21.

Feinstein, J. S., M. K. Block, and F. D. Nold. (1985). "Asymmetric information and collusive behavior in auction markets." *American Economic Review, 75*, 441–60.

Fellner, W. (1960). *Competition among the Few.* New York: A. M. Kelley. (Reprints of Economic Classics)

Fisher, F. M. (1970). "Quasi-competitive price adjustment by individual firms: a preliminary paper." *Journal of Economic Theory, 2*, 195–206.

Forsythe, R., Palfrey, T., and C. R. Plott. (1982). "Asset valuation in an experimental market." *Econometrica, 50*, 537–68.

Fouraker, L. and S. Siegel (1963). *Bargaining Behavior.* New York: McGraw-Hill.

Frahm, D. S. and L. Schrader. (1970). "An experimental comparison of pricing in two auction systems." *American Journal of Agricultural Economics*, November, 528–34.

Fried, D. (1984). "Incentives for information production and disclosure in a duopolistic environment." *Quarterly Journal of Economics, 99*, 367–81.

Friedman, J. W. (1963). "Individual behavior in oligopolistic markets: an experimental study." *Yale Economic Essays, 3*, 359–417.

Friedman, J. W. (1969). "On experimental research in oligopoly." *Review of Economic Studies, 36*, 399–415.

Friedman, J. W. (1970). "Equal profit as a fair division." *Beiträge zur Experimentellen Wirtschaftsforschung*, Volume 2 (H. Sauermann, ed.), pp. 19–22. Tübingen: J. C. B. Mohr and Paul Siebeck.

Friedman, J. W. (1971). "A non-cooperative equilibrium for supergames." *Review of Economic Studies, 38*, 1–12.

Friedman, J. W. (1972). "On the structure of oligopoly models with differentiated products." *Beiträge zur Experimentellen Wirtschaftsforschung* (H. Sauermann, ed.) Tübingen: J. C. B. Mohr and Paul Siebeck.

Friedman, J. W. (1977). *Oligopoly and the Theory of Games.* Amsterdam: North-Holland.

Friedman, J. W. (1979). "On entry preventing behavior." *Applied Game Theory*, pp. 236–53. (S. J. Brams, A. Schotter, and G. Schwödiauer, eds.), Vienna.

Friedman, J. W. (1983). *Oligopoly Theory.* Cambridge: Cambridge University Press.

Friedman, J. W. and A. C. Hoggatt (1980). *An Experiment in Non-Cooperative Oligopoly.* Greenwich, Conn.: JAI Press.

Fudenberg, D. and E. Maskin. (1986). "The folk theorem in repeated games with discounting or with incomplete information." *Econometrica, 54*, 533–54.

Fudenberg, D. and J. Tirole (1986a). *Dynamic Models of Oligopoly.* New York: Harwood Academics.

Fudenberg, D. and J. Tirole. (1986b). "A 'signal-jamming' theory of predation." *Rand Journal of Economics, 17*, 366–78.

Gabszewicz, J. J. and P. Garella. (1986). "'Subjective' price search and price competition." *International Journal of Industrial Organization, 4*, 305–16.

Gabszewicz, J. J. and P. Garella. (1987). "Price search and spatial competition." *European Economic Review, 31*, 827–42.

Gal-Or, E. (1985). "Information sharing in oligopoly." *Econometrica, 53*, 329–43.

Gaskins, D. (1971). "Dynamic limit pricing: optimal pricing under threat of entry." *Journal of Economic Theory, 2*, 306–22.

Geroski, P., L. Phlips, and A. Ulph. (1985). "Oligopoly, competition and welfare: some recent developments." *Journal of Industrial Economics, 33*, 369–86. (A Symposium on Oligopoly, Competition and Welfare)

Giles, D. E. A. and B. A. Goss. (1980). "Futures prices as forecasts of commodity spot prices." Monash University Working Paper 5/80.

Giran, J.-P. (1979). *Recherche d'information et déséquilibres.* Paris: Economica.

Glazer, A. (1984). "The client relationship and a just price." *American Economic Review, 74*, 1089–95.

Gordon, R. J. (1981). "Output fluctuations and gradual price adjustment." *Journal of Economic Literature, 19*, 493–530.

Graham, D. A. and R. C. Marshall. (1984). "Bidder coalitions at auctions." Duke University, Mimeo.

Graham, D. A. and R. C. Marshall. (1985). "Collusive behaviour at a single object English auction." Working Paper 85-01, Duke University.

264   **References**

Green, E. J. (1982). "Non-cooperative price taking in large dynamic markets." *Non-Cooperative Approaches to the Theory of Perfect Competition* (A. Mas-Colell, ed.). New York: Academic Press.

Green, E. J. and R. H. Porter. (1984). "Noncooperative collusion under imperfect price information." *Econometrica, 52,* 87–100.

Green, J. and J. J. Laffont (1978). *Incentives in Public Decision Making.* Amsterdam: North-Holland.

Greer, D. F. (1979). "A critique of Areeda's and Turner's standards for predatory practices." *The Antitrust Bulletin, 24,* 233–61.

Grossman, S. (1976). "On the efficiency of competitive stock markets where traders have diverse information." *Journal of Finance, 31,* 573–85.

Grossman, S. (1978). "Further results on the informational efficiency of competitive stock markets." *Journal of Economic Theory, 18,* 81–101.

Grossman, S. and J. E. Stiglitz. (1976). "Information and competitive price systems." *American Economic Review, 66* (May), 246–53.

Grossman, S. and J. E. Stiglitz. (1980). "On the impossibility of informationally efficient markets." *American Economic Review, 70,* 393–408.

Hallagan, W. and W. Joerding. (1985). "Equilibrium price dispersion." *American Economic Review, 75,* 1191–4.

Hamada, K. (1976). "Liability rules and income distribution in product liability." *American Economic Review, 66,* 228–34.

Hänchen, T. and T. von Ungern-Sternberg. (1985). "Information costs, intermediation and equilibrium price." *Economica, 52,* 407–19.

Hansen, R. G. (1985). "Auctions with contingent payments." *American Economic Review, 75,* 862–5.

Hansen, R. G. (1985). "Empirical testing of auction theory." *American Economic Review, 75* (Papers and Proceedings), 156–9.

Harris, M. and A. Raviv. (1978). "Some results on incentive contracts with applications to education and employment, health, insurance, and law enforcement." *American Economic Review, 68,* 20–30.

Harris, M. and A. Raviv. (1979). "Optimal incentive contracts with imperfect information." *Journal of Economic Theory, 20,* 231–59.

Harris, M. and A. Raviv. (1981). "A theory of monopoly pricing schemes with demand uncertainty." *American Economic Review, 71,* 347–65.

Harsanyi, J. C. (1967–68). "Games with incomplete information played by Bayesian players." *Management Science, 14,* 159–82, 320–34, 486–502.

Heal, G. (1976). "Do bad products drive out good?" *Quarterly Journal of Economics, 90,* 499–502.

Heal, G. (1977). "Guaranties and risk sharing." *Review of Economic Studies, 44,* 549–60.

Hellwig, M. (1982). "Rational expectations equilibrium with conditioning on past prices: A mean-variance example." *Journal of Economic Theory, 26,* 279–312.

Hellwig, M. (1987). "Some recent developments in the theory of competition in markets with adverse selection." *European Economic Review, 31,* 319–25.

Hendricks, K., R. H. Porter and B. Boudreau. (1987). "Information, returns, and bidding behavior in OCS auctions: 1954–1969." *Journal of Industrial Economics, 35,* 517–42.

Hey, J. D. (1979). *Uncertainty in Microeconomics.* Oxford: Martin Robertson.

Hirschleifer, J. and J. G. Riley. (1979). "The analytics of uncertainty and information – an expository survey." *Journal of Economic Literature, 17,* 1375–421.

Hoffman, E. and C. R. Plott. (1981). "The effect of intertemporal speculation on the outcomes in seller posted offer auction markets." *Quarterly Journal of Economics, 96,* 223–41.

Hoffman, E. and J. R. Marsden. (1986). "Empirical evidence on competitive bidding, some surprising results." *Economics Letters, 22,* 15–21.

Hoggatt, A. C. (1959). "An experimental business game." *Behavioral Science, 4,* 192–203.

Hoggatt, A. C. (1967). "Measuring the cooperativeness of behavior in quantity variation duopoly games." *Behavioral Science, 12,* 109–21.

Holahan, W. L. (1978). "Cartel problems: comment." *American Economic Review, 68,* 942–6.

Holt, C. A. (1979). "Uncertainty and the bidding for incentive contracts." *American Economic Review, 69,* 697–705.

Holt, C. A. (1980). "Bidding for contracts." *Bayesian Analysis in Economic Theory and Time-Series Analysis, The 1977 Savage Dissertation Awards* (C. A. Holt and R. W. Shore, eds.). Amsterdam: North-Holland.

Hotelling, H. (1929). "Stability in competition." *Economic Journal, 39,* 41–57.

Hughart, D. (1975). "Informational asymmetry, bidding strategies, and the marketing of off-shore petroleum leases." *Journal of Political Economy, 83,* 969–85.

Isaac, R. M. and V. L. Smith. (1985). "In search of predatory pricing." *Journal of Political Economy, 93,* 320–45.

Jaffe, J. F. and R. L. Winkler. (1976). "Optimal speculation against an efficient market." *Journal of Finance, 31.*

Jaffee, D. M. and T. Russell. (1976). "Imperfect information, uncertainty, and credit rationing." *Quarterly Journal of Economics, 90,* 651–66.

Johansen, L. (1982). "On the status of the Nash type of noncooperative equilibrium in economic theory." *Scandinavian Journal of Economics, 84,* 421–41.

Jovanovic, B. (1982). "Favorable selection with asymmetric information." *Quarterly Journal of Economics, 97,* 535–9.

Jung, A. F. (1960). "Price variations among automobile dealers in metropolitan Chicago." *Journal of Business, 83,* 31–42.

Kagel, J. H. and D. Levin. (1985). "Individual bidder behavior in first-price private value auctions." *Economics Letters, 19,* 125–8.

Kagel, J. H. and D. Levin. (1986). "The winner's curse and public information in common value auctions." *American Economic Review, 76,* 894–920.

Kambhu, J. (1982). "Optimal product quality under asymmetric information and moral hazard." *Bell Journal of Economics, 13,* 483–92.

Kamien, M. I. and N. Schwartz. (1971). "Limit pricing under uncertain entry." *Econometrica, 39,* 441–54.

Kihlstrom, R. E. and L. J. Mirman. (1975). "Information and market equilibrium." *Bell Journal of Economics, 6,* 357–76.

Kim, J.-C. (1985). "The market for 'lemons' reconsidered: a model of the used car market with asymmetric information." *American Economic Review, 75,* 836–43.

Kofi, T. A. (1973). "A framework for comparing the efficiency of futures markets." *American Journal of Agricultural Economics, 55,* 584–94.

Kohlberg, E. and J.-F. Mertens. (1986). "On the strategic stability of equilibria." *Econometrica, 54,* 1003–37.

Kohn, M. G. and S. Shavell. (1974). "The theory of search." *Journal of Economic Theory, 9,* 93–123.

Koller, R. H. (1971). "The myth of predatory pricing: an empirical study." *Antitrust Law and Economics Review, 4,* 105–23.

Kreps, D. M. and J. A. Scheinkman. (1983). "Quantity precommitment and Bertrand competition yield Cournot outcomes." *Bell Journal of Economics, 14,* 326–37.

Kreps, D. M. and R. Wilson. (1982a). "Reputation and imperfect information." *Journal of Economic Theory, 27,* 253–79.

Kreps, D. M. and R. Wilson. (1982b). "Sequential equilibria." *Econometrica, 50,* 863–94.

Kyle, A. S. (1978). "Continuous auctions and insider trading." *Econometrica, 53,* 1315–35.

Laffont, J. J. (1985). *Cours de Théorie Microéconomique, Vol. II – Economie de l'Incertain et de l'Information.* Paris: Economica.

Laffont, J. J. and E. Maskin. (1983). "The theory of incentives: an overview." *Advances in Economic Theory* (W. Hildenbrand, ed.), Cambridge: Cambridge University Press. (Econometric Society Monographs in Quantitative Economics)

Laffont, J. J. and E. Maskin. (1987). "Monopoly with asymmetric information about quality: behavior and regulation." *European Economic Review, 31* (Papers and Proceedings), 483–9.

Landsberger, M. and I. Meilison. (1985). "Intertemporal price discrimination and sales strategy under incomplete information." *Rand Journal of Economics, 16,* 424–30.

Layard, R. and G. Psacharopoulos. (1974). "The screening hypothesis and the returns to education." *Journal of Political Economy, 82,* 985–98.

Lee, L.-F. and R. H. Porter. (1984). "Switching regression models with imperfect sample separation information – with an application to cartel stability." *Econometrica, 52,* 391–418.

Leland, H. (1980). "Minimum quality standards and licensing in markets with asymmetric information." *Occupational Licensure and Regulation* (S. Rothenberg, ed.). Washington: American Enterprise Institute.

Li, L. (1985). "Cournot oligopoly with information sharing." *Rand Journal of Economics, 16,* 521–36.

Lippman, S. A. and J. J. McCall. (1976). "The economics of job search: a survey." *Economic Inquiry, 14,* 155–89.

Lippman, S. A. and J. J. McCall (1979). *Studies in the Economics of Search.* Amsterdam: North-Holland.

Luce, R. D. and H. Raiffa. (1957). *Games and Decisions.* New York: Wiley.

MacLeod, W. B. (1984). "The core and oligopoly theory." *Revised Version of CORE Discussion Paper 8331.* Louvain-la-Neuve: Université Catholique de Louvain.

MacLeod, W. B. (1985). "A theory of conscious parallelism." *European Economic Review, 27,* 25–44.

MacLeod, W. B., G. Norman, and J.-F. Thisse. (1984). "Competition, collusion and free entry in spatial or differential product markets." *CORE Discussion Paper 8436.* Louvain-la-Neuve: Université Catholique de Louvain.

Manning, R. and P. B. Morgan. (1982). "Search and consumer theory." *Review of Economic Studies, 49,* 203–16.

March, J. G. (1978). "Bounded rationality, ambiguity, and the engineering of choice." *Bell Journal of Economics, 9,* 587–608.

Marschak, J. (1954). "Towards an economic theory of organization and information." *Decision processes* (R. M. Thrall, C. H. Coombs, and R. L. Davis, eds.). New York: Wiley.

Marschak, J. (1955). "Elements for a theory of teams." *Management Science, 1,* 127–37. (Reprinted in J. Marschak 1974)

Marschak, J. (1974). *Economic Information, Decision, and Prediction.* Dordrecht: Reidel. (Selected Essays)

Marschak, J. and R. Radner. (1972). *Economic Theory of Teams.* New Haven: Yale University Press.

Marvel, H. P. (1976). "The economics of information and gasoline price behavior: an empirical analysis." *Journal of Political Economy, 84,* 1033–60.

Marvel, H. P. and S. McCafferty. (1984). "Resale price maintenance and quality certification." *Rand Journal of Economics, 15,* 347–59.

Maskin, E. S. and J. G. Riley. (1984). "Monopoly with incomplete information." *Rand Journal of Economics, 15,* 171–96.

Maskin, E. S. and J. G. Riley. (1985). "Auction theory with private values." *American Economic Review, 75* (Papers and Proceedings), 150–5.

Mathewson, G. F. (1983). "Information, search, and price variability of individual life insurance contracts." *Journal of Industrial Economics, 32,* 131–48.

McAfee, R. P. and J. McMillan. (1986). "Bidding for contracts: a principal-agent analysis." *Rand Journal of Economics, 17,* 326–38.

McAfee, R. P. and J. McMillan. (1987). "Auctions and bidding." *Journal of Economic Literature, 25,* 699–738.

McCall, J. J. (1970). "The simple economics of incentive contracting." *American Economic Review, 60*, 837–46.

McGee, J. S. (1958). "Predatory price cutting: The Standard Oil (N.J.) case." *Journal of Law and Economics, 1*, 137–69.

McGee, J. S. (1960). "Ocean freight rate conferences and the American merchant marine." *University of Chicago Law Review, 27*, 191 sq.

McGee, J. S. (1964). "Government intervention in the Spanish sugar industry." *Journal of Law and Economics, 7*, 121 sq.

McGee, J. S. (1980). "Predatory pricing revisited." *Journal of Law and Economics, 23*, 289–330.

Menze, H. (1963). "Markttransparenz in Theorie und Wettbewerbsrecht." *Wirtschaft und Wettbewerb, 13*, 578–90.

Mestmäcker, E. J. (1952). *Verbandsstatistiken als Mittel zur Beschränkung und Förderung des Wettbewerbs in den Vereinigten Staaten und Deutschland.* Frankfurt.

Milgrom, P. R. (1979a). "A convergence theorem for competitive bidding with differential information." *Econometrica, 47*, 679–88.

Milgrom, P. R. (1979b). *The Structure of Information in Competitive Bidding.* New York: Garland.

Milgrom, P. R. (1981). "Good news and bad news: representation theorems and applications." *Bell Journal of Economics, 12*, 380–91.

Milgrom, P. R. (1985). "The economics of competitive bidding: a selective survey." *Social Goals and Social Organization, Essays in Memory of Elisha Pazner* (L. Hurwicz, D. Schmeidler, and H. Sonnenschein, eds.). Cambridge: Cambridge University Press.

Milgrom, P. R. and J. Roberts. (1982a). "Predation and entry deterrence." *Journal of Economic Theory, 27*, 280–312.

Milgrom, P. R. and J. Roberts. (1982b). "Limit pricing and entry." *Econometrica, 50*, 443–59.

Milgrom, P. R. and J. Roberts. (1986). "Relying on the information of interested parties." *Rand Journal of Economics, 17*, 18–32.

Milgrom, P. R. and J. Roberts. (1987). "Informational asymmetries, strategic behavior and industrial organization." *American Economic Review, 77* (Papers and Proceedings), 184–93.

Milgrom, P. R. and N. Stokey. (1982). "Information, trade and common knowledge." *Journal of Economic Theory, 26*, 17–27.

Milgrom, P. R. and R. J. Weber. (1982). "A theory of auctions and competitive bidding." *Econometrica, 50*, 1089–122.

Modigliani, F. (1958). "New developments on the oligopoly front." *Journal of Political Economy, 66*, 215 sq.

Morard, B. (1981). "Sur les équilibres informationnels au sens de S. Grossman." *Analyse du Déséquilibre* (G. Bramoullé and J. P. Giran, eds.), pp. 229–54. Paris: Economica.

Mortensen, D. T. (1970). "Job search, the duration of unemployment and the Phillips curve." *American Economic Review, 60*, 847–62.

Nelson, P. (1970). "Information and consumer behavior." *Journal of Political Economy, 78,* 311–29.

Nelson. P. (1974). "Advertising as information." *Journal of Political Economy, 82,* 729–54.

Nelson, P. (1975). "The economic consequences of advertising." *Journal of Business, 48,* 213–41.

Nermuth, M. (1982). *Information Structures in Economics.* [Lecture Notes in Economics and Mathematical Systems, No. 196]. Berlin: Springer-Verlag.

Neven, D. and L. Phlips. (1985). "Discriminating oligopolists and common markets." *Journal of Industrial Economics, 34,* 133–49.

Newbery, D. M. G. and J. E. Stiglitz. (1981). *The Theory of Commodity Price Stabilization.* Oxford: Clarendon Press.

Novshek, W. and H. Sonnenschein. (1982). "Fulfilled expectations Cournot duopoly with information acquisition and release." *Bell Journal of Economics, 13,* 214–8.

Okada, A. (1982). "Information exchange between oligopolists." *Journal of the Operations Research Society of Japan, 25,* 58–75.

Osborne, K. D. (1976). "Cartel problems." *American Economic Review, 66,* 835–44.

Palfrey, T. R. (1982). "Risk advantages and information acquisition." *Bell Journal of Economics, 13,* 219–24.

Palfrey, T. R. (1983). "Bundling decisions by a multiproduct monopolist with incomplete information." *Econometrica, 51,* 463–83.

Pascall, A. H. and J. J. McCall. "Agglomeration economics, search costs and industrial location." *Journal of Urban Economics, 8,* 383–8.

Patinkin, D. (1947). "Multi-plant firms, cartels, and imperfect competition." *Quarterly Journal of Economics, 61,* 173–205.

Peterman, J. L. (1979). "The international salt case." *Journal of Law and Economics, 22,* 351–64.

Phlips, L. (1964). "Markttransparenz in Theorie und Wirklichkeit." *Wirtschaft und Wettbewerb, 14,* 205–11.

Phlips, L. (1983). *The Economics of Price Discrimination.* Cambridge: Cambridge University Press.

Phlips, L. (1986). "Price discrimination: a survey of the theory." *Journal of Economic Surveys* (forthcoming).

Phlips, L. (1987). "Information and collusion." *The Economics of Market Dominance* (D. Hay and J. Vickers, eds.), pp. 89–104. Oxford: B. Blackwell.

Phlips, L. and J.-F. Richard. (1986). A dynamic oligopoly model with demand inertia and inventories. *Journal of Mathematical Social Sciences* (forthcoming).

Phlips, L. and J.-F. Thisse. (1981). "Pricing, distribution and the supply of storage." *European Economic Review, 15,* 225–43.

Plott, C. R. (1982). "Industrial organization theory and experimental economics." *Journal of Economic Literature, 20,* 1485–527.

Plott, C. R. and S. Sunder. (1982). "Efficiency of experimental security markets with insider information: an application of rational expectations models." *Journal of Political Economy, 90,* 663–98.

Plott, C. R. and L. L. Wilde. (1982). "Professional diagnosis vs. self-diagnosis: an experimental examination of some special features of markets with uncertainty." *Research in Experimental Economics, 2* (V. L. Smith, ed.). Greenwich, Conn.: JAI Press.

Polinsky, A. M. and W. P. Rogerson. (1983). "Products liability, consumer misperceptions, and market power." *Bell Journal of Economics, 14,* 581–9.

Ponssard, J. P. (1977). *Logique de la Négociation et Théorie des Jeux.* Paris: Les Éditions d'Organisation.

Ponssard, J.-P. (1979). "The strategic role of information on the demand function in an oligopolistic market." *Management Science, 25,* 243–50.

Ponssard, J.-P. (1981). *Competitive Strategies.* Amsterdam: North-Holland.

Porter, R. H. (1983a). "Optimal cartel trigger price strategies." *Journal of Economic Theory, 29,* 313–38.

Porter, R. H. (1983b). "A study of cartel stability: the joint executive committee 1880–1886." *Bell Journal of Economics, 14,* 301–4.

Posner, R. A. (1976). *Antitrust Law: An Economic Perspective.* Chicago: University of Chicago Press.

Pratt, M. D. and G. E. Hoffer. (1984). "Test of the lemons model: comment." *American Economic Review, 74,* 798–800.

Pratt, J. W., D. A. Wise, and R. Zeckhauser. (1979). "Price differences in almost competitive markets." *Quarterly Journal of Economics, 93,* 189–211.

Pyatt, G. (1971). "Profit maximization and the threat of new entry.'" *Economic Journal, 81,* 242–55.

Radner, R. (1983). "The role of private information in markets and other organizations." *Advances in Economic Theory, Econometric Society Monographs in Quantitative Economics* (W. Hildenbrand, ed.). Cambridge: Cambridge University Press.

Rea, S. A., Jr. (1981). "Workmen's compensation and occupational safety under imperfect information." *American Economic Review, 71,* 80–93.

Reece, D. K. (1978). "Competitive bidding for offshore petroleum leases." *Bell Journal of Economics, 9,* 369–84.

Rees, R. (1985). "Cheating in a duopoly supergame." *Journal of Industrial Economics, 23,* 378–400.

Riley, J. G. (1975). "Competitive signaling." *Journal of Economic Theory, 10,* 174–86.

Riley, J. G. (1976). "Information, screening and human capital." *American Economic Review, 66,* 254–60.

Riley, J. G. (1979). "Informational equilibrium." *Econometrica, 47,* 331–59.

Riley, J. G. and W. F. Samuelson. (1981). "Optimal auctions." *American Economic Review, 71,* 381–92.

Roberts, J. (1986). "A signaling model of predatory pricing." *Oxford Economic Papers, 38* (Suppl.), 75–93.

Roberts, K. (1985). "Cartel behaviour and adverse selection." *Journal of Industrial Economics, 33,* 401–13. (A symposium on oligopoly, competition and welfare)

Rockwood, A. (1983). "The impact of joint ventures on the market for OCS oil and gas leases." *Journal of Industrial Economics, 31,* 453–68.

Rosenfield, D. B. and R. D. Shapiro. (1981). "Optimal adaptive price search." *Journal of Economic Theory, 25,* 1–20.

Rosenthal, R. W. and A. Weiss. (1984). "Mixed-strategy equilibrium in a market with asymmetric information." *Review of Economic Studies, 51,* 333–342.

Rothschild, M. (1973). "Models of market organization with imperfect information: a survey." *Journal of Political Economy, 81,* 1283–1308. (Reprinted in Diamond and Rothschild 1978)

Rothschild, M. (1974a). "A two armed bandit theory of market pricing." *Journal of Economic Theory, 9,* 185–202.

Rothschild, M. (1974b). "Searching for the lowest price when the distribution of prices is unknown." *Journal of Political Economy 82,* 689–711. (Reprinted in Diamond and Rothschild 1978)

Rothschild, M. and J. Stiglitz. (1976). "Equilibrium in competitive insurance markets: an essay on the economics of imperfect information." *Quarterly Journal of Economics, 90,* 629–50. (Reprinted in Diamond and Rothschild 1978)

Rothschild, R. (1981). "Cartel problems: note." *American Economic Review, 71,* 179–81.

Sakai, Y. (1985). "The value of information in a simple duopoly model." *Journal of Economic Theory, 36,* 36–54.

Salant, S. (1977). "Search theory and duration data: a theory of sorts." *Quarterly Journal of Economics, 91,* 39–57.

Salop, S. C. (1973). "Systematic job search and unemployment." *Review of Economic Studies, 40,* 191–201.

Salop, S. C. (1976). "Information and monopolistic competition." *American Economic Review, 66,* 240–245.

Salop, S. C. (1977). "The noisy monopolist: imperfect information, price dispersion and price discrimination." *Review of Economic Studies, 44,* 393–406.

Salop, S. C. (1979). "Strategic entry deterrence." *American Economic Review, 69,* 335–38.

Salop, S. C. (1981). *Strategy, Predation, and Antitrust Analysis.* Washington, D.C.: Federal Trade Commission, Bureau of Economics, Bureau of Competition.

Salop, S. C. (1985). "Practices that (credibly) facilitate oligopoly coordination." *New Developments in the Analysis of Market Structure* (J. Stiglitz and I. Matthewson, eds.). London: Macmillan.

Salop, S. C. and J. E. Stiglitz. (1977). "Bargains and ripoffs: a model of monopolistically competitive price dispersion." *Review of Economic Studies*, 44, 493–510.

Salop, S. C. and J. E. Stiglitz. (1982). "The theory of sales: a simple model of equilibrium price dispersion with identical agents." *American Economic Review*, 72, 1121–30.

Salop, S. C. and L. J. White. (1988). "Private antitrust litigation: an introduction and framework," in L. J. White (ed.), *Private Antitrust Litigation: New Evidence, New Learning*. Cambridge, Mass.: MIT Press, 1988.

Satterthwaite, M. (1979). "Consumer information, equilibrium industry price, and the number of sellers." *Bell Journal of Economics*, 10 (Autumn), 483–502.

Sauermann, H. and R. Selten. (1967). Ein Oligopolexperiment. *Beiträge zur experimentellen Wirtschaftsforschung*, pp. 9–59. Tübingen: J. C. B. Mohr and Paul Siebeck.

Scharfstein, D. (1984). "A policy to prevent rational test-market predation." *Rand Journal of Economics*, 15, 229–43.

Scherer, F. M. (1964). "The theory of contractual incentives for cost reduction." *Quarterly Journal of Economics*, 78, 257–80.

Schmets, G. (1985). *Ventes publiques expérimentales*. Université Catholique de Louvain. (M.A. thesis)

Schwartz, A. and L. L. Wilde. (1979). "Intervening in markets on the basis of imperfect information: a legal and economic analysis." *Pennsylvania Law Review*, 127, 630–82.

Schwartz, A. and L. L. Wilde. (1982a). "Competitive equilibria in markets for heterogeneous goods under imperfect information: A theoretical analysis with policy implications." *Bell Journal of Economics*, 13, 181–93.

Schwartz, A. and L. L. Wilde. (1982b). "Imperfect information, monopolistic competition, and public policy." *American Economic Review*, 72 (May), 18–23.

Seidmann, D. J. (1987). "Incentives for information production and disclosure: comment." *Quarterly Journal of Economics*, 102, 445–52.

Selten, R. (1965). "Spieltheoretische Behandlung eines Oligopolmodells mit Nachfrageträgheit." *Zeitschrift für die Gesamte Staatswissenschaft*, 121, 301–24, 667–89.

Selten, R. (1978). "The chain store paradox." *Theory and Decision*, 9, 127–59.

Selten, R. (1979). "Experimentelle Wirtschaftsforschung." *Rheinisch Westfälische Akademie der Wissenschaften Vorträge*, 287, 41–72.

Selten, R. (1982). "Einführung in die Theorie der Spiele mit unvollständiger Information." *Information in der Wirtschaft*. Berlin: Duncker and Humblot. (Schriften des Vereins für Socialpolitik, Gesellschaft für Wirtschafts- und Socialwissenschaften, Neue Folge Band 126)

Shaked, A. and J. Sutton. (1987). "Product differentiation and industrial structure," *Journal of Industrial Economics*, 34, 131–46.

Shapiro, C. (1982a). "Consumer information, product quality, and seller reputation." *Bell Journal of Economics, 13*, 20–35.

Shapiro, C. (1982b). *Optimal Pricing of Experience Goods.* Princeton University: Woodrow Wilson School of Public and International Affairs.

Shapiro, C. (1986). "Exchanges of cost information in oligopoly." *Review of Economic Studies, 53*, 433–46.

Shefrin, H. M. (1979). "Spot trading, efficiency and differential information." *Journal of Economic Theory, 20*, 281–99.

Shubik, M. (1982). *Game Theory in the Social Sciences, Concepts and Solutions.* Cambridge, Mass.: MIT Press.

Simon, H. A. (1955). "A behavioral model of rational choice." *Quarterly Journal of Economics, 69*, 99–118.

Simon, H. A. (1956). "Rational choice and the structure of the environment." *Psychological Review, 63*, 129–38.

Slade, M. E. (1987). "Interfirm rivalry in a repeated game: an empirical test of tacit collusion." *Journal of Industrial Economics, 35*, 499–516.

Smallwood, D. E. and J. Conlisk. (1979). "Product quality in markets where consumers are imperfectly informed." *Quarterly Journal of Economics, 93*, 1–24.

Spence, A. M. (1974). *Market Signaling: Information Transfer in Hiring and Related Processes.* Cambridge, Mass.: Harvard University Press.

Spence, A. M. (1976). "Competition in salaries and signaling prerequisites for jobs." *Quarterly Journal of Economics, 90*, 51–75.

Spence, A. M. (1977). "Consumer misperceptions, product failure, and producer liability." *Review of Economic Studies, 44*, 561–72.

Spence, A. M. (1978). "Tacit co-ordination and imperfect information." *Canadian Journal of Economics, 11*, 490–505.

Spence, A. M. (1981). "Competition, entry and antitrust policy." In Salop (1981), pp. 45–88.

Stahl, K. (1982). "Differentiated products, consumer search, and locational oligopoly." *Journal of Industrial Economics, 31*, 97–113.

Stahl, K. and P. Varaya. (1978). "Economics of information: examples in location and land-use theory." *Regional Science and Urban Economics, 8*, 43–56.

Stark, R. M. and M. H. Rothkopf. (1979). "Competitive bidding: a comprehensive bibliography." *Operations Research, 27*, 364–90.

Stigler, G. J. (1961). "The economics of information." *Journal of Political Economy, 69*, 213–85.

Stigler, G. J. (1962). "Information in the labor market." *Journal of Political Economy, 70*, 94–105.

Stigler, G. J. (1964). "A theory of oligopoly." *Journal of Political Economy, 72*, 44–61.

Stiglitz, J. E. (1977). "Monopoly, non-linear pricing and imperfect information: the insurance market." *Review of Economic Studies, 44*, 407–30.

Stiglitz, J. E. (1987). "The causes and consequences of the dependence of quality on price." *Journal of Economic Literature, 25*, 1–48.

Stiglitz, J. E. and A. Weiss. (1981). "Credit rationing in markets with imperfect information." *American Economic Review, 71*, 393–410.

Stoecker, R. (1980). *Experimentelle Untersuchung des Entscheidungsverhaltens im Bertrand-Oligopol.* Bielefeld: Pfeffersche Buchhandlung.

Streit, M. E. (1983). "Modelling, managing and monitoring futures trading: frontiers of analytical inquiry." *Futures Markets* (M. E. Streit, ed.), pp. 1–26. Oxford: Blackwell.

Stuart, C. (1979). "Search and the spatial organisation of trading." *Studies in the Economics of Search* (S. A. Lipmann and J. J. McCall, eds.). Amsterdam: North-Holland.

Telser, L. G. (1960). "Why should manufacturers want fair trade?" *Journal of Law and Economics, 3,* 86–105.

Telser, L. G. (1966). "Cutthroat competition and the long purse." *Journal of Law and Economics, 9,* 259–77.

Telser, L. G. (1973). "Searching for the lowest price." *American Economic Review, Proc., 63,* 41–49.

Tomek, W. G. and R. W. Gray. (1970). "Temporal relationships among prices on commodity futures markets: their allocative and stabilizing roles." *American Journal of Agricultural Economics, 52,* 372–80.

Varian, H. R. (1980). "A model of sales." *American Economic Review, 70,* 651–9.

Veendorp, E. C. H. (1984). "Sequential search without reservation price." *Economics Letters, 6,* 53–57.

Vickrey, W. (1961). "Counterspeculation, auctions, and competitive sealed tenders." *Journal of Finance, 16,* 8–37.

Viscusi, W. K. P. (1978). "A note on lemons markets with quality certification." *Bell Journal of Economics, 9,* 277–9.

Vives, X. (1983). *Duopoly information equilibrium: Cournot and Bertrand.* Unpublished doctoral dissertation, University of Pennsylvania, Department of Economics.

von Ungern-Sternberg, T. (1982). "Equilibrium prices in a model with differentiated goods and search." *Zeitschrift für die gesamte Staatswissenschaft, 138,* 22–35.

von Ungern-Sternberg, T. (1984). *Zur Analyse von Märkten mit unvollständiger Nachfrageinformation.* Berlin: Springer-Verlag.

von Ungern-Sternberg, T. and C. C. von Weizsäcker. (1981). "Marktstruktur und Marktverhalten bei Qualitätsunsicherheit." *Zeitschrift für Wirtschafts-und Sozialwissenschaften. 101,* 609–26.

von Ungern-Sternberg, T. and C. C. von Weizsäcker. (1985). "The supply of quality on a market for 'experience goods'." *Journal of Industrial Economics, 33,* 531–40.

Weitzman, M. L. (1980). "Efficient incentive contracts." *Quarterly Journal of Economics, 44,* 719–30.

Wilde, L. (1979). "An information-theoretic approach to job quits." *Studies in the Economics of Search* (S. A. Lippmann and J. J. McCall, eds.). Amsterdam: North-Holland.

Wilde, L. (1980a). "The economics of consumer information acquisition." *Journal of Business, 53,* 143–58.

Wilde, L. (1980b). "On the formal theory of inspection and evaluation in product markets." *Econometrica, 48,* 1265–80.

Wilde, L. and A. Schwartz. (1979). "Equilibrium comparison shopping." *Review of Economic Studies, 46,* 543–54.

Williamson, A. W. (1979). "Intertemporal competitive equilibrium: On further experimental results." *Research in Experimental Economics, 1* (V. L. Smith, ed.). Greenwich, Conn.: JAI Press.

Williamson, O. E. (1976). "Franchise bidding for natural monopolies in general and with respect to CATV." *Bell Journal of Economics, 7,* 73–104.

Williamson, O. E. (1977). "Predatory pricing: a strategic and welfare analysis." *Yale Law Journal, 87,* 284–340.

Wilson, C. (1977). "A model of insurance markets with incomplete information." *Journal of Economic Theory, 16,* 167–207.

Wilson, C. (1979). "Equilibrium and adverse selection." *American Economic Review, 69* (Papers and Proceedings), 313–17.

Wilson, C. (1980). "The nature of equilibrium in markets with adverse selection." *Bell Journal of Economics, 11,* 108–30.

Wilson, R. (1969). "Competitive bidding with disparate options." *Management Science, 15,* 446–8.

Wilson, R. (1977). "A bidding model of perfect competition." *Review of Economic Studies, 44,* 511–8.

Wilson, R. (1979). "Auctions of shares." *Quarterly Journal of Economics, 93,* 675–98.

Wolinsky, A. (1983a). "Prices as signals of product quality." *Review of Economic Studies, 50,* 647–58.

Wolinsky, A. (1983b). "Retail trade concentration due to consumers' imperfect information." *Bell Journal of Economics, 14,* 275–82.

Wolinsky, A. (1984). "Product differentiation with imperfect information." *Review of Economic Studies, 51,* 53–61.

Yamey, B. S. (1972). "Predatory price cutting: notes and comments." *Journal of Law and Economics, 15,* 129–42.

Index

277